THE BLACK FLAG OF JIHAD STALKS LA RÉPUBLIQUE

authorship international

Published by authorship international
Paris, France
authorshipintl@gmail.com

Cover photo: Jiro Mochizuki
Design: Aaron Levin

ISBN 9780-9887119-7-6

NIDRA POLLER

THE BLACK FLAG OF JIHAD STALKS LA RÉPUBLIQUE

Contents

Introduction

In Greek mythology, the god Apollo bestows Cassandra with the power of prophecy. When she rejects his love, he takes revenge by casting a spell on her so that even as she foresees the future, no one will believe her. Enter Nidra Poller. The seasoned writer connects the elusive dots— those bits and pieces of news that are half heard, poorly comprehended or lost to sound bites obfuscating antisemitic bias and missing context.

> *You can't think it through in 24 hours, you can't grasp it properly from a distance. If my work has any value it is because of my way of assimilating tons of information over long periods of time, organizing it, using it where others have forgotten or never noticed. (p 119)*

She and a handful of scholars are correct. Future generations looking back at the first decade of the 21st century will note the exceptional behavior of the Western intelligentsia that identified itself as liberal and progressive and that held unusual sway over discourse in the public sphere during that time, notes colleague Richard Landes.[1] Poller reminds us of this:

> *The Western mind is softened and remodeled. The courage to defend liberty has been choked up with adulterated human rights grease, and dissolved in crocodile tears. Undercurrents of old-fashioned Jew hatred swept up by torrents from the Islamic source have rendered the West incapable of defending its interests. Essential values are reduced to flotsam and jetsam. The connection between antisemitism and Western surrender to Islamic jihad is not circumstantial; Judaism is the origin of our civilization. (p 139)*

...and the consequences of the ubiquitous "lethal narrative" to emerge, calling all things Israeli (and by association all things Jewish) evil—e.g. baby killers, intransigent peace blockers, land grabbers, then on to the endless stereotypes of Jews as universal saboteurs undermining God, the social good, through their well-known heartless, soulless, money grubbing, world dominating ways.

Reporting from ground zero on Europe's jihad against the Jews, this compilation marks Paris smoldering and burning over the past years. The author begins with the events of March 2012 and closes in November 2015. What transpires in between is an analysis rarely echoed in the mainstream news media i.e. Operation Protective Edge, the July 2014 pogrom, *Charlie Hebdo* and events rarely reported. Even if we wanted to know, most of what Poller describes has been sanitized in the mainstream news media, never quite allowing readers to capture the force let alone the history of Islamic antisemitism. Point in fact, a survey of news source coverage during Protective Edge found one national Canadian news source (*Globe and Mail*) inconsistently reporting facts while another (*Al Jazeera*) wholly omitted 3 of 11 facts and the entire Israeli narrative.[2]

Had four Jews been killed at the Hyper Cacher Porte de Vincennes in January 2015, it may have gone unnoticed, except for the Jewish press. Muslim-perpetrated attacks maiming or killing French Jews had been occurring for at least two decades. But this time was different. The jihadis gunned down Jews, a Muslim and several Christians —among those who made the beloved progressive satire *Charlie Hebdo* so très français. The death toll from *Charlie Hebdo* was twelve. Eight staff, one free-lancer, one visitor, a bodyguard and one policeman—recipients of retributive justice, Islamist style. The reasons for their murder ranged from protecting public safety to insulting Islam or being a Jew, but they had in common kufir status aka nonbeliever/Infidel so their guilt had already been established.

An estimated 100,000 spontaneous demonstrations occurred throughout France the next day followed by a Sunday march of an estimated 2.5 million in Paris led by sixty heads of state. Contrasting the left's assertions of media controlling Jewish Lobby, Poller offers evidence to the contrary, inferring the plangently unfair Palestinian bias dominates the mainstream with one intention in mind.

And when the Palestinians or assorted Iranian proxies launch military attacks against Israel, legitimate criticism switches to: excessive force, killing children, destroying property, starving civilians, committing war crimes and crimes against humanity. Take away these endlessly repeated barbs and what's left to say about Israel? Nothing. It doesn't exist in the popular imagination. Look squarely at this so-called legitimate criticism and it boils down to one thing: submit. Surrender to jihad. It's not legitimate criticism, it is the confluence of the underground spring and the over-arching jihad masterminds. It is an injunction aimed at leaving Israel as defenseless as a village in northern Nigeria or a Yazidi town in Syria. (p 142)

We share Nidra Poller's sense of betrayal when *L'Express* editor Christophe Barbier decries France's Jews for leaving. He and many Frenchmen seem to forget the Republic's decade's long failure to protect its Jewish citizens from Islamic-perpetrated assaults. This harassment, intimidation, bombings, rape, knifings, murder is not addressed by Barbier. Instead he brings a novel stroke of literary legerdemain, combining sociological blaming the victim with anti-Dreyfussard politics. By abandoning ship early, writes Barbier, you provide the enemy with the wrong information. This is treason—conduct unbecoming a Frenchman, and your fellow Frenchmen will grow more suspicious of Jews. Poller's interpretation is simpler. "French Jews shouldn't give in to fear, shouldn't run for safety to Israel, shouldn't clump together to defend themselves here and Israel there, shouldn't be too Jewish lest they be perceived as not enough French."

Poller deplores and distrusts those who start their arguments with "Israel has a right to defend itself but... Personne n'a le droit de l'accorder, ni de la nier, ni de la limiter"—Nobody has the right to grant or deny or limit Israel's right to self-defense. Noting that the French government can't seem to rescue its own society from a massive influx of "unqualified unsatisfied hostile immigrants," Nidra Poller asks and rightfully so— where is our collective dignity? "While the Caliphate is slicing, the world is waffling .... Instead of proclaiming that we're not going to put up with hostage taking and beheading anymore, world leaders are pushing Israel to take its daily rockets and turn the other cheek. But the beheaded can't turn the other cheek!"

When reading manuscripts, one might occasionally highlight a noteworthy passage here or there. In most cases, this occurs infrequently. But when reading Nidra Poller, you'll find a noteworthy passage on almost every page. Her innovative terms—lethal narrative, punk jihadis, caliphators— and her sardonic style have a way of entertaining one's mind, like bonbons while watching a good movie.

You have the opportunity to read a writer's writer cutting through mainstream news media obfuscation, denial, conciliatory fluff, and pointing her finger towards the disinformation and bias pervading the news accounts as she did in her *Al-Dura: Long Range Ballistic Myth*.

"Despair is a tribute to fatality," states Poller, "it is a misconception." She reminds us that "we have reached the tipping point and the tables can be turned." A few more Nidra Pollers and maybe we can wake from the social amnesia Apollo cast upon Cassandra and her followers.

Steven K Baum, Editor
Journal for the Study of Antisemitism
www.jsantisemitism.org

Chapter 1/ Prelude

FLASHBACK

January 2013

The graphics of jihad in its early days featured pyramids of severed heads of unbelievers who refused to submit to Islam. Though nothing proves this motif will not make a comeback, the outstanding feature of the jihad against Israel today is dead children. Not, of course, the dead Israeli children targeted individually or collectively by savage killers; they have no graphic value in the contemporary warscape. Dead children like Mohamed al Dura, "targeted by gunfire from the Israeli position," in the words of his so-to-speak godfather, *France 2* Jerusalem correspondent Charles Enderlin. Ashen dead children with squeaky clean cuddly toys gathered, who knows how, in Kfar Qana to form a barrage against Israeli forces in the aborted 2006 Lebanon incursion. Dead Syrian children recycled and launched against Israel in a crucial phase of the brief Pillar of Defense operation.

So far, no equivalent to the Iron Dome has been devised to protect the Jewish state from this weapon of mass destruction. Who can be blamed? Certainly not Israeli hasbara troops, pinned down by relentless fire from the media, academics, NGOs, the EU, the UN, and a Golem that goes by the name of International Opinion. Should Israel be blamed for not realizing what is hitting it when the whole free world sits dumbfounded on the sidewalk like evicted tenants as its precious values are hauled out and thrown into dumpsters?

The close up poster image of a man and a boy cringing in the face of non-existent gunfire disseminated as a news report on September 30, 2000 has left an indelible mark in the collective public mind. Totally divorced from any legitimate journalistic reality, the staged death scene is inextricably connected to a larger hoax—the "Second Intifada"—and in progressively widening circles to the peace process, the 2-state solution, the Mideast conflict, and intervening stages of a comprehensive attack against Israel and the West whose name is jihad. This is what I have described as the lethal narrative strategy of 21st century jihad.[1] Mistaken as familiar techniques such as propaganda and asymmetrical warfare, lethal narratives are operating with greater scope and deeper impact than anything that has been imagined. Attempts to deal separately with any particular "chapter" of the narrative are stumped by the interlocked force of the strategy as a whole. This is why, after years of analyzing the al Dura hoax and covering the legal battle fought by France 2 and Charles Enderlin against Philippe Karsenty, I have widened the field of my analysis.

Today, twelve years after the earth-shaking broadcast, the al Dura myth is back in the news. Its poisonous hatred flowed through the bloodstream of France's latest Jew-killer, Mohamed Merah, who introduced the gruesome video of his murder spree with a selection of images of dead Palestinian children. The al Dura "news report" figures of course in this justification of his evil acts. They kill our children [Israelis in "Palestine"], I kill their children [Jews in Toulouse].

In a Canal + broadcast aired shortly after the Merah murders, French-Congolese slammer Rost unashamedly pulls out the al Dura card. His description of the scene—"the boy is shot up right before our eyes"—faithfully reproduces the narrative that effectively overrides the total absence of visual evidence. Those who have viewed Merah's horrifying reality show can testify that the visual evidence is, on the contrary, overwhelming.

6

Another aspiring jihadi, the French-Congolese Yann Nkusa, arrested with his mates in October 2012, is also reported to have a video of Palestinian child victims (of Israeli cruelty of course) in his film library. Yasser Arafat's widow Suha just calmly announced that her husband planned and implemented the "2nd intifada" after the failure of the Camp David talks in the summer of 2000. Did this give rise to a cascade of reevaluations? Did the Mitchell Commission reconvene to revise its attribution of shared responsibility for the allegedly spontaneous popular uprising? Was there any squeak from the journalistic choir that has been weaving and embroidering and packaging and selling its twisted tales ever since? Has the revelation stimulated any curiosity about its broad implications? If it has, I must have missed it. So let me do the heavy lifting for all the lazy minds.

The intifada was not planned in a one-line memo to three trusted collaborators. It was planned like what it is: jihad. One of many such jihad campaigns disguised in one of an inexhaustible wardrobe of costumes. Charles Enderlin is fond of asking how the Palestinians could concoct a staged scene in the midst of a fierce gun battle. Now it is our turn to ask how Arafat could concoct a jihad-intifada without engaging his troops and putting his executives to work on specific projects... such as the al Dura scene. When I began to catch on to how this strategy works, I made a guess at who was the direct mastermind of this al Dura hoax: Marwan Barghouti. I stick to that guess today. The strategy was immediately apparent: manipulate children—in fact youths— bringing them to the front lines, crafting the image of the courageous little stone thrower facing down Nazified Israeli tanks and heavily uniformed soldiers. Armed men hiding behind the youths fired at Israeli soldiers that, sooner or later, had to return fire. Youths fell and these casualties were transformed into high power weapons. This is something far more vicious than human shields. Every political encounter meant to bring a halt to the violence was torpedoed by the dead-children weapon. Palestinian officials and so-called negotiators claimed they could not quell the popular violence because x number of children had been killed. Meanwhile, more children were placed on the firing line and Arafat was already claiming that the Palestinian children would march and fight and fall and march until they would take Jerusalem.

The staged al Dura scene was the keystone of this combat strategy. It established, before the fact, direct unambiguous Israeli responsibility for the deaths that would be tallied as conclusive proof of Israeli and, by extension, Jewish guilt. Charles Enderlin didn't hesitate to use this argument, giving the figures of subsequent deaths as validation of the authenticity of the al Dura scene. The emotional shock of the staged scene created the myth whose power obscured the sordid reality of the "2nd Intifada" Islamic war.

In a rational world, the failure of the Camp David talks, initially and correctly attributed to Yasser Arafat, would have put an end to the peace process illusion. But the al Dura hoax filled TV screens, filled the public mind, filled the landscape from top to bottom and obscured the ineluctable reality of the Oslo fiasco. Still today, dead children are used to abort self-defense operations and, on a regular basis, to maintain the negative image of Israel. The peace process illusion is still covering up the reality, Israel is still blamed for the failure to create a Palestinian state and, as with the al Dura video itself, no amount of hard evidence can change that configuration.

And our *résistance*? How are we doing? To put it kindly, we are learning. Gradually. But time is running out. Confronted with a global strategy operating on so many levels with such a variety of tactics, we have not yet devised an adequate strategy. Rather than criticize others, I am trying to refine my own. I think the only objective that can succeed is to convince the majority of citizens in democratic nations that they have the means to be informed, to recognize their own interests, resist, and prevail. The barrier that separates them from those means is not impenetrable. If, however, the goal is to demonstrate their ignorance and ill will, there is no chance of convincing them.

If the *résistance* is organized with a romanticized commando mentality harking back to other times, if it turns into a self-perpetuating merry go round of commentary, we won't reach the people who have the power to reverse the dangerous trend.

ATTACKING ISRAEL WITH GENOCIDAL INTENTIONS

25 July 2012

From the first stirrings of Judaism to the present day the war against the Jews has been pursued with variations in methods, scope, and intensity. It would be foolish to sum up in a few sentences the brilliant work of a host of thinkers who have analysed this process and examined its underlying causes. We can no more ignore their thought than rest on their conclusions. We have to integrate their wisdom into fresh thinking based on the contemporary situation. What stands in the way of an early twenty-first century genocide of the Jews? Compared to the previous genocide, Jews today are healthier, wealthier, and wiser. Honest human beings the world over are sincerely horrified by the Shoah and more or less aware of the dangers of a repetition. The democratic nations in which the Diaspora lives in relative peace and prosperity are well-armed to defend themselves against attack and the Jews against potential exterminators. But all of these safeguards would crumble if not for the State of Israel.

Therefore, one could say with near scientific precision that the State of Israel stands between the Jews and a twenty-first century genocidal plot. How clever, then, to labour away at destroying Israel while denying the slightest anti-Semitic intentions. The range of weapons is limitless. The combinations are devilish. A peace process seasoned with Intifadas, martyrdom operations coupled with invocations of international law, humanitarian flotillas armed to the teeth, rocket attacks in tandem with UN recognition bids, and of course the construction of a tight-knit international network of sympathizers extending from the grassroots to the halls of power. While Israel's neighbours pound away at its existence, Muslims in Europe and the Americas blithely attack Jews to 'avenge' their Palestinian 'brothers'. Again, freedom to harm Jews has been granted along with immunity from the anti-Semite label. Domestic and foreign enemies of the Jews collaborate to conduct attacks that terrorize large populations into granting whatever is demanded in the name of Islam, Palestine, peace, and adulterated civil rights. The leavening agent of this recipe is a compound of the good, obtained by a reverse chemistry that transforms the moral lessons of the Holocaust into the amoral values by which Jews can once more be pursued and exterminated.

In the name of the good, Jews can be harassed on university campuses, elbowed out of professional and commercial activities, vilified in lowbrow and highbrow media, abandoned to thugs and murderers and, conversely, glorified if they outspokenly reject Israel. Cartoonists win prizes with Nazi style caricatures where Jews are recycled as Israelis. Arab-Muslim intellectuals are invited to speak in high places and given tenure in prestigious universities for justifying the persecution of Jews identified as Israelis. Outreach operations promote the narrative that Jews, Christians, and Muslims are mutually guilty of/victims of prejudice. Idealists wave the coexist banner. People of all colours and creeds can live together harmoniously as long as the Jews turn their backs on the outlaw state of Israel – under its present government, of course. The genocidal plot aims to divide and conquer: divide Diaspora Jews from Israel, Israeli Jews from their government, Israelis living inside the green line from 'colonists,' and so on.

Here and there, the 'evils of Zionism' give permission to break the post-Auschwitz taboo and stir up old-fashioned anti-Semitic stereotypes. The hue and cry against Wall Street speculators and billionaires names emblematic targets of Jew hatred that would be unleashed if the bulwark of Israel were ever to collapse.

Nevertheless it is counterproductive to label as 'anti-Semitism' the will to destroy the State of Israel by all means possible and impossible. On the one hand this old vocabulary that we have not been able to update leads to outdated reactions and outworn strategies; on the other, it drags into dead-end debate with a new kind of enemy that will swear to the heavens and to the end of time 'I am not an anti-Semite.' Furthermore, with or without the hyphen, the term implies that it has something to do with being against Jews. Does it?

Yes and no. The genocidal plot is not a reaction to the evil deeds or noble acts of Israel or the Jews, but to the notion of the good upheld by Judaism. Ironically, the irrepressible impulse to commit genocide without hindrance from the prohibition inscribed in Judaic values leads to the hatching of genocidal plots against the Jews. In common language this would be: get out of my way so I can really do what I am falsely accusing you of doing.

This brings us full circle to the comprehensive programme – the will to destroy life – of which the destruction of Israel by specious arguments is an essential but partial element. Only when we have perceived the outer reaches of this project can we understand and combat its concrete on-the-ground manifestations. Otherwise we assume a defensive position that feeds the animosity directed against us. Rather, we should take heart from the fact that the genocidal plot is not moving forward as quickly as planned. Neither armed invasion, nor shahid operations, nor subversion, nor BDS (Boycott, Divestment, Sanctions), nor the combined forces of the United Nations General Assembly have come anywhere near to defeating Israel. Israel is flourishing. The genocidal plot persists, however, in a hair trigger configuration: an Iranian nuclear weapon over Israel's head, and a detriment to all humanity. We have to dismantle it.

What should be done with the specious arguments used to attack Israel? They are no more valid than the ones used to attack the Jews over the centuries. And yet we seem to be fooled every time into answering lies with facts. Not that the facts are worthless. On the contrary, they are helpful to those who defend Israel, the Jews, and civilized values. When used, however, to counter destructive lies they paradoxically give weight to the accusations. Reasonable arguments inadvertently imply that there might be some truth to the accusation, and lead to quibbling over details. Since the accusers have no scruples, they will twist every single detail, constantly adding weight to the lie, never answering any objection, never conceding a point, and eventually slamming a door in the Zionist's face: 'It's impossible to discuss anything with you, you're an unconditional supporter of Likud and the colonists. So what's the solution? Do you want to kill all the Palestinians?'

The lies – I call them 'lethal narratives' – have kinship with earlier versions of Jew hatred: 'Israel stole the land from the Palestinians' functions in the same way as 'the Jews killed Christ'. No number of historical documents, deeds, multi-coloured maps, or population statistics can make a dent in that argument because, like the Christ-killer accusation, it is essential, not circumstantial. 'Stole the land' defines Israel. It does not stand upright as a three-dimensional reality which one could examine by going behind it, around it, underneath it.

'Israel is an apartheid state' does not mean that Israel treats Arab-Muslim-Palestinians like South Africa treated Blacks. It means the Israelis, who are intruders, can be forced by BDS to hand over power to the rightful inhabitants of Palestine. A few years ago a French journalist reporting from Israel translated a shabat elevator for haredim into an apartheid elevator reserved for Blacks. The whole rubbish heap of Israel apartheid charges is of the same low quality, and its long term success is not guaranteed. Israel Apartheid Week (IAW) was nipped in the bud this year in France. The major event, a colloquium scheduled at the Université de Paris 8, a hotbed of Palestinianism a stone's throw from the sky-scrapers of La Défense, was cancelled by the president, Pascal Binczak, on the grounds that the organization could not ensure public order on campus and did not respect the 'intellectual and scientific independence of the university where the pluralism of scientific and critical approaches and free analytic debate must be seen as intangible academic obliga-tions.'[1] Efraim Karsh penned a head-on collision for the IAW slander convoy.[2] The 15 April 2012 Flytilla was grounded, provoking outrage on the French BDS site *Europalestine.org*, where the intention to defeat the 'illegitimate' state of Israel is broadcast in every way, shape, and form. When the Bienvenu en Palestine operation was thwarted, the organiza-tion accused European airlines, police, and military of collaborating (as in 'Vichy collaborators') with the Israeli secret services to deny them their rights – to go to Bethlehem and inaugurate a school. The move-ment invents international laws to condemn Israel, flouts French law that prohibits their anti-Israel boycotts, and denies the existence of in-ternational law that allows sovereign nations to require visas, establish no-fly lists, and requires airlines to repatriate unwanted passenger at the airline's expense. Duly informed that their reservations were cancelled, the Flytillistas publicly promised to cause trouble at the airports, then shrieked when met by law enforcement. Their real intention is to erase Israel's borders and strangle its sovereignty by inventing a sovereign Palestine whose borders can be defined by will or whimsy. The geopoliti-cal fait accompli of the designation 'Palestine' is reinforced by the ex-citement it offers, as if it were a new sexual organ promising unspeakable orgasms.

These ugly lies are best countered with the contempt they deserve. Much progress has been made in this direction over the past 12 years. Israel is increasingly skilled at deflecting barrages of inflammatory alle-gations. The more Israel shows itself to be indifferent to false charges – responding sharply in international instances, deflating ludicrous accu-sations with lively humour,[3] repelling stunts like the Million March to

Jerusalem, fighting back against 'humanitarians' armed to the teeth, exposing the hypocrisy of UN organizations – the less harm they can do. Though they will always subsist in the shadows, morph into endless variations, sustain the image of Israel as the Bad Guy, and stand ready to poison the atmosphere and justify violence against Jews when the occasion arises.

Ugly lies are a danger but beautiful lies are far more dangerous and difficult to counter. Ugly lies are the meat and potatoes of mean people who want to do bad deeds. They don't really care about Palestinians; they aren't really shocked by the plight of Muslims; they have no noble values to honour. But beautiful lies are a treasure held dear by masses of well-meaning people. Anyone who dares to challenge the beautiful lie of the peace process risks being relegated to the margins of public discourse, branded 'extremist' by some, accused of war crimes by others, shunned by prestigious colleagues and editors. Why should commentators or political leaders bring opprobrium on their heads by declaring that the two-state solution is just as false as 'Israel is an apartheid state' or 'the Jews killed Christ'? Since there is no chance of a Palestinian state being established in the near future it may seem easier to give lip service to the two-state solution and get on with one's career. This isn't cynical. It's a strategic choice. But I will argue that it is harmful.

The purpose of the peace process is to make war against Israel by demonstrating that Israel doesn't want peace. The term 'peace process' is a semantically self-justifying trick that confounds 'peace process' with the ways that peace can effectively be made in the real world. It follows that if Israel won't accept the terms of the process, then it is the obstacle to peace. That failure is the success of the process. The proof is that Palestinian rejection of the process is not defined as an obstacle but as further justification for placing the blame on Israel. By virtue of the peace process, certain Jewish neighbourhoods are declared to be illegal because they are located in 'occupied' territories. International law is invoked like a pagan god to bellow flames on the illegal occupiers and reduce them to ashes. Those who accept the principle of a Palestinian state living peacefully side by side with Israel on secure borders are considered to be moderates. Ostensibly free to debate details, modalities, and timing, they are in fact sucked up into 'the solution that everyone knows': retreat to the 1967 borders adjusted by land swaps, division of

Jerusalem, and solution of the refugee problem. The more obvious it has become that none of this could, should, or will happen, the more the solution is reiterated. Another massive block of affirmation that cannot be examined from all or any sides.

What is the role of the peace process in the twenty-first century genocidal project as compared to the earlier version, the Shoah that we have recently commemorated? It functions like the series of proto-legalistic measures that gradually stripped European Jews of their rights, their strengths, and their capacity to resist extermination. How many people would have obeyed the laws and decrees if they knew where they were being led? Register as a Jew or you'll be arrested, leave your profession, turn over your company to an Aryan, turn in your radio, pick up your Jewish badge and sew it on your clothes or you'll be jailed, stay out of the parks and libraries, come with us or you'll be shot... Every step was legalized; the documents drafted in beautiful old-fashioned bureaucratic penmanship are lined up on the walls of Holocaust Memorials like the sharp teeth of man-eating beasts.

Today's equivalent measures are: respect international law, end the illegal occupation, surrender your sovereignty and life-saving protection, create the Palestinian state that will exterminate you, don't make us attack you, do it to yourselves.

Heads of state who have no desire to see the Jewish people exterminated periodically promise to roll up their sleeves and get the peace process going. They assure us that this time the solution that everyone knows will finally prevail. Jews who definitely do not want to be massacred or see their Israeli brethren exterminated reiterate their devotion to the peace process and, too often, grab Israel by the ear and scold it for not making the painful concessions that will, as everyone knows, bring peace.

Does this mean that Jewish survival depends on convincing the multitudes that the peace process is in fact a war and the friendly criticism of Israel fosters a genocidal project? How? What hasn't been tried yet? How do we break the stranglehold? Deny that there is a plot to exterminate the Jews and all the humanism seems to fall on the other side of the equation. You sound heartless if you say you don't want a Palestinian state. You sound alarmist if you say Israel is facing an existential threat and Jews everywhere will be in danger if Israel can't resist. You sound pretentious if you say the survival of the free world depends on Israel. European Jews of the World War II generation are often torn between gratitude for the decisive American intervention that defeated Nazism and disappointment with the failure, in their eyes, of American Jews to pressure their government to specifically target the killing machine, to bomb Auschwitz. In fact, Jews in those days were not far removed from their greenhorn origins, subject to domestic anti-Semitism, quota systems, and other forms of discrimination. Now comfortably rich, powerful, and well-integrated, many American Jewish citizens, leaders, and donors seem to take pride in their 'independence' from Israel. They believe that gay marriage, abortion rights, and redistribution of wealth are the crucial issues of our times, the moral slide-rule by which we should be judged. Eschewing partisan support of Israel, they reach out to defend Muslims, designated as victims of prejudice and discrimination.

While Israel's score in popularity polls soars in the United States, voters chose a president whose hostility to Israel was already revealed during the Democratic primaries, later demonstrated in the Cairo speech, and repeatedly displayed in policies and attitude thereafter. The president's popularity among Jewish voters is reportedly still flying high, undisturbed by a foreign policy that belies his claim to 'have Israel's back'. (The phony street talk betrays the speaker.) The disparity between the popularity of Israel and enduring support for an anti-Zionist president demonstrates once more the complexity of the genocidal plot. Americans love Israel in a t-shirt kind of way. What becomes of this puppy love when, as it seems, citizens and their representatives are unable or unwilling to influence the administration's bizarre approach to Iran – an outstretched hand and blindfolded eyes? Iran is given all the elbow room it needs to develop the genocidal weapon par excellence, the *New York Times* leaks Israeli war plans like a divinely ordained blabber, and Israel's best friends speak in enigmas: an Iranian bomb would be a disaster, an Israeli attack will be a catastrophe. Or vice versa.

How did we, at this crucial time, lose America? From the first Democratic primaries, at the end of 2007, the protective shield formed around the candidate Barack Hussein Obama was respected by mainstream and, with rare exceptions, alternative media. Criticism of the candidate was muted, understated, or censored. Reliable information about Obama's anti-Zionist ideas and friends was suppressed by the mainstream and diluted by the alternatives. The tyrannical mode was in place from the very beginning. No one wanted to offend unconditional Obama supporters among the readership and benefactors. Everyone was afraid of being called a 'racist'.

The rise of anti-Semitism in Europe in the past decade was misinterpreted as a replay of the 1930s and 1940s. Europe was going rotten again. Jews should immigrate en masse to the United States. Not to Israel? No, they considered Israel too dangerous. Europe was finished, collaborating once again with the Nazis, this time in an Islamist version. The images were telling: torched synagogues, battered rabbis, smashed windows, murdered Jews, swastikas. While attention was focused on the fall of Europe into its final episode of anti-Semitism, Muslim Brotherhood front organizations in suits and ties were weaving their web in the vast United States of America. Today, Jewish organizations are swimming like little fish into the nets cast by CAIR (Council on American–Islamic Relations) and its multiple front organizations. Paradoxically, the tons of garish anti-Zionist garbage dumped in Europe since September 2000 has mobilized some European Jews, particularly in France, to greater vigilance and stronger defence of Israel, while the honeyed chants of the Brotherhood are lulling American Jewry into self-destructive outreach and cosy ecumenism. (Not to suggest that we are totally immune to this kind of thing.) It is not a question of transatlantic competition but of lucidity. The misconception that the United States is a refuge today as it was in the days of Nazism weakens support for Israel and lulls American Jews into a false sense of security. If an analogy must be made, could the US be compared to Germany in the 1920s?

Above and beyond the ugly lies and the beautiful lies is the ultimate lie: blood libel. The Jews as Christ-killers are child-killers (Christ as the child of God). The Muhammad al-Dura scene broadcast by state-owned France 2 TV on 30 September 2000, has functioned as blood libel on an international scale in the age of instant mass communication. A fabrication purporting to show a Palestinian youth killed in real time by Israeli soldiers opened the floodgates to a torrent of Jew hatred buoyed up by and justified by merciless criticism of the state of Israel. The Dura controversy has come forward once again in France, in the aftermath of the

2012 murders at Ozar Hatorah school in Toulouse. Muhammad Merah's declaration that he was avenging the killing of children in Gaza was mentioned, among other information, but did not resonate as it would have just a few years ago. France 2's Jerusalem correspondent Charles Enderlin, responsible for the Dura broadcast, has as usual leapt to his own defence and reiterated against all evidence the accusation that the boy was killed and the shots were fired from the Israeli position. Filmmaker Pierre Rehov, who was one of the first to contest the Dura broadcast, reminds us in a forceful open letter to Charles Enderlin that he interviewed the Israeli soldiers who manned the checkpoint on the day of the alleged incident.[4] They happen to be Druze. It does not make them any the less Jewish child-killers for the blood libel.

The polite dismissal of Israel by a cocktail of harsh criticism, snide remarks, inflammatory images, twisted documentaries, EU statements and UN resolutions is amplified by a chorus of crude Jew hatred from an Islamic world in a state of paroxysm. The revolt or reform (as in Salafist return to the origins) billed as the 'Arab Spring' is a retrograde movement leading to the domination of parties with different names and similar platforms based on the imposition of sharia law. Accomplished with elaborate scenarios in the Maghreb and Mashrek and brutally in sub-Saharan Africa it has met with determined resistance in Syria, where Bashar Assad's forces have killed an estimated 11,000 Syrians, most of them civilians. The international community that stamps its feet and throws its weight around when Israel is involved has by turns entreated, pleaded, summoned, ordered, requested Assad to put an end to the killing. The hallowed United Nations expressed all forms of consternation, named an emissary, brokered a truce of sorts, and is now sending in unarmed blue-helmeted observers. Turkey reprimanded, the Arab League finger-wagged, the ECOWAS (Economic Community of West African States) threatened to send troops and President Assad is still there, doing what comes naturally. No one expects him to respond to human rights arguments.

Why would we be defeated by an enemy that is militarily, technologically, and intellectually weak, disorganized, and torn with internecine strife – an enemy that wherever it exerts its dominion has nothing good to offer its people? The only way we could be defeated is if we act as if the decision is not in our hands. We will not prevail by stretching our necks to the outermost reaches and convincing the inveterate Jew hater to change his ways, but by reaching inside ourselves and forging the utmost conviction of our right to live and prosper, forging it with such fire and light that it gradually ignites those closest to us and in an ever widening circle reaches the misguided.

The lightning speed of information offers advantages that no other generation enjoyed. The lapse of time between the premise and the conclusion is so brief, the facts are in, the tricks are unmasked, the pros and cons worked out in real time in concrete reality; we have the discourse, the debate, and the consequences in a bit more than a tweet. That's why we can do what has not been done before. We have a nation, a land, an army, and the information needed to stymie the genocidal plot.

What will calm the ardour of the genociders is not painful concessions, apologies, admissions of guilt, bending over backward to mollify critics, giving 10% credit to ugly lies and heart-sinking validity to the beautiful 'everyone knows the solution' lie; no, what throws ice-cold water on the genociders is when Israel stands firm, strikes when attacked, and strikes pre-emptively when existentially threatened, fulfilling the promise of a land of refuge and fulfilment for the Jewish people and throwing the hatred back where it came from, back to the dark hearts of those who want to kill Jews so they can destroy humanity. Western civilization is not lost, it is staggering. As Jews we have a responsibility to defend ourselves so that free people everywhere can rediscover the courage to defend their freedom and highest values. That is the upright humanitarian position that reaches out to all decent human beings. It is not the phony outreach posture of throwing ourselves into the jaws of the purveyors of sharia.

Clean up the static, and the blood-curdling cry rings out loud and clear: Kill the Jews! Some think it is nothing but background noise. It's a question of fine-tuning.

— *Israel Affairs Volume 18, Issue 3, 2012*

DEATH LAG

7 July 2014

Keeping love company, I was watching the France-Nigeria soccer match that evening ... as my mind wandered from Boko Haram to the next game—if Algeria beats Germany and then gets eliminated by France in the next round, they'll make an all-out bash... on our heads. Between two matches —between two wars— I dipped into my inbox. Breaking news from *Metula News Agency*. "They are dead." All three. Eyal Yifrah, Gilad Shaar, Naftali Frenkel. When were they killed? Last week journalists on *i24 News* remarked a shift in official declarations: authorities say they are doing everything possible to find the kidnappers ...not the kids. Two weeks ago at a UPJF event, Gladys Tibby admitted with tears in her voice that one of the boys— they don't know which one— was dead. Now we learn that their hasty execution was recorded right after the phone call to the police. "I've been kidnapped." Followed by murderous Arab voices! Gunshots! Moans. Happy killers rejoicing. "Three!" The parents knew already. That's how it's done in Israel. They had all the evidence. But hope against hope prevailed. You don't mourn the living.

Eighteen days. A whole nation lived and breathed with the anguished parents. Emmanuel Navon wrote: "It could have been my kids."[1] Yes, I had thought of my Efrat family ... without realizing that two of them are adolescents now. The French press was busy as usual separating us from our humanity. Children delivered up to the savagery of wild beasts became *colons* [colonizers]. Youths devoted to their studies were dismissed as "*colons* going to school in occupied territory." This world that doesn't know how to draw a red line between barbarity and civilization delights in drawing green lines to hide the forest of sharpened trees aimed at us.

Sébastien Sélam, slaughtered and mutilated in the underground garage of his building in the 10th arrondissement of Paris by his Muslim neighbor. With what accomplices and what complicity? Ilan Halimi kidnapped, tortured for 24 days in a Parisian banlieue in the heart of a project subsidized by French taxpayers in a territory occupied by worthless brutes and heartless onlookers. Myriam Monsonego, Jonathan Sandler, his sons Arieh and Gabriel executed by Mohamed Merah in Toulouse, France. What side of the green line is Toulouse, Messieurs the surveyors? Emanuel and Miriam Riva, Dominique Sabrier, Alexandre Strens, shot by Mehdi Nemmouche who has only one regret: the bummed out GoPro didn't immortalize his *beau geste*. Who are they? Adel Amastaibou, Fofana et cie, Merah, Nemmouche? Noble *Gaulois* defending the fatherland?

We stumble from the special edition on *i24 News* to the Germany-Algeria match. I size up the shape and volume of Salafist beards, coldly dismiss Algerian agility, just wondering if their fans here in our occupied French cities will torch more or fewer cars if they lose instead of winning. No infidels and just one Black, the superstar bearded goalie, on the Maghrebi team. They leave us the benefits of diversity and snuggle up with their own. As for me, I'm counting on those sturdy Germans. Forgive and forget *achtung*, give us *blitzkrieg* tonight.

Last stop at my inbox before lights out. A message from X, who watched the game in a café in a city somewhere in the south of France morphed into the north of the Maghreb: "I left before the game was over." *Ouf*!

Soccer genius Lionel Messi lifted his jersey to show a ≠*Bring Back our Boys* t-shirt. No echo from Michelle Obama. Her United States President Husband calls for restraint on all sides. Hamas threatens to open the gates of hell if Israel dares to react with anything more than a whimper to the execution of the "three *colons*." *Ah bon*? I didn't know hell's gates had ever been closed in the territories occupied by Hamas. Meanwhile Boko Haram merrily pursues its danse macabre—miscellaneous kidnapping, barbecues of Christians in their churches, fresh bombs in colorful markets... The spectacular grab of 200 girls is old news, the hashtaggers discarded their look-at-me cause like clothes donated to charity. Don't be too hard on them. Just understand why we Jews are not a dish for compassionate consumption.

The world followed the World Cup; the mothers of the kidnapped youths went to Geneva to plead their case before a sneering UN Human Rights Commission. Elsewhere, interminable talks are giving Iran all the space-time needed to perfect its nuclear arsenal. 2,400 dead in Iraq in June. How many thousands added to the toll in Syria, spiraling up to 200,000? The caliphate, straddling Syria and Iraq, has the hots for Jordan, raging to get its sting into the heart of Israel while the democratically elected president of my native land, a double triple friend of the Muslim Brotherhood, churns up devious isolationism that reaches all the way to the anti-jihad contingent. Let them kill each other! It's not our problem, we have no business butting in, what nonsense, thinking you could give them democracy like you give flour to the starving (then again it ends up on the black market).

Americans, we're told, are tired of war. And Europeans? They can't stomach it. That's why French troops, truly engaged in Mali and the Central African Republic, are invisible to the general public. It's crazy how our media can hide a regiment behind the dumb blonde smile of an anchoress, behind the false face of an amoral press corps.

Israeli soldiers just a few years older than the kidnapped kids are dispatched to search for them. The population, like one conglomerated Jewish mother, mobilizes to bring the soldiers some comfort— lasagnas, tooth brushes, a clean bed in a spare room. We see, in passing, the well-equipped comfortable homes of Hebron's Muslims. We don't find the teenagers— at the time we hoped they were still alive— but we discover that Hamas has a foothold in Hebron, where 800 stubborn Jews sojourn among a hundred thousand Arabs. Extremists! Who? Arabs laboring for the total destruction of the State of Israel and the extermination of the Jews? No, the "extremists" are Jews who believe the cave of Machpela, paid in full, is all ours (even though we share it with the Muslims). Arms caches, tunnels, basements, and computers are searched or seized. The father of one of the kidnappers, Marwan Kawasme, reigns over a clan of 10,000 Hamasniks.

This isn't about double standards; it's about no standards. Even a journalist should know how to get the whole picture. Instead, they block the light. Mahmoud Abbas condemns the kidnapping [official PA media delight in it], his security forces work shoulder to shoulder with the Israelis [his propaganda forces publish a cartoon of three rats branded with the *magen David* hanging from a fishing line]. Mahmoud Abbas [who has recently formed a national union government with Hamas] warns the Israelis against collective punishment. The American government, the UN, the EU [that had applauded this promising reunification] let it be understood that their patience is limited. Military boots stomping through homes, mass arrests, baseless accusations [dixit the families of the culprits], and then these muffled threats against Hamas or worse, against the entire population of Gaza and the West Bank, all that fuss over three *colons*, it's getting to be a bit too much.

It would take more than a whole lifetime to tell the story of one single life, even the life of a 16 year-old. Infinitude of small acts, solicitude of every instant from conception onward, all day every day, the warmth, the light of a human being, his miraculous singularity, the physiology of a living being and the millions of signs scrutinized by a studious *yeshiva bocher*, the heart to heart that binds us, the rhythms and the music of hope in flesh and bones... annihilated in one single gunshot. Instantly. Evil, armed, acts, pam! Straight line from the diabolical plan to its fulfillment. We can't do anything about it. Retroactively.

Then, by ricochet, comes a different murder that tears us from our foundations.

Hope, disappointment, the atrocious announcement, support from a nation united as one family, the nobility of the bereaved, the winding-sheet, the lifeless body, the kaddish... We know how to do all that.

A Muslim youth. From Jerusalem. Kidnapped. Assassinated. It could be an act of vengeance.

Committed by Jews.

No! Not that. Not a stupid filthy deed.

No.

We pray it's not that.

Unverifiable information is circulating. It could be an honor killing ... there are precedents... Burned? No, a Jew wouldn't do that.

9-11 July 2014

We tried so hard to put it together with the al Dura affair, the Torah, codified Islamic honor killings, but the truth is implacable. Mohamed Abu Kheidr was burned alive. The one or ones who did it are not characters from a work in progress. They exist. We grit our teeth and read, "The police suspect a nationalist crime." Equals: the perpetrators are Jews.

It's unbearable. Why? Not because of a posture of moral superiority, not because of a guilt complex. It's unbearable because Judaism is not a historical monument, it's not an edifice, it's a system of values that lives by the active commitment renewed with each breath by Jews in flesh and bones, each one totally responsible.

Jews grab a 16 or 17 year-old Muslim Israeli, knock him out, sprinkle him, and set him on fire and it's supposed to be vengeance for the death of three Jewish Israelis kidnapped and assassinated? Don't believe it. It's a pretext. Like those Arab or Palestinian Israelis that throw rocks and firebombs at the police, vandalize streets, buildings, and tramway stations in Jerusalem, smashing the rails put there to include them in the collectivity, and it's all motivated by the murder of the young Abu

Kheidr? That touches them to the core? More likely thrilled at the chance to explode in destructive energy.

But what was cousin Tariq doing in this mess? The American cousin, beat up by Israeli policemen—the video proves it, if it's really him. Really bashed, that's for sure. With his swollen face and black eyes, he testifies: " I wasn't doing anything, just watching, that's all, the police came running, I tried to escape, they caught me, beat me senseless, I woke up in the hospital." His American as apple pie mother in hijab adds: "The Israelis do it every day to Palestinians, and they can't get lawyers, they can't defend themselves. I want it to be known: what my son endured is inflicted on Palestinians day in and day out." Tariq is a student at the Universal Academy of Florida, an Islamic school connected to the Tampa Bay Islamic Center, a notorious foothold of the CAIR/Hamas/ Muslim Brotherhood persuasion. How did the typical American boy who came in June to visit family in Israel feel about the tragic murder of his cousin? We're not told. They are about the same age and look like twins. According to the police, the American was running with a gang that attacked them. Two of his buddies were armed with knives, Tariq was using a slingshot, he ignored a warning ... Whatever the case may be, our young Tariq, who plays on the Tampa Bay Islamic Society team that sports the colors of CAIR = Hamas= Muslim Brotherhood, considers himself an innocent victim of notorious Israeli brutality. Equals= I have the right to promote your extermination; you don't have the right to touch a hair on my head.

In fact, no, they weren't "price to pay" activists, not right wing or hilltop extremists... the guys who savagely murdered Mohamed Abu Khdeir are "soccer hooligans." One week later their forfeit became the Kristallnacht of the planned extermination of the Palestinians. What team does Mahmoud Abbas, whose official media accuse Israel of genocide, play on? Genocide is 37 killed in Gaza, almost all of them *mujahidin* and their kin. They're already starting to throw logs on the fire— children of Gaza happy to die to protect the home of a Hamas chief. Not really to protect the house. Proof: it was destroyed. The purpose is to unleash a well-oiled scenario. Incursion, kidnapping, murder, rain of rockets, promise of final solution; then some losses on the side of the aggressors that scream bloody murder, appeal to the international community, the UN, demanding the immediate imposition of a ceasefire

...that will give them the deserved victory. Our harbingers of peace tweet-tweet "political solution" while their scavengers toss an enormous black winding sheet stamped with the *allahu akbar* logo over our heads and invite the international instances to grab the other end.

They are preparing a massacre. Are we ready? Do we have a rhetorical iron dome to shield us from their lethal narrative? Remember Qfar Qana in 2006? They need a battalion of dead children to rev up the machine of imposed surrender. You have to understand that we are still in the al Dura sphere of influence. Palestinian children unearthed, buried alive in a Hamas HQ, dragged in from other battlefields, from Syria, Iraq, a jackpot of dead children will be poured on the screen. We'll have to climb over them and pursue the defensive operation.

We, who follow the confrontation closely but from a distance, resist the temptation to scream at every barb of disinformation. Mildly pleased to note that our French media are not bursting with enthusiasm for the Hamasian cause this time. The "Arab Spring" has come and gone, jihad has entered the vocabulary, the beheaders are bursting out all over, the shadow of the caliphate dampens giddy orientalism, European jihadis back from the slaughterhouse are breathing down our necks and everyone knows that Jews are not their only prey. So let's not waste energy pointing out the media howlers one by one. And Israeli leaders should turn a deaf ear to the siren calls of the "international community."

Because, if I'm not mistaken, the dike has already broken. A little visit on the third day of the operation (July 10th) to the bright lights of *Sky News*, the *BBC*, *France 24*, *LCP* ... the threshold of tolerance is crossed. Of course Israel has the right to defend itself, but not like that! *Get the garbage bags ready, yahud, we're going to make mincemeat of you.* Oops, that's a Palestinian voice. We're looking for sobs. The dead and the wounded. All civilians, all innocent. Ah, here they are. What a relief. We are finally on familiar ground. You're strong, Israel, you have that iron dome. Will you please get your hands off those poor disarmed occupied Palestinians!

Muslims go to pray in their mosque on Temple Mount—their religious rights protected by the State of Israel— then walk out on the esplanade by the hundreds to rejoice in the show of rockets fired on Jerusalem from the Gaza Strip. After the iron dome we need a giant vacuum cleaner that will suck them up, whoosh, and drop them gently ...in Aleppo, for example.

The friends of my friends are there, my friends are the target of rockets, their children, their grandchildren are massed on the border ready to move into the hell of Gaza, my family is there, the grown children of my French friends are there, my memories are there, the hospitality, the meals, human warmth, warm sun, *nuit blanche* in Tel Aviv, shabbat in Jerusalem, conferences, conversations, gardens, the delicious intelligence of fine minds, open air weddings, dinner on the terrace, the hills of Judea, dead sea and more-than-alive people, how can I help you now?

We depend on you. You are the democracy of all democracies. It's not "the Palestinians" bearing down on you, it's jihad.

The Syria-Iraq caliphate will be the Gaza of the Western World.

ANTI-ISRAEL PROTESTERS ATTACK PARIS SYNAGOGUES
July 15, 2014

Traditionally French people dance in the streets and fire stations on the eve of the Quatorze Juillet, known in English as Bastille Day. This year, however, anti-Israel demonstrators took control of the monument in the center of the Bastille circle on Sunday, brandishing Palestinian flags and cardboard replicas of scimitars and Kassam rockets. Described in *AFP* releases as a well-mannered demonstration except for a few incidents, it was in fact a hate-fest against Israel and the Jews. "Death to the Jews," "Murderous Israel," "One Jew Some Jews All Jews are Terrorists" figured loudly among the slogans hurled by kefiyyeh-clad marchers.

According to the police, the 7,000 demonstrators (organizers claimed 30,000) started in the northern quartier of Barbès, which has a large African and Maghrebi population, and marched to the Bastille, where they remained for several hours. A small contingent started to attack the police, and was quickly brought under control. At the same time, hundreds of protesters raced up rue de la Roquette [street of the rocket] and surrounded the Don Isaac Abravanel[1] synagogue, which is protected by a tall metal gate. Security guards from the SPCJ (Service de Protection de la Communauté Juive), Beitar, and the Jewish Defense League faced assailants reportedly armed with knives, axes, and iron bars.

Five riot policemen stationed in front of the synagogue, where some 200 congregants happened to be attending a prayer service for Israel's safety, were unable to handle the crowd. It took a half hour for reinforcements to arrive, and another two hours during which law enforcement combed the surrounding streets before members of the congregation were told it was safe to leave. The chief rabbi of Paris, Michel Guggenheim, was at the synagogue during the incident.

Another synagogue, on the rue des Tournelles near the Place des Vosges, was also targeted, though details of that incident have not yet emerged. Two weeks ago I attended a joyful ceremony there for the more than 1,500 French Jews making aliyah this summer, in the presence of Natan and Avital Sharansky, as well as the Israeli ambassador to France and the newly elected chief rabbi of France, Haim Korsia.

Jewish radio stations were abuzz Sunday evening and Monday with testimony from people who had been inside the synagogue and statements from Jewish community leaders. Mainstream media coverage, however, focused largely on the 14 Juillet military parade, with the day's "death to the Jews" chants neatly overlooked.

Roger Cukierman, president of the CRIF, the umbrella organization of French Jews, and Joël Mergui, president of the Consistoire, met with Interior Minister Bernard Cazeneuve yesterday, and asked for an outright ban on anti-Israel demonstrations due to their blatant disregard for law and order.

Local Jewish community leaders have excellent relations with President Francois Hollande's government, as they did with the previous Sarkozy administration. During the incident at the Don Isaac Abravanel synagogue, Jewish leaders were in contact with the Interior Minister, Prime Minister Manuel Valls, and the chief of police. No one questions the government's sincere sympathy for the Jewish community, or its fervent wish to bring a halt to the incidents, which are alienating French Jews and giving France a bad reputation internationally. The problem is that French authorities are overwhelmed, outrun, cornered, and caught in their own contradictions.

Violent demonstrations under various pretexts have taken place in France since the early 2000s. In 2003, participants in a peace march beat up two young men from Hashomer Hatzair, then tried to break into a locale in the Marais where more than 100 young Jews were gathered.

There were massive, violent anti-Israel rallies during the 2009 conflict between Israel and Hamas. Sunday's incident, however, signifies a heightened threat against French Jews. Anti-Israel protestors are more heavily armed and more defiant than before. French Jews, however, are not cringing. They are standing firm and demanding appropriate government measures. Still, there is a sinking feeling that one day soon the doors will not resist, the mob will enter, the intolerable will occur.

— *Tablet*

GAZA-ISRAEL: IT DOESN'T ADD UP
16 July 2014 (anniversary of the rafle du Vel d'Hiv)

Israel, they say, harumph, has the right to defend itself, but... But not entirely. Both sides are asked to act with restraint. Not exactly both. Because the conflict is lopsided: 37 then 58, 102, and now more than 200 Palestinians killed. The vast majority, according to Palestinian sources, are civilians. Women, children and the elderly, to say nothing of the thousands of wounded. On the other side, zilch. That's it, the stage is set, the lethal narrative has wheels and it's going to be fueled daily, automatically, unapologetically.

How might Hamas act with restraint? Its goal is to kill all the Jews and occupy all the territory from the Jordan to the sea. Whereas the Israelis want zero dead, zero wounded, and the pursuit of a productive life in an intact nation. So what would restraint amount to? Hamas would kill half the Jewish Israelis? There is no justification for this cooking-the-books vision of a confrontation with worldwide ramifications: The frontier between civilization and savagery runs along the Gaza-Israel border.

The Israeli army could crush Hamas in the space of 24 hours, simply by disregarding the fate of civilians caught in the interstices of a war machine built instead of a decent place for living creatures. Israel doesn't use its power that way.

If the heroic Iron Dome were struck with a malediction and all eight batteries suddenly went dead, if ever Hamas got the upper hand, the

THE BLACK FLAG OF JIHAD

rockets launched from Gaza could quickly balance the books. Would that be okay? 200 victims on each side. A draw? The competing teams shake hands and go home happy to have played a good game? No. Hamas would pursue its genocidal enterprise without the slightest restraint. What would they say then? The president of the United States, his secretary of state, European leaders, the General Secretary of the United Nations, journalists and readers eager to comment on the "conflict." If ever Israel became weak like the helpless people of Iraq or Nigeria, what would public opinion say? Sorry, guys. It turns out you should have hit the enemy with all your might. Contemporary public opinion has taken a strong stand on that old-fashioned genocide, the Shoah. It doesn't take a genius to figure that one out: it was a terrible tragedy that is sincerely regretted. Or almost.

Thirty-seven killed on the Palestinian side in the first days of the operation and nothing on the opposite team, how dare they? Genocide, dixit Mahmoud Abbas. From then on, every day has its lot of tribulations, the toll is rung up at the end of each newscast on channels all over the world, the proportion of civilians increases from many, to more than half, to almost all. Where do these figures come from? Palestinian sources. Who can verify them? Don't bother. Every confrontation involving Israel uses the same accounting methods. A man who launches a rocket—from someone's patio— aimed at civilians in Israel becomes, if hit by the counter-attack, a civilian. While all Israelis, all Jews, including the three students assassinated in June, are soldiers.

Hamas is not a terrorist organization, it's a jihad fighting force. It has the same Islamic faith and ideology, the same slogans, banners, uniforms, and methods as the forces that occupy a large swath of Syria and Iraq where they have laid the foundations of the caliphate that must spread over the whole earth. The fact that Hamas is in murderous rivalry with other jihad factions doesn't make a nick in their common trunk. All of them—Al Shabab, Boko Haram, ISIS, Jabhat Al Nosra, diverse and varied Salafists, Wahabis, Muslim Brotherhood, and down to the so-called lone wolves— are manifestations of one and the same force that is exploding in the face of the world today.

The parents of hundreds of young women kidnapped three months ago in Chibouk weep; Syrian, Iraqi, Libyan, Pakistani Christians tremble; Egyptian Muslims revolted, and the Kurds of Kirkuk proudly defend their land against mujahidin determined to impose submission. Like Hamas in Gaza, like Hamas against Israel. Like the jihadis that laid siege to the Don Isaac Abravanel synagogue on rue de la Roquette in Paris on the 13th of July.

There too, restraint on both sides? The locals shouted loud and clear, like the Hamas they support: Kill the Jews! Should the president of the synagogue have let them in to discuss the terms of a ceasefire? Or were the Beitar, Jewish Defense League and unaffiliated braves justified in fighting with all their might against those Sunday jihadis until riot police, empowered by la République, finally arrived? Their aim was zero dead on the Jewish side.

Since the unilateral withdrawal from Gaza in 2005 a total of 11,000 rockets have been fired into Israel. These rockets are eminently concrete. They have to be manufactured or smuggled in. They use raw materials and financial resources, take up space, require mobile or stationary launching pads installed in schools and private homes, hidden in underground tunnels. It's an elaborate enterprise, freely chosen. Our [French] foreign affairs minister pleads for an immediate ceasefire.

Our president reminds us that France always seeks compromise, mutual understanding, peace. [The mayor of Bordeaux] Alain Juppé asks what is the use of "brutal repression [by Israel]." And Hamas demands, the last we heard, draconian conditions: unfettered opening of border crossings into Israel and Egypt, release of all the prisoners set free in the exchange deal for Gilad Shalit and re-arrested during the search for the three kidnapped students.... Once the fire has ceased Hamas will certainly demand abundant fruits of their jihadish victory such as reparations, condemnation... Ah, I almost forgot... and the end of the Occupation, from Eilat to the Golan.

In other words, as a reward for having shot more than 1000 rockets at Israel this week, Hamas insists on a return to the status quo ante that will give it a chance to replenish and improve its stock of arms in view of the next round and so on and so forth until the final victory.

Who could satisfy these demands? The international community, my friend! Composed, on the one hand, of Hamas' Islamic brothers and paymasters and, on the other, of those who, after Israel, as well as Israel, are in the crosshairs of Hamas or its comrades in arms, or its more jihadist, more powerful, even more brutal rivals, any or all of the above fighting under the black banner of jihad, shouting slit the throats of the Jews, slaughter the kuffars, allahu akbar.

It is obscene to say "Israel has the right to defend itself, but..." That's not a right, it's a permission. No one has the right to grant it, refuse it, or limit it.

— *New English Review*

Chapter 2 / Gaza-Israel Dateline Paris / July

DISPATCH N° 1

20 July 2014

LETHAL NARRATIVES

I know you are drowning in floods of information, can't keep up with your email correspondence, don't have time to read the best compilations let alone the middling ones, not even time for the "must reads" sent by trusted sources... But I encourage you to buy and read my book, *Al Dura: Long Range Ballistic Myth*. It sheds original light on events that are turning our world upside down, with the Middle East as the pivot. While Israeli civilians run for the bunkers to escape the murderous intentions of Hamas rockets, and Israeli soldiers confront Hamas mujahidin on their own territory in the confines of the Gaza Strip, "international opinion" has mobilized for another round of lethal narrative warfare. On the third day of an all-out Hamas offensive against Israeli civilians, the lethal narrative kicked in. Today it has reached the height of frenzy. And Western media have gone berserk, in step with the raging crowd.

Metula News Agency[1] reports today that several journalists that wanted to leave Gaza were blocked at the Eretz Crossing by Hamas operatives. Why? Might they fear that once outside Gaza, journalists would report the truth about what is happening there? Western media fervently defend the fighting forces of a jihad movement that would just as easily behead them as enslave them but would never ever allow them to report freely as they are doing today. Even though they abuse that freedom, they enjoy it.

The question is not "why do they act against their own interests"? It's like asking a gun why it shoots bullets at this or that target. A gun is a weapon in the hands of a gunman. The media, academia, international organizations, charities...the list is endless of entities and institutions that have become weapons of 21st century jihad conquest. Israel, a democratic nation, is the target of an all-out genocidal assault from the Hamas branch of the Muslim Brotherhood, and one week after Israel mobilizes in self-defense, Kill-the-Jews stampedes are on the march worldwide, and the facts have disappeared from mass media. We are assailed by something that is not reportage. It is not biased, one-sided, twisted; it is non-existent, and it fills the eyes and ears for hours on end. It's not news, not journalism, it's lethal narrative. A weapon. And it works.

KILL-THE-JEWS STAMPEDE IN PARIS ON JULY 13, 2014

My brief article published in *Tablet* was based on information available at the time. When the *14 juillet* holiday weekend ended I started to receive eyewitness accounts from Web sites, Jewish radio, and my own sources. It became apparent that the original *Agence France Presse* release, used by outlets worldwide, was concocted in lethal narrative format. Now we have videos of the "demonstration" from start to middle to semi-finish at Place de la Bastille that reveal its true nature. It was not a peaceful gathering slightly tarnished by a few rowdies at the last minute (see annotated links to videos).[2] Distinguished members of the Jewish community who were in the synagogue, including the Chief Rabbi of France, testified to the violence of the attempted intrusion. A [bad] translation of a text by a member of the congregation is posted on the *Tablet* site.

Interviewed on *Radio Communauté Juive*, a peace & love novelist, Valerie Zeccati, eloquently described the mobs that fanned out from the

Bastille into the nearby Marais: they were filled with murderous rage, they wanted to kill, they were thrilled by their own blood lust, the masses of demonstrators applauded them as they ran screaming, "We're going to smash the Jews!" The "imam" on the sound truck declared,"No provocation," and immediately segued to a resounding *allahu akbar* followed by other blood lust cries.

A widely circulated video shows the young men who were in fact protecting the synagogue from the mob that was trying to break in. I haven't been able to find out who shot the film, but it is emblematic of the vision of the Hamas attack on Israel: the attackers have been edited out, making the Jews look like the aggressors. And that's the purpose of the film.

One of the organizers of that stampede (they called it a demonstration) ingenuously explains that the contingent that went up rue de la Roquette [in fact they ran, screaming their heads off] were just on their way to a métro station. A member of a Jewish pro-Palestinian [and now pro-Hamas] organization claims the roughnecks from the Jewish Defense League started the fight. Four of them sitting on a bench somewhere along the route insulted the demonstrators and threw things at them. She doesn't explain how they lured the mob of hundreds all the way up rue de la Roquette to the synagogue, 400 meters from the Place de la Bastille. Or why, once they got there, the mob decided to attack the synagogue instead of taking the métro.

These apologists have a lot of explaining to do. Why did the mob first try to break into the synagogues on Rue des Tournelles and Place des Vosges? They couldn't get in because there were enough riot police there to stop them. How about the horde that chased a young couple walking their four month-old son in his stroller? They had to run for their lives. The harrowing tale is posted on the *Metula News Agency* Facebook page. Did the over-enthusiastic "pro-Palestinians" mistake them for Jewish Defense League adversaries?

The bobo weekly *Nouvel Observateur* ratcheted up and hammered out the revisionist version that, when you think of it, undermines the *Agence France Presse* whitewash.[3] Yes, there was violence, but it was all the fault of the Jews. Subsequently, in a *France 24* debate, a German freelancer with a steely smile took a ride with the revisionist version: not only are the Israelis merciless in Gaza, the Jews are persecuting pro-Palestinians in Paris.

33

Subsequent developments here in France should put that story out of commission. First, the government is not fooled by media tricks this time around. Particularly Prime Minister Manuel Valls, who until recently was Minister of the Interior. He knows what kind of volcano is boiling up in France, and what kind of people are behind these so-called pro-Palestinian demonstrations. His successor, Bernard Cazeneuve announced that local *préfets* will deny permits to demonstrations that are likely to disturb the peace.

The demonstration scheduled for Saturday July 19th was banned. Unless I am mistaken, France is the only country that took this step. The organizers appealed, their appeal was rejected. So what did they do? Stay home and write op-eds? Send pizzas to the harassed citizens of Gaza? No, they proudly and publicly declared that they would demonstrate anyway. Loudly proclaiming their democratic right to march, they trampled on the duty incumbent on law-abiding citizens.

This time the stampede didn't get far past its starting point in Barbès.[4] Riot police hemmed them in [they are complaining about police brutality]. They weren't rounded up and sent to jail for breaking the law. So they showed their appreciation by going wild, tearing up the asphalt and throwing chunks at the police, injuring 15. They set fire to cars, garbage cans, wooden pallets, and Israeli flags, smashed whatever was in reach, wreaked havoc for hours on end. And there were no Jewish Defense League boys to blame it on. An informative article in *Le Point* describes the assault on the Lariboisoière Hospital. The security guards, outnumbered [disproportionate force?], ran for cover. An elderly man shouted at the mob, "Are you crazy, that's a hospital." "It's a Zionist hospital," they shouted. But didn't burn it down...this time around.[5]

Today, they did a repeat performance in Sarcelles, known as little Jerusalem because a large contingent of the Sephardic Jews chased from the Maghreb settled there in public housing. For which they were grateful. From which many moved on to successful careers. And those who still live in neat and clean Sarcelles are constantly harassed by their Muslim neighbors in Garges-les-Gonesses. Many Jewish men have been attacked in the train station that serves the side by side communities.

Again, riot police were locked in battle for five hours while residents hunkered down in their homes. How is the government going to deal with this flagrant and ever more violent disrespect? What will be the consequences for the NPA, the extreme radical far left anti-capitalist party that got about 1% of the vote in the last municipal elections, and suddenly appears as an organizer of these stampedes?

In 2005 the insurrection was almost exclusively confined to the banlieues, on the other side of the *péripherique* [ring road]. This time it penetrates to the center of Paris and it is fired with murderous hatred of Jews. Many who fled the Maghreb say it reminds them of those times. Some observers are saying this looks like the early stages of "pogroms" but I think the appropriate term would be "farhud."

— *New English Review / The Iconoclast*[6]

DISPATCH N°2

July 21, 2014

Fourteen years after the al Dura blood libel, France discovers bare faced anti-Semitism in its midst

It's on all the lips, in all the media: burning Jewish shops in Sarcelles is anti-Semitic. Prime Minister Manuel Valls declared, in an excellent speech at the commemoration of the rafle du Vel d'Hiv [mass roundup of Parisian Jews in July 1942], that anti-Semitism was trying to hide behind anti-Zionism. Florian Philippot, Vice President of the Front National accused the Prime Minister of promoting French self-hatred because he acknowledged the dishonor of Vichy France compliance with orders from the German occupant that resulted in the deportation of 76,000 Jews from France to the death camps: 2,000 returned alive. Valls added a long tribute to the honor of the Résistance and courageous French people who risked their lives to hide Jews. Why would Philippot, speaking for the party that was supposedly going to liberate France from Islamization, prefer to lash out at Manuel Valls than to condemn the Islamic thugs? Valls defended the decision to ban further pro-Palestinian demonstrations that deteriorated into attacks on synagogues, precisely in the Marais, where Jews had been rounded up and sent to the death camps, and on rue de la Roquette, not far from the Japy Gymnasium where Jews were held before being sent to the Vel d'Hiv. Making the junction between the dishonor of 1942 and the intolerable assaults of 2014, the Prime Minister accurately measured the level of the threat hanging over the French Republic today.

Why is the Front National so skittish? Who is the blatantly pro-Putin anti-American FN trying to protect? At the other end of the political spectrum, aging militants from the anti-capitalist NPA or even more obscure fringe groups pop up in the media to defend the right to demonstrate. While videos of the authorized July 13th operation are freely available to refute all apologetics, these gentlemen place the blame on a repressive government. By denying the right to demonstrate they kept us from providing our own security service that would have prevented these unfortunate marginal acts of violence [like you did when they rushed to the synagogues last week?] No journalists were on screen to question the rationality [sic] of this discourse thrown at the public like a rock. The balding apparatchik warns us: You have to understand their anger.

The other day, Foreign Affairs Minister Laurent Fabius flew to the region with stops in Jordan, Egypt, and Israel, determined to impose an immediate ceasefire. He emerged, disappointed, from a half-hour conversation with Israeli Prime Minister Netanyahu. The French plan apparently is based on some kind of security guarantees that would reassure the Israeli government and convince it to lay down its arms and retreat, leaving Hamas victoriously intact. French forces can guarantee security at the Eretz Crossing? Riot police in Paris can't even thwart a crowd of 3,000 punk jihadis in Sarcelles! Dozens of police were wounded, a pitiful handful of assailants have been arrested, shops were looted and torched. French authorities cannot prevent a punk anti-capitalist party from defying a perfectly legal ban and ringleading violent attacks on French citizens, their property, and law enforcement.

GAZA-DONETSK

Lethal narratives from Gaza alternate in the world's media with coverage of the MH17 crash scene in the eastern Ukraine. The bereaved, side by side with billions of media-invited bystanders, watch as men described as "pro-Russian separatists" mishandle the bodies and belongings of crash victims, systematically destroy the evidence and cart off the wreckage to an unknown destination. No Ukrainian forces, no world leader, no international institution, no public opinion can stop them. It's happening before our eyes.

Unlike Prime Minister Valls who intelligently linked the roundup of Parisian Jews in 1942 to attacks on Parisian Jews in 2014, commentators are not making the junction between demands for a ceasefire in Gaza and the spectacle in the Ukraine: this is the way the world looks when legitimate forces are either helpless or hogtied. Hamas not only dreams of shooting down passenger planes landing at Israel's Ben Gurion airport, they are gearing up to be able to do it. When a state does not mobilize its forces to defend itself, the civilian population is immobilized. Passengers boarding a Malaysian Airlines flight from Amsterdam to Kuala Lampur belong to a fast disappearing world where ordinary people are free to do business, attend conferences, visit family, or frolic in a global playground. Lack of disclosure on the disappearance of flight MH370 coupled with under-reporting of the conflict in the eastern Ukraine may well have contributed to the feeling of normality in boarding that flight.

French citizens, not only Jews, are wondering what next, where next? Turn any corner, walk into any shop, drive down any street and you might find yourself face to face with one of those enraged mobs. In Israel, 75% of the territory, under daily attack by Hamas rockets, is partially immobilized. In one failed state after another, maniacal tyrants immobilize terrified populations. If this movement is not stopped, how many countries will become no-go zones for commercial aviation?

SCENES OF DESTRUCTION IN GAZA

Does anyone remember that these bombed buildings didn't exist media-wise? The people of Gaza lived in hovels in miserable refugee camps. Now the buildings are discovered just in time to be reduced to rubble. The same kind of rubble we've seen in Libya and Syria, for example. Gaza has come of age, it finally has the death and destruction of its Muslim neighbors. Not in the same proportions of course. The "heartless Israelis" committing "war crimes" have opened a field hospital at the Eretz Crossing to treat the injured from Gaza. Media-wise the field hospital doesn't exist. No room for it in the lethal narrative. Indecent exposure of the dead and wounded in Gaza—innocent victims, all.

Then Hamas boasts of capturing an Israeli soldier (Israel denies the claim); a jubilant crowd of the innocent citizens of Hamas-occupied Gaza explode in joy. Thirteen Israeli soldiers are killed in three separate incidents in the Sharjiya neighborhood but somehow no Hamas fighters show up in the casualty toll last night.

REACTIONS CUT ACROSS PARTY LINES IN FRANCE

Reactions to the violent outbreaks in Paris and Sarcelles cut across party lines, with some political figures in the right wing opposition criticizing the government decision to allow people to demonstrate their outrage at the situation in Gaza, and others calling for more vigorous action, including the deportation of all dual nationals participating in the violence. Many politicians in the governing coalition object to the ban on "pro-Palestinian demonstrations" and what they see as the government's excessive support for Israel in this conflict. Christian Estrosi, mayor of Nice and outspoken friend of Israel, has transferred to the appropriate authorities CCTV footage that will allow them to identify and prosecute law breakers in his city.

SOME DETAILS ON THE SARCELLES ATTACK

[My translation of excerpts from the richly illustrated *Figaro* article.][1]

4 PM: standoff between demonstrators and the police in front of the synagogue on avenue Paul Valery; access to the synagogue in Garges is blocked.... Then a string of attacks: a Simply Market store right behind the Garges police station is torched, three people are grabbed by police as they were trying to hold up a tobacco shop, rioters target a bank in Sarcelles, demonstrators try to set fire to the Garges station and rip up the tramway rails. Several shops are looted... the police fire rubber-coated bullets at the rioters.

In front of the main Sarcelles synagogue, the atmosphere is tense. They just heard that the [Naouri] kosher grocery store was burned to the ground... In 2012 it was attacked with a grenade. "They burned pharmacies that belong to Jews and a bar that belongs to Chaldeans, they have no respect, all they want to do is smash Jews!"

Note that Jewish Defense League and other Jewish self-defenders, with the help of the police, successfully protected the synagogues in Garges and Sarcelles during the five hour demi-*farhud*; riot police were not able to protect the shops, pharmacies, cars, etc. They were able to foil an attempted incursion into the Garges police station. This time.

DISPATCH N°3

24 July 2014

The Christians of Mosul had 24 hours, the infidels of the West have a bit more time

The just and merciful caliph gave the Christians of Mosul 24 hours to convert, leave, or die. The payment of the jizya (= dhimmitude tax) option initially included in the multiple choice injunction was withdrawn. A church dating back 1800 years, before the advent of Islam, was burned to the ground before the Christians left. The infidels of the West were too busy decrying the "massacre" in Gaza to ask for whom the bell tolls.

Ali Khamenei proposes the elimination of Israel by referendum. Former French Foreign Affairs Minister Dominique de Villepin thinks an imposed peace plan enforced by UN peacekeepers would do the trick. Hamas leaders, safely hunkered down in tunnels or in 5-star hotels abroad, exult in victory. Western media launch lethal narratives from morning to night and Jews look for the nearest shelter. Israel's bosom buddy, the United States of America, wants an imposed ceasefire, presumably before joining in on an imposed peace plan, while slapping a brief but telling blockade on air travel to and from Israel. Did you get the message, haverim? Do unto the blockaders as they do unto Gaza.

In the aftermath of the shocking violence unleashed last weekend in Barbès and Sarcelles, benevolent French judges smiled upon the meager handful of culprits arrested after the Barbès operation. Suspended sentences of 4, 6, or 10 months were handed down like feeding candy to the wolves. The justice ministry has exercised its right to appeal these lenient sentences. Those arrested for mayhem in Sarcelles will theoretically go to jail, but perhaps not. Short sentences rarely lead to actual imprisonment here. It's hard to prove that a given actor in an enraged mob actually committed this or that infraction. And it's hard to have confidence in the government when thousands of punk jihadis show up for a banned demonstration and are not immediately dispersed. All the more so when a political party, the anti-capitalist NPA formerly led by the phony mailman Besancenot, brazenly maintains its call to demonstrate.

62% of French people polled said the pro-Palestinian demonstrations should be banned. But who's listening?

Under pressure from interested parties, the Hollande government decided to authorize demonstrations on the 23rd and 26th of July...

because every possible guarantee had been given by the organizers that there would be no *débordements* [literally, "overflow"]. The Communists had by then joined the NPA in fronting for the Brotherhood. Jean-Luc Mélenchon was there under the banner of the Front de Gauche that is part of the governing coalition, along with a handful of Socialist deputies. Prime Minister Manuel Valls had tried to stick to his guns. All last week he defended the ban, refuting claims that the ban was the cause of the violence. Note the lethal narrative: An authorized demonstration on July 13th replete with Death to the Jews culminates in attacks on synagogues. Therefore, demonstrations banned the following weekend yield 50 times more incitement and violence. Logical, *n'est-ce pas?* If I park in a no-parking zone and you tow my car away, it's only to be expected that I will burn down the city hall and invite the assassination of the mayor.

Lethal narrative, cont'd. The authorized pro-Palestinian demonstration, majestically escorted by riot police, marched from Place Denfert-Rochereau to les Invalides—in the shadow of Napoleon's tomb— via Montparnasse where artists and intellectuals, refugees from tyrannical regimes, used to gather and enrich Parisian life.

Lo and behold, it worked. All these 14,000 blessed souls needed was the freedom to wrap themselves in Hamas keffiehs, brandish Israel-assassin posters, and confide to complaisant microphones their heartfelt concern for Palestinian victims of a massacre. "They're killing Palestinians for no reason, for the fun of it." "We see the images every day, it's unbearable, we had to do something."

Print and audiovisual media fell over themselves oohing and ahing over the concerned darlings. No anti-Semitic slogans, no threats, no destruction. When a few punks moved in on a France 2 correspondent doing his stand-up routine in the field and covered his face with a big Palestinian flag, the incident was packaged as "demonstrators (nicely) interrupt a France 2 newscast." A few years ago, near Cairo's revolutionary Tahrir Square, a similar maneuver ended with a sexual assault on the French journalist that had been (nicely) interrupted during her newscast. Nothing objectionable in this *bon enfant* demonstration where the good-natured, friendly citizens of France expressed (nicely) their grievances against "Israel Assassin, Hollande complice," some dressed in soft green BDS t-shirts, others holding up horrible photos of massacred chil dren and shouting in unison *"Palestine vaincra* [will triumph]."

Last night, *Le Monde Juif Info*[1] filled in some of the missing details. Fine-tuned ears picked up Death to the Jews that had escaped the attention of mainstream media. A camera filmed the burning of an Israeli flag. A *BFM TV* correspondent had proudly claimed that a woman immediately went over and stopped the unruly gesture. *Monde Juif Info* says she told them not to do it because it would be all over the evening news. In fact, it wasn't. And the cameraman noticed a group of men clearly saying "Let's go to the Marais Jewish Quarter and fight the Jewish Defense League." For these experienced stone-throwers, the Marais is NOT a stone's throw from les Invalides You have to really be motivated to make the detour!

This morning a Jewish radio station reported that some 40 individuals had tried to attack a restaurant in the Marais.

Riposte Laïque[2] has an eloquent photo gallery of posters the mass media didn't see. The restaurant that was attacked, the Pitzman, is on rue Pavée next door to the synagogue and across the street from the yeshiva. Just a half block away from a main thoroughfare, rue de Rivoli, it was probably easier to hit than the shops and restaurants on rue des Rosiers.

Breaking news: a plane flying from Ouagadougou to Algiers disappeared from radar screens somewhere near northern Mali. Many, perhaps the majority of the passengers were French.

Flashback: the day the French troops landed in Bangui, the capital of the Central African Republic, 1,000 people were killed in what is described as "ethnic conflict" between Muslims and Christians. French forces gradually imposed relative calm. Remember Sabra and Chatilla?

DISPATCH N°4

Friday, 25 July 2014

According to a report in *Le Figaro*[1] the UN is disturbed by a fatwa from the Caliphate ordering excision (genital mutilation) for all women. Don't expect the world's cameras to take positions inside the clinics—or above dirty blankets spread on the ground—to witness the mutilation of a potential 4 million victims. Unless and until Western media, civil rights organizations, thinkers, and governments understand that this fatwa will spread like the jihad conquest of the Middle Ages and put the knife to the cherished sexual freedom of the free world, there will be no peace worthy of the name. Not in the Middle East, not in London, Paris, New York or Tokyo.

From the general to the particular: there was no cluster of journalists in front of the Pitzman restaurant Thursday morning. No visible police presence either. On the surface, everything was back to normal. I stopped by to verify the information heard that morning on *Radio J*, one of the best Jewish radio stations broadcasting from Paris. Yes, that's how it happened. About 40 men apparently split off from the "good-natured" demonstration that dispersed at les Invalides on Wednesday and headed for the restaurant. Warned by someone who saw them running down the rue de Rivoli, the personnel lowered the metal shutter that protects the front door. The windows are bullet-proof. I asked how much time they had to batten the hatches. "Two minutes."

The restaurant was filled. Diners could hear the raucous cries for Jewish blood as the assailants hammered the shutter with iron bars and baseball bats and tried to pry it open. One of the owners slipped out the back and came out through the synagogue where he was able to rescue two Jews trembling in fear.

Think of it: if or when these Jews make Aliyah and the young men don the uniform of the Israeli Defense Forces, they will become the heartless monsters portrayed in the soap opera that has been running successfully for 14 years. They will not cower, they will not wait for French riot police. They will defend themselves. And the media, and this and that human rights league, and the UN, and the pro-Hamas proto-caliphators will deplore their use of "disproportionate force." Supplications will mount to the high heavens. Ceasefire! Immediate ceasefire. Humanitarian ceasefire.

The crash of an Air Algérie plane on its way from Ouagadougou to Algiers and points north with 54 French citizens on board was a coincidence, unrelated to the FAA ban on flights to and from Israel. There is no reason to believe that the passengers tragically killed on that flight would have gone to Tel Aviv instead. That would be ridiculous. So there is no reason to believe that the city of Paris decided to repair the botched paving on the rue des Rosiers this very week, when the heart of the old Jewish quarter is the target of those "good-natured pro-Palestinian demonstrators."

Half the length of the street is closed off from vehicle traffic by flimsy metal hoardings. Uprooted paving stones, wooden planks and metal grids are stacked up in easy reach. Pedestrians—and assailants—can make their way to shops and restaurants. But the circulation of police cars would be difficult. Thursday evening the police were stationed at the corner of rue des Ecouffes and rue des Rosiers, facing l'As du Falafel, the most fantastic falafel joint this side of rehov Ibn Givarol [falafel street in Tel Aviv]. Hefty police ready for almost anything, not the good-natured types in shirt sleeves that usually patrol the neighborhood. At 11 PM, business was not booming as usual but the eateries were far from empty.

What will happen tomorrow (Saturday 26 July)? If, as I suspect, Wednesday's relatively non-violent authorized demonstration was staged to make way for a full-fledged assault on Saturday, with its focal point at la République, a sort of launching pad for multidirectional attacks in the area known, before the mass deportations of WW2, as the Pletzel, that extended from la République to St. Paul, heavily populated with French Jews and Jewish refugees from other European countries.

Last week France discovered contemporary anti-Semitism. When I published an article about it in *Commentary* ["Betrayed by Europe," March 2004] then French ambassador to the U.S. Jean-David Levitte wrote a letter to the editors denouncing my dishonest portrayal of his country that had rehabilitated Dreyfus, elected Leon Blum, and saved 75% of its Jews from extermination. Now that anti-Semitism has become a household word, I've moved on. I prefer to focus on lethal narrative as a strategy of 21st century jihad conquest.

If we were dealing with biased reporting we could counter it with the facts. They are abundantly available on the Net. Any journalist anywhere in the world can know as much as you or me about what is really happening in Gaza today. They even report some of it. And then proceed to launch another lethal narrative rocket. Rockets were discovered last week in two UNWRA schools. Yesterday, 15 people were killed and 200 wounded in an as yet unidentified hit on an UNWRA school where some 8,000 Palestinians had reportedly sought refuge. We were treated to an obscene display of gore and hysteria in the hospital while the notorious Chris Guinness unequivocally condemned Israel. "Massacres" deliberately provoked by launching rockets from UN compounds in Lebanon and Gaza have been effective in the past.

It isn't working this time. One reason is the discovery of some 34 tunnels from Gaza into the backyards of kibbutzim and moshavim on the other side of the frontier, along with an alleged plan for a Rosh Hashanah [Jewish New Year] massacre that is being compared to the surprise attack of the 1973 Yom Kippur war.

Disinformation can be countered by hard contradictory evidence ...but the jihad strategy forges ahead. From the al Dura blood libel that set the scene for this drama, in which Israelis are cast as merciless child killers, to the cats-in-heat calls for a ceasefire, an invitation to mass suicide is broadcast as the highest aspiration of decent human beings everywhere. Hopes for a ceasefire, chances for a ceasefire, Kerry tirelessly seeking a ceasefire, anchormen and women looking into the entrails of Palestinian victims for signs of an impending ceasefire...

Hamas has been trying in vain to hit Ben Gurion airport. Finally the debris of a rocket pulverized by the iron dome lands on a house in nearby Yehud and the FAA shows us how the United States of Obama "has Israel's back." A ban on flights, a stab in the back, another ceasefire pressure point. And reasonable people all over the world are saying the solution [to the "Mideast conflict"] is not military. Israel must make a sincere effort to negotiate with the moderate Abbas [president of a Fatah-Hamas unity government] to conclude the everyone-knows agreement, end the colonization, offer the Palestinians a proper state [from which they can really truly bomb Ben Gurion airport to their heart's content.]

The only ceasefire possible with jihad warriors is a hudna. Its purpose is to extricate the mujahidin from an inconclusive foray, cut the losses, buy time to regroup and reinforce their offensive capacity and strike again the next time the iron is hot.

The al Dura blood libel unleashed murderous rage against Jews in the Diaspora. Here in France synagogues were burned, people and property were brutally attacked, Israel was dragged through the mud, murders were committed, and the anti-Semitism that drives it (call it Jew hatred, Judeophobia, Koranic genocidal hatred) was denied. The Muslim killer of Sébastien Selam was "mentally disturbed," 26 of the 27 jailers who tortured Ilan Halimi were misguided underprivileged youths, Mohamed Merah killed Muslims too, did Mehdi Nemmouche really target the Jewish museum of Brussels because it was Jewish...etc. Shahid [martyrdom] operations murdered more than a thousand civilians in

44

Israel without provoking calls for a humanitarian ceasefire. The al Dura effect is Pavlovian: if a Palestinian child is killed it is exclusively the fault of Israeli cruelty, a war crime.

Today we have irrefutable concrete proof that Hamas, following Israel's unilateral withdrawal from Gaza, seized control of the Strip and constructed a border-to-border above and underground army base sheathed with a civilian protective shield. Gaza exists for the sole and unique purpose of exterminating the Jewish State of Israel.

Israel has the will and the means to defend itself. Consequently, after three days of defensive military action, the lethal narrative kicked in. Hamas disappeared. Nothing but Palestinians in Gaza. All civilians. Israeli combat victims were felled by three year-olds. No fighters in Gaza. And this "asymmetry" serves as an excuse for attacks against Jews throughout the Western world.

If North Korea attacked South Korea would Western journalists move into Pyongyang and deliver periodic news bulletins based on information supplied by North Korean sources? If South Korea had the will and the means to liberate the population of the open-air death camp to the north, would the UN demand an immediate ceasefire?

Breaking news: the prime minister announces that the government has decided to ban the "pro-Palestinian" demonstration scheduled for Saturday. The organizers, including the NPA [anti-capitalists], the PCF [Communists], les Indigènes de la République [virulent ethnic diversity party], are furious. They predict/promise violent incidents in reaction to this "unjustified" repression of their right to demonstrate solidarity with the Palestinians.

A 19 year-old Jewish boy was attacked by a gang of 15 wannabe Jew-killers in Bobigny. They said "we're going to give you what Ilan Halimi got." There is reportedly a kill-the-Jews Facebook group that fishes for profiles of Jews and then stalks them.

When I hear the word "ceasefire" I draw my weapon—the written word. When I hear the hysterical demands for a ceasefire, I whisper *am yisroel chai*. The Jew-haters went too far. Jews are united, people who want to be free know where to place their bets.

The tide has turned.

DISPATCH N° 5
Saturday, 26 July 2014

PART 1

What is the difference between a banned and an authorized demonstration in Paris?

So far, none.

Crudely scrawled poster caught by a cameraman at Place de la République:

Israel, your G-d is not your strength

Meaning, your G-d doesn't give you strength anymore

Burly, aggressive keffieh-clad demonstrators surround a *BFM TV* cameraman on location, waving flags and hollering "Israel Assassin"!

4:30 PM the mob starts fanning out from Place de la République [*Le Figaro*] and mixing with traffic allowed to flow as usual. After all, the demonstration was banned, so nothing could disturb the peace, right?

PART 2

Interior Minister Bernard Cazeneuve set forth, in a solemn address to the nation, a severe warning to organizers and potential demonstrators. The right to demonstrate is indeed respected in France. Over 60 demonstrations of support for the Palestinians have been held in France, only 5 have been banned. The ban is based on a thorough examination of all available evidence from social media and other sources. The risk of disturbing the peace is too great. The organizers have not given convincing proof of their ability to control the crowd. The ban was upheld by the court. It is the law of the land. We cannot tolerate expressions of anti-Semitism masked in support for Palestinians. Synagogues were attacked, Jewish property was destroyed, public property was smashed and riot police were attacked.

Approximately one half hour later the crowd started to gather at Place de la République. By 3 PM it was estimated at 3,000 and at the height of the demonstration, at 5,000. Journalists tweeted, cameramen filmed, riot police stood firm, and nobody rounded up the lawbreakers and carted them away. As the story always goes, it started out as a good-natured gathering, lots of women and children, nothing objectionable, well almost nothing. A jihad flag is clearly visible at the foot of the monument to the République alongside the "moderate" Palestinian flag. Israel was called dirty names. The media were accused of pro-Israel bias. You have to understand jihad to know that these guys are dead serious.

Unless you present their Islamically pure version, unless you display the same slogans, repeat the same war cries, show the same hatred as they demonstrate, you are a pro-Zionist puppet. They cap Prime Minister Valls with a kippa and show President Hollande waving an Israeli flag. As the afternoon wore on journalists were kicked, threatened, pushed around. Mike and camera were grabbed away from an *I-Télé* crew.

That was the good-natured part of the demonstration. It went on for about two hours and, surprise, as it was dispersing, some 500 (maybe it was more like a thousand?) tough guys started to attack the police. A rumor reportedly triggered the change in temper—the Jewish Defense League was on its way. Or already there. In which case it would be logical to attack the police, don't you see?

The battle went on for two hours. The security detachment provided by the organizers was a pushover. The usual smashing was enjoyed by all. Teargas filled the square. It is reported that 50 people were pulled aside and about 30 of them actually detained.

The police surrounded the mob, pushing them gradually...to the metro station. Yes, that is how it was described. They evacuated the smashers by sending them into the metro station. And on their merry way.

Hours later the Marais was itself again. A beautiful summer evening with a gentle breeze. Sounds of joyful singing wafted from the windows of the synagogue on the Place des Vosges while in a corner under the arcades someone played *hatikvah* on a tingly instrument. Languages mixed on the quiet streets, cafés and restaurants pulsed with life, people lined up to buy Italian ice cream at Amorino's. It was hard to believe that the caliphators had been making obscene quenelle gestures and lusting for Jewish blood just a few hours before and a few blocks away.

Friendly imams, intellectuals, and common ordinary pundits have been assuring the public that the pro-Palestinian demonstrations just like the Arab-Israeli conflict that provokes them have nothing to do with religion. Here are more photos of the kickoff of today's banned event.[1]

By the way, you might be wondering what the Front National has to say about all of this Islamic disturbance of the peace. You expect the FN is in the forefront, more outspoken than the prime minister and the interior minister put together. The supposedly anti-Islamization party would be shaking the gates of the Republic, calling for swift and stern action, denouncing the wimpish administration that permits what it has banned and lets the *allahu akbars* drown out the Marseillaise.

Not at all. Marine Le Pen, who never hesitates to speak out when she has something to say, is inaudible on the issue of Palestine. Her silence should be deafening to her allies at the EU Parliament.

DISPATCH N°6
July 28 2014

In Paris as in Gaza, human shields are the way to go!

Journal du dimanche correspondent Paul Guyonnet, reporting from the 5,000-strong banned demonstration at Place de la République on Saturday July 26 noted, at 5 PM: "Many peaceful pro-Palestinians have left the Square despite pressure from the more virulent, who tried to block their way." The JDD reporter says the prayer session [that other sources place at the beginning of the rally] called by an imam at 6:30 PM, magically calmed the assembled mass.

Shortly afterward the violence resumed as punk jihadis pelted riot police with fire bombs, stones, paper bags filled with broken glass, and the rest of their standard arsenal. A video by Guy Sauvage embedded in an editorial on the site of *Riposte Laïque* shows the early stages of the demonstration. The best footage I've seen so far of the insurrectional climax was posted by *LTL News*.

Talk about misreporting—mainstream journalists who were on the spot when these videos were shot somehow managed to estimate the unruly element at three to five hundred. It looks more like one thousand to me. This selective tally is part of the narrative. The demonstration is always good-natured, the violence is always on the edges, never in the center, always disconnected never an integral part, necessarily paradoxical not squarely in the logic of everything that went before, and committed by a minority rejected by the good-natured majority.

Guyonnet picked up and tweeted this slogan, "Hamas résistance, jihad résistance"[1] What is "jihad résistance?" Might it be this exhibition of severed head on stakes, posted by Walid Shoebat?[2] Does it include the destruction of Jonah's tomb in Mosul? The planned Rosh Hashanah massacre in southern Israel? The murder of four civilians at the Jewish Museum in Brussels? Public executions in the squares of Iraqi cities and towns brought under the black flag of the Caliphate? Is that the "jihad résistance" these people are preparing for us? France, a nation so proud of its Résistance to the brutal Nazi occupation now stands down as the Hamas/jihad résistance violates the Marianne, symbol of the République. Unopposed, this neo-résistance would deliver us into the hands of the Caliphate.

Where is the Front National when Islam assaults the Republic? Following up on my comment about the Front National at the end of Dispatch N° 5: VP Florian Philippot clearly states FN's position in a TV interview [Les 4 vérités:] It was wrong to ban pro-Palestinian demonstrations; stifling the expression of legitimate concerns leads to violence. (Philippot, who is systematically hostile to Manuel Valls, also opposed the ban on Dieudonné's anti-Semitic road show last winter.) Never pronouncing the terms "Muslim" or "Islam," Philippot deplores the repeated outbursts of violence in France, due to mass immigration and "*communautarismes*" [clannishness, tribal politics, or the sense of belonging to a community, such as Muslim or Jewish.]. There should be an immediate cease fire in Gaza to end this unacceptable death and destruction of Palestinians, he says. The only solution is two states. It is incumbent on Israel as the stronger party to back down and stop this armed conflict.

Widening the frame: now who's disproportionate?

How can savage beheaders inspire such benevolent denial, here in the 21st century, when their gory exploits are abundantly filmed and broadcast? Any idiot can see what "jihad résistants" do when they get power over people. Is the collective conscience paralyzed by fear? Fear, yes, if you find yourself face to face with a mob or even a single one of them geared up for a killing spree. But how can citizens of well-armed democracies believe collectively that the way to deal with these mujahidin, when they have a gripe against you, like Hamas with Israel, is give-and-take negotiation? Put yourself in their shoes. [But they want to put your head on their pike!] You have to offer the population attractive prospects. Hamas, for example, is asking for an airport, a seaport, open borders, reconstruction billions, release of prisoners, hands off what's left of their tunnels, and that's for starters.

These are approximately the terms of the cease fire agreement hammered out in the gilded salons of the Quai d'Orsay the other day, under the auspices of French Foreign Affairs Minister Laurent Fabius and U.S. Secretary of State John Kerry, apparently acting under the direction of Qatari and Turkish ministers, with meek approval from the bit players. This, reportedly, is the proposal John Kerry stuck to Israel's security cabinet like a diplomatic quenelle.

The Israeli government rejected it, but we always wonder what threats are being stabbed into Israel's back behind the scenes by its main man over there in America.

Terms like guerilla warfare, urban guerilla, asymmetric conflict, and disproportionate force are bandied about in the Western world like cries of despair from confused dhimmis. In fact, the disproportionate force is Islam, its doctrine of superiority, its limitless ambitions, its uninterrupted state of warfare, its unethical way of fighting, its genius for hiding behind its masses, its relentless assault on Western thought.

Poor little Gaza, like a fingernail on the map, battered and beaten by the superrpowerful Israel. Hapless civilians in an open-air prison, at the mercy of tanks, airplanes and uniformed monsters. Enlarge the frame: in the name of Gaza, Muslim fighters all over the Western world attack Jews, the government, the native population, law enforcement, public property. They, too, are victims, underprivileged Muslims, unfairly confused with the handful of rowdies who "instrumentalize" their religion. In the name of the "moderate majority" Islam is acquitted of responsibility for the violence it inculcates.

Acquitted, like the assailants who tried to pry open the shutter and massacre the Jews in the Pitzman restaurant, next door to the synagogue on rue Pavée. Recognized by the victims. Acquitted by the judge. Insufficient evidence. Acquitted, like the 5,000 "jihad résistants" who gathered in the very square of the République and participated in a violent anti-Semitic insurrectional banned demonstration. Perhaps a hundred were rounded up, about 40 are in custody, and most will fly out of the courtroom on a carpet of insufficient evidence.

The disproportionate force in this conflict is Islam. No matter the objective circumstances, Islam always wins, always prevails, always dominates. Deliberately misinterpreted as another ho-hum round of tit for tat fighting between Hamas and Israel, this acute crisis on the fault line between Islam and the West, is kneaded and shaped to yield a mounting wave of collective exasperation. Rubble in the Sharjiya neighborhood is a mine of virtual rocks thrown at Israel. The image is repeatedly broadcast, engraved in the doped-up minds that drink it in and moan, in chorus with Ban Ki Moon, "Israel must stop the violence!" The humanitarian plight of Gaza is a victory. Ali Waked (*i24 news*) gives an ingenuous summary of Hamas accomplishments: They shot rockets at Tel Aviv, Dimona, ben Gurion and points north and south. They killed 43 Israeli soldiers, penetrated into Israeli territory through tunnels, restored their lost esteem in the Arab world, attracted handsome financial donations, closed down Ben Gurion airport, achieved a death toll close to 1,000 of their own, almost all civilians [their breakdown], thereby creating a mass international movement in their favor.

From the heights of its rubble, victorious Hamas dictates the terms of a cease fire. And John Kerry carries water for Hamas?

With a combination of forays like the current Hamas escapade, and lethal narratives that warp the Western mind, Islam imposes its law: Islam can strike you, you are not allowed to fight back. Instilling the belief that only Israel and the Jews are guilty of crimes against humanity, Islamic jihad entices world populations to submit to its law. The French government, entangled in the web of Qatari investments, lacks the determination to stop these disgraceful pro-Hamas bashes that undermine its legitimate democratic power. Israel is not the obstacle to peace, it is the example of the courage to resist against a totalitarian system that is knocking on every door.

COMIC RELIEF

The nominally conservative *Figaro* daily has outdone itself in the lethal narrative department with this bomb from Frédéric St. Clair, advisor to PM Dominique de Villepin from 2005-7.[3] The idea, concocted during the British occupation of Palestine in 1917, of creating a Jewish national homeland to save these populations from pogroms was "a major act of theological-political blindness." The future state was built on a religious foundation, confirmed by the UN in 1947, and the choice of location was based on the Bible, "offering the 'Promised land' to the 'Chosen People.'"

Consequently, legitimate revolt against oppression of the Palestinians "takes an anti-Jewish tone." Until Israel adopts *la laïcité à la française* there is no hope for peace in the region.

When Palestinians are identified with Muslims, he says, Israel's encroachment on Palestinian territory is equivalent to "the expansion of Judaism's pretentions over Islam." Then Israeli army oppression of Gaza becomes Jewish oppression and, if it is compounded by Jewish solidarity, rebellion against those exactions naturally becomes a combat against the Jews.

However, monsieur Saint Clair does not condone brutal riots in the streets of France or genocidal attacks on Jews in Israel. He offers friendly advice. The State of Israel has to do like 20th century France, shake off its religious shackles and become a modern non-denominational State.

Merci, monsieur, vous êtes trop aimable.

According to the most recent Israeli government estimates: Hamas fighters account for 750 of the reported 1,000 deaths in Gaza.

Watch this video[4] of an exchange between Ron Dermer, Israeli ambassador to the United States, and *CNN* journalist Erin Burnett, distraught over (reported) casualties in an UNWRA school—15 dead and 200 wounded by Israeli tank fire: "Couldn't you have gone into the school to find out if there were people there before attacking," she scolded, as if she were the voice of humanity personified. The army has now published the results of its investigation.[5] There was fierce fighting around the area, an errant Israeli mortar did fall into the schoolyard. But there was no one in the schoolyard when it landed.

The UN is still claiming 15 dead, 200 wounded, and demanding an impartial (UN) investigation.

Chapter 3/ Gaza-Israel Dateline Paris / August

DISPATCH N°7

Saturday, 9 August 2014

"Never again" isn't working. Let's try "Don't you dare."

Don't you dare solemnly declare your intention to kill all the Jews. Don't you dare vote for a party that promises genocide and tools up for action. Don't you dare hand out sweets when Jews are murdered, don't you dare wave the flag of Islamic mass murder, don't you dare sit humbly like a frog on a log while the mujahidin dig tunnels under your butt. When the day of reckoning explodes on your poor head and reduces your camouflaged military base to ruins, and your evil taskmasters make you climb over the rubble pretending to gather a few miserable belongings, don't come crying to me. It's your rubble, you wanted it, you got it. As for your hospital passion plays, howling ambulances unloading bit players while your mangled warriors are slipped in by the back door, please be informed that I do not look. I will not participate. Don't play games with me.

More than 500 journalists were posted in Gaza this month and all they saw was hospital performances, selected rubble, wailing women in hijab, almond-eyed children in UN schools before & after staged massacres, and Hamas information sheets stamped with the UN logo. The same footage was reeled out on every channel from the *BBC* to *Sky News*. They could have mentioned, with readily available illustration, that those refugee kids were deprived of the summer camps where they dress up in battle fatigues and practice killing Jews with cute replicas of lethal arms. Footage of ferocious Hamas warriors decked out to kill, jogging Indian file through their state of the art tunnels, shown on the Israeli channel *i24 news* was available to any journalist who cared to know the whole story.

On the home front, the ground is littered with victims of lethal narrative warfare: commentators, analysts, specialists, elected officials, heads of state and big chiefs of international organizations are moaning, holding their heads, shrieking with indignation. Even as the concrete evidence topples into the public domain—the Hamas manual of underhanded warfare, the multimillion dollar tunnel network complete with plans for a joyous high holiday massacre, tunnel entrances and weapons caches in homes, schools, hospitals, and mosques—the frenzied condemnation of Israel rises in crescendo. It has nothing to do with the facts. It is entirely disconnected from the pace of the action, the situation on the ground. It is like pre-recorded background laughter for a stand-up comedian.

The height of outrage erupts with the "massacre" at an UNWRA school in Rafah. B. Obama, L. Fabius, D. Cameron, and the orchestra leader B.K. Moon sing out in unison: this is too much, it's worse than a massacre, it's a carnage, a massive bloody slaughter. "International opinion" joins in the choir. Enough is enough. Inexcusable. Granting that weapons had been discovered in several "abandoned" UN buildings, the puppet-faced General Secretary of the UN rewrites the rules of war and decrees that it is illegal to strike a civilian site used for military purposes.

It seems that the last-straw massacre (that I predicted weeks ago) follows the hallowed tradition of the staged al Dura death scene and other massacre hoaxes, including Jenin, Kfar Qana, the Gaza Beach etc. It was apparently a Pallywood production, with all the familiar tricks, convinc ingly analyzed frame by frame by Thomas Victor.[1] Unless someone can provide a serious refutation, we can conclude that no one was massacred in the UN school at Rafah. But the UNSG puppet has to whine louder than everyone else put together because UN(WRA) is Hamas-compliant down to the last stretch of tunnel, the last inch of a launch pad, the last letter of a manual on how to wage war by getting your civilian population killed and their homes destroyed. By the way, many homes in Gaza were destroyed by Hamas booby-traps installed to kill Israeli soldiers. And 25% of the rockets aimed at Israel fell short.

There is no assurance at this writing that the ongoing 3-day ceasefire will be extended. But the "wrapping up" mood already prevails in punditry land. They all know "there is no military solution." So the destruction of some 31 offensive tunnels, control and command headquarters, weaponry, and approximately 900 fighters may be military but it's not a solution. Hamas rocket launchers are at least temporarily silent, Hamas killers have lost their free-entry tunnels into Israel, the population governed by Hamas is bombed out and distraught, and even if it looks like a military solution, the fact is, they say, Israel has lost the international opinion battle. How do they know? Because they are the ones who run that show.

For example: *CNN* anchor Jim Clancy to his correspondent in Gaza—Israeli sources claim they were sending food, medical supplies, basic necessities into Gaza, even at the height of the battle. Is it true? [Update: Clancy resigned from *CNN* after accusing Israel, in nasty tweets, of using the *Charlie Hebdo* massacre for its own propaganda purposes.] The correspondent goes silent. It's the equivalent of censorship strips on a written document. When he gets his voice back, he sidesteps the question and relays the severe scolding meted out to Israel by BKM, BHO, and everyone who is anyone, condemning the unforgivable carnage at the UN school in Rafah. Now the studio wants to know if it's true, as Israelis are saying, that Hamas keeps journalists from telling the truth about what's going on. Not so, replies the correspondent. He is free to show and tell as he sees fit. A real journalist! Granted, he admits, he's never seen a Hamas fighter, but... Sometimes if they approach a hot spot they hear warning shots and back off. And it's true, some crews have been expelled, but..."But" is enough to suggest it was their own fault. On an earlier occasion the correspondent was asked if it is true that Hamas uses human shields. Nope. He speaks to all kinds of people. No one ever said he'd been used as a human shield.

Back in the fall of 2000, al-Dura hoax producer Charles Enderlin flatly stated that he trusts Palestinian sources over Israelis. Behold the confidence-building measures of the lethal narrative. Then and now, official Israeli statements are "PR," Israeli army investigations are "whitewash," photos of launch pads in mosques and kindergartens are a bore. Hamas tells the truth, Israel spins. Today's journalists, who probably never heard of "the ineluctable reality of the visible," think they can smudge the simple reality of Hamas out of the picture? Take a good look at some interviews with Osama Hamdam, a fat-faced Hamas spokesman living it up in Dohar, and then ask yourself how a Western journalist can conclude that Israel spins and Hamas tells it like it is.[2]

August 8, 2014

Ceasefire expires. As promised, Hamas resumed rocket attacks on Israel at 8 AM. In spite of yesterday's raucous victory parade in Gaza, neither Egypt nor Israel has caved in to the "victor's" maximalist demands for the spoils, including a seaport, airport, prisoner release, money to rearm and rebuild the tunnels, open borders, etc. The etcetera is actually the jackpot. "From the river to the sea, Palestine will be free." Excuse me for repeating myself but it's important to understand that this is jihad and the Islamic party always wins. That explains how Hamas, backed in fact by Fatah, can wail and display its wounds while simultaneously sticking out its chest, stomping its feet, and demanding submission. They play by the rules of jihad. What, then, explains the journalistic amen corner, echoing Hamas demands?

Are they leftist anti-Semites? Generous humanitarians? Fair-minded peace-lovers? Or dhimmis! Dhimmis of course. Why do journalists cave in? Why does a shovel dig into the ground? Because it's a tool in the hands of the digger. And it's not just journalists. The narrative weaves in and out from jihad sources to media to public officials and experts, to "public opinion" and their divinity, the "international community." The narrative pops up here and there like dog poop on the streets of Paris. Those knowing smiles, those tired clichés, those lost souls damning Israel from the depths of their own depravity. Israel, they say with a smirk, won the ground battle but lost the "war of ethics." Or the "war of images." Ha! They're the ones peddling Hamas-approved images. As for ethics, watch out for the boomerang. It only takes a few honest reporters safely out of Gaza to confirm what we all know and unmask the hundreds of worker bees who have been lying through Hamas teeth for a month. "International opinion" swears that the people of Gaza cannot be expected to endure another day of that heartless blockade. US President Obama agrees. What blockade? Hamas has spent the last two years blissfully arming itself to destroy the Jewish state of Israel. Give them credit for proving the blockade was totally ineffective.

The puppet show will soon be over. Reality always prevails. It will sweep away the battalions of correspondents standing in the rubble praising Hamas to the top of the toppled minaret, parroting Hamas demands as if they were liberty and justice for all, betraying their profession, their fellow citizens, their own freedom of speech.

Gaza, I said, is the toenail of the Caliphate. The feet are stomping into the north of Lebanon now. The legs are crushing Shias, Christians, Yazidis, miscreants, lukewarm Muslims, and miscellaneous disobedient daredevils in Syria and Iraq while pushing to join up with mujahidin near and far. The torso is in the bowels of Iran's nuclear arms program. And the head is planning great exploits in Europe and the United States.

In the pernicious twist of contemporary jihad conquest, the international community pressures Israel to pull its punches so that Hamas can boast of standing up to the disproportionate Israeli war machine for one whole month. What would happen to undefeatable Hamas if Israel attacked full force?

Meanwhile in Paris a man identified as a 32 year-old Algerian (not Franco-Algerian) has been sentenced to three years in prison, effective immediately, for smashing and burning a transport authority truck during the July 19th insurrection at Barbès. There's been some languid talk about banning the Jewish Defense League and, fair's fair, the "Cheik Yassine brigade" and "Gaza Firm." Would the government stoop so low as to ban the JDL for protecting synagogues against bloodthirsty punk jihadis? Or is it a case of second string summer replacement journalists whirling up some cotton candy just for fun? We won't know until mid-August at the earliest. The caliphators have settled into a routine of regular Saturday pro-Hamas bashes, *Agence France Presse* trots along beside these "relatively uneventful pro-Palestinian demonstrations," the population gets used to seeing the black flag of jihad and all the keffieh'd trimmings. While Da'esh barrels its way through Syria and Iraq harvesting severed heads, the black flag of jihad flies in Europe and America. Never in the history of humanity have the facts been so easily available and so stubbornly denied. I repeat from the rooftops: you think you're defending the poor l'il Palestinians, no, you're acquiescing to the triumph of the black flag of jihad in your public squares. You mumble nonsense like a slobbering senile wreck and they raise the black flag of jihad in your streets. They mean it.

1969 WOODSTOCK 2014 HASHTAG GAZA
August 20, 2014

What's left of that flower power? Heads lopped off like daisies in the field and hashtag Gaza fashionistas ripe for the slaughter.

My generation spent its childhood on the Home Front while fathers, uncles, and older brothers fought on the front lines. We were patriotic, united in fear for our loved ones and hatred of the enemy. The V for Victory was a question of life and death, not a silly gesture or substandard jihad boasting. Victory was a blessed relief: No more shortages, no more anxious waiting for news from European and Pacific battlefields. The energy mobilized in wartime was pumped into civilian life. New products hit the market: plastics, nylon, ball point pens, and television. It was the beginning of commercial air travel.

For us, first generation Jewish immigrants, the Shoah was an essential dimension. Our parents witnessed from an anguished distance the extermination of those that stayed behind. In our daily lives we experienced a milder form of anti-Semitism that began to dissipate after the war. For Blacks, too, the civil rights movement was getting underway.

There was a hunger for freedom and justice. We expected the values our men had defended with their lives on dreadful battlefield to be more fully applied at home in peacetime. The booming economic success story was shaping the man in the grey flannel suit...who would soon be decried. But the immediate postwar period was a time of consensus. A terrible challenge had been met with honor and courage.

When I went to the University of Wisconsin in the early fifties, we got a fortune in learning and paid virtually nothing for tuition. Today it's the reverse: kids get virtually nothing in learning and tuition costs a fortune. In those days, the University of Wisconsin was a hotbed of radicals in a coast to coast landscape of academic conservatism. I hung out with leftist bohemians in turtle neck sweaters and hand crafted sandals. Once a year we made a pilgrimage to our capital, Greenwich Village. Our guiding star was psychoanalysis, Fidel Castro's muchachos were our heroes, our Communist buddies visited the Soviet Union.

Some remained true to the cause to their dying day, others slid into professional and family responsibilities and became "squares." Due to personal circumstances that I have amply explored in fiction, I ducked out of my own generation in the mid-Sixties and hitched a ride on the new wave. Beyond the hipsters came the hippies. Nothing would ever be the same again. Whatever the critical distance I had at the time, being half in & half out, both mature and responsible and more than a bit wild, I cannot imagine a reversal of the fundamental changes that took place in our society in those years. Unless, of course, the forces of jihad should prevail.

Woodstock was the culmination of the psychedelic music current, one among several streams in that bursting open world of the Sixties. It was not my "trip." I was in the literary, third-world, soul and Afro-beat division that was skeptical if not downright hostile to the psychedelic wing, dismissed as a cheap commercial rip-off of African rhythms. Woodstock left us cold. My only memory of Woodstock at the time was— MUD. The Black putdown went like this: white boys play at being hip, dropping out, and doing drugs but when they see the misery it brings they cut their hair, put on a suit, and get a job from some friends of their daddy. White boys expropriate black music, pretty it up, sell it by the millions, white men make the money, black musicians do the real thing and get nothing.

That's where I was when Woodstock happened. I don't think I ever saw the film. The 6-day war passed me by the same way. I wasn't a Zionist in those days. Our problem was the Vietnam War. It wiped out the memory of WW2 heroism and overturned the notion that the United States uses its military might to liberate people from tyranny. We were the bad guys. It was almost a pleasure to shout it from the rooftops, whisper it in poetry readings, march it in the streets, wear it like stardust in our eyes.

Though dreams of unbridled sexual pleasure have somewhat soured into single motherhood, same-sex marriage, divorce, loneliness, and Aids, the radical change in fashion and physique acquired in the Age of Aquarius has never really been overturned. But it seems that the strongest survival of those days is the anti-war fervor nourished by the certainty that we in the West are the bad guys.

In Europe and the United States, the children and grandchildren of the Woodstock generation are poised on a brink that could drop them into a world with no peace & love flowers, no warm cuddly fraternity, no free for all sex, no civil rights, gay rights, abortion rights, no diversity, no music... A world in which the naked breasts of Woodstock would not be strapped into a bra and covered with a demure blouse, no, they would be buried in a niqab. If not stoned to death. The Woodstock generation and its children that revolted against those self-satisfied squares who won the war against the 20th century fascists have been left with a vulnerability that could throw them back... not back to those pre-war days, not back to the hilarious revolt against the bourgeoisie, back to the Middle Ages, to a savagery they cannot see through their flower power eyes.

Greens hopping onto Gaza Flotillas, erstwhile feminists joining the sisterhood of the genitally mutilated, inveterate leftists marching arm in arm with their allahu akbar brothers in keffieh are a trickle compared to the masses transformed by the Woodstock culture of the Sixties but the antiwar mentality fostered back then persists despite all evidence to the contrary. The mindless "values" of those strawberry fields have become by twists and turns a poisonous hatred of the State of Israel with the Palestinians cast in the role of the flower children, the downtrodden, the helpless victims of a merciless war machine. The antiwar movement of the Sixties has permeated every level of Western nations though they are assailed on all sides by an implacable enemy. Americans, living in business-as-usual luxury, enduring no shortages, no restrictions, not drafted into military service, have been convinced by opinion-makers that they are war weary. The spirit of Woodstock abides in mushy hand-holding with imams and celebrations of "Abrahamic" religions. Schoolchildren are taught to love Islam the way their grandparents loved marijuana. The illusion of a cozy non-conflictual world is still there but the joy is gone.

France's newspaper of record, *Le Monde*, outdid itself this summer with a two-page spread on the hashtag- Gaza fashionistas. The skilled hand of the trendy journalist turned those pro-Hamas stampedes— where thousands of bloodthirsty caliphators rampaged down the streets of Paris looking for Jews to stomp and bash, destroying Jewish shops, attacking synagogues—into little modern day Woodstocks. Everyone who is anyone had to be there. No cheap Chinese prints for the most sophisticated hashtaggers. They got their keffiehs imported directly from the last authentic craftsman in Hebron. An authentic two-color weave, *mon ami*. Muslim traders in fashionable suits literally danced out of the office and hopped over to Place de la République where the black flag of jihad was giving an up-yours to the monument to the French Republic. Of course they didn't throw firebombs at the police, but they didn't leave the party either. Humanitarians for Hamas chanted side by side with the Jew-killers and young ladies wearing Palestinian flags as hijab participated in the hallowed French tradition of *droits de l'homme*. Wasn't it called consciousness-raising back in the Sixties?

When I think of Woodstock I think of the mud. I think of the mindless self-destruction that was manifest, even at the height of those glorious years when a spirit of liberation gave us wings and it felt like life was made for pleasure. If you didn't dig it, you had hangups. Some went along and some went over the top. Young men on speed aged and died in two short years. Promising students lived in filth and spent their days beating cardboard drums on the sidewalks of Berkeley. Nice middle class girls lived like whores and got hooked on heroine. Today, in France, the forlorn grandchildren of Woodstock are covered in gangsta tattoos.

But there's something sweet in that heritage, something lyrical that we haven't lost. Youth's hopeful bountiful energy will come up with new configurations. There's no end to surprises in this all too human story. And no end to mistakes...to be corrected by future generations.

— *Midah (Hebrew translation)*

DISPATCH N°8

Wednesday, 27 August 2014

The truth is hanging by a thread. Beheaded journalist's father: "I didn't know how brutal they were."

This is what I wrote a month ago, in the first dispatch in this series:"Western media fervently defend the fighting forces of a jihad movement that would just as easily behead them as enslave them but would never ever allow them to report freely as they are doing today. Even though they abuse that freedom, they enjoy it."

This week we were treated to the stark beheading video of American reporter James Foley. It is normal that the bereaved family would pay tribute to Foley's courage maintained "up to the last minute." He was on his knees. His last words were an indictment of his native land for conducting offensive air strikes against the Caliphate. It is fair to assume that if he had stood tall and faced the man who was preparing to saw off his head the video would not have been broadcast. If he had tried to wrest the knife out of the hands of his executioner we would never have known. Only videos of submissive victims are offered for the world's contemplation.

That's Da'esh [I don't use ISIS or IS, I call them what they call themselves]. In another frame, in Gaza, we have surly black-hooded Hamas executioners pushing around some pathetic men accused of collaborating with the Israelis and shot on the spot. The condemned have what looks like paper bags on their heads.

The truth hangs by a thread from Da'esh to Hamas. But the journalists, who could find themselves one day on their knees, mouthing accusations, ready for beheading, won't make the connection. They are already parroting the words of their eventual captors. Western journalists in Gaza, submissive to Hamas, report on the summary executions with eerie approval. For example, Ian Lee for *CNN*. Yup! Collaborating in wartime is serious business. Some of the executions were public. Hmph! It's a warning to anyone that might think of giving information to the Israelis.

The anchoress asks why they would do it. Well, there's the financial angle (Jews=money=corruption) and then maybe some of them are blackmailed. So, somehow, even as the camera focuses on the thick blood of the summarily executed, it turns out to be the fault of the Jews.

And why are their heads covered? Maybe it's to protect their families, he surmises. Then again, some of them, says the bright guy, might be Hamas commanders.

In fact they're all down-at-the-heels low level henchmen. You think a Hamas commander would be at the mosque in a stretched out t-shirt and shabby sandals? Even the killers, though dressed in black, look like nobodies. But the correspondent has never seen a proper Hamas fighter so how would he know? In Rafah, says a self-satisfied Lee, there was enthusiastic support for the killings. One man said they shouldn't shoot them they should burn them alive.

Da'esh is classier. They provided a gentleman from London to wield the knife. (Though recent reports suggest the video was staged and the actual butchering was done by a stand-in or a pro). The in-your-face role played by the London bloke has caused some embarrassment to the British government. And led to the brutal interruption of President Obama's golf outing. The Brits put an A-team of forensic experts on the case, and may have already identified the chap that disgraced the Queen's English. The prime suspect, Abdel-Majed Abdel Bary, is the son of an Egyptian extradited to the U.S. for his alleged implication in the 1998 embassy bombings.[1] Douglas Murray summed it up beautifully: "Just a bit more beheading than we are used to."[2]

Is it reasonable to add to the fearless journalist's kit the risk of being kidnapped and beheaded? With an added probability of sexual assault for the female of the species? War correspondents are a special breed, they willingly share the risks of soldiers and many have died on the battlefield. But hostages are humiliated, treated like dogs, exploited, and in some cases publicly beheaded to make an advertisement for the Caliphate. More often than not these captured reporters were there to tell the "other side" of the story, not hiding their sympathies with this or that "rebel" group or their antipathy to their own country. The French are notorious for bailing out their hostages, often with the help of Qatari intermediaries who already have their bank details, because they're directly funding the hostage-takers.

Where is our collective dignity? Why do they get away with this?

The truth hangs by a thread. While the Caliphate is slicing, the world is waffling, threatening to charge Israel with war crimes at the ICC. The West is on its knees. And telling Israel to swallow the medicine. Instead of proclaiming that we're not going to put up with hostage taking and beheading anymore, world leaders are pushing Israel to take its daily rockets and turn the other cheek.

But the beheaded can't turn the other cheek!

THE GAZA-ISRAEL LETHAL NARRATIVE IS UNRAVELING

Here in France, the virulent pro-Hamas stampedes were followed by a flutter of pseudo-intellectual kill-the-Jews essays. Otherwise presentable journalists like Christophe Barbier fell into the snake pit. Western governments don't know what to do about the thousands of passport-bearing "citizens" now fighting with the Caliphate, some of whom will inevitably return with plans for small and big massacres. They don't know what to do about the pro-Hamas foot soldiers in Europe, tearing up the pavement, flying the black flag of jihad on our treasured monuments, attacking police, screaming unadulterated Jew hatred. They can't rescue society and the economy from a massive influx of unqualified, unsatisfied, hostile immigrants. So the likes of Barbier set up the last concentric circle of the Gaza-Israel lethal narrative: it's all the fault of the Jews. It's the domestic variation on the theme "Israel has to make courageous concessions." Friends like Nicolas Sarkozy sang the tune as they set foot on the landing strip at Ben Gurion airport. "Israel cannot be secure unless the Palestinians have a state." Barbier's variation goes something like this: French Jews shouldn't give in to fear, shouldn't run for safety to Israel, shouldn't clump together to defend themselves here and Israel there, shouldn't be too Jewish lest they be perceived as not enough French. As far as I can tell this kind of sniffling has also been heard in US and other European media.

Elsewhere, the dawning recognition of the reality of Hamas, Da'esh, and jihad conquest leads to "mermaid discourse" that begins with the cold facts and ends with a writhing fishtail. Some Israeli leftists do the dance, granting that Hamas is intractable to any sort of civilized arrangement; everything has been done and repeated for more than a month to arrive at a pure and simple ceasefire that would have spared innocent Gazan civilians the hardships that befall them. It is common knowledge—ignored by most media—that Qatar has threatened to expel Khaled Mashal if Hamas agrees to an unconditional ceasefire. We know that Hamas had been planning to assassinate PA president-for-life

Mahmoud Abbas…after entering into a unity government with him. Israelis, whatever their political persuasion or geographical location, won't put up with any more rocket attacks from Gaza. Not at the present rate of more than a hundred a day, not at the previous rate of a dozen here and fifteen there. Hamas must be defeated, say the mermaids, and then… ah, well then we have to get down to the serious business of creating a State of Palestine. Gaza must be demilitarized, sing the mermaids, and who will take care of the store? Oh, that's easy: the international community. The UN? The EU? Or maybe the police force of Ferguson Missouri.

The media were floundering. Hamas broke the last truce, Da'esh showed its sharp teeth, US Defense Minister Chuck Hagel suffered a premature Hallowe'en moment: Hey, those guys are really mean! They're worse than al Qaida. Four year-old Daniel Tragerman was killed by a mortar shell fired into his kibbutz close to the border with Gaza. CNN "rose" to that occasion with a brief exchange between anchor and correspondent on the same wave length. Sad, yes, you feel for the parents, of course, their personal loss but… But of course the death toll on the Palestinian side is a hundred times more.

And you're surprised that Hamas is celebrating its victory?

Sky News, the BBC, and France 24 dipped into a bottomless barrel of moderate Muslims, adept at tongue lashing the West. My favorite was British MP Yasmin Qureshi, former aide to Ken Livingstone, who was allowed to speak from a genteel English garden background, with no contradiction within earshot. First, the facts: the Foley beheading has nothing to do with Islam. One of your contributors said it is an extreme form of sharia. That's not true. It has nothing to do with sharia. The ISIS people should be treated like enemy combatants. 99.9% of Muslims (in the world? in the UK? in her circumscription?) are against this disgraceful beheading. If they don't express themselves specifically as Muslims it's because it has nothing to do with Islam. However, many (most? 99.9%? all?) Muslims here in the UK are terribly upset by our government's policies in the Middle East over the past 30 years. They wouldn't kill people, they wouldn't behead anyone…We have to deal with all extremisms—Zionist extremism, neoconservative extremism, that's what created the problem we have now.

The truth hangs by a thread. Israel can't solve the Hamas problem, the West can't solve the Da'esh problem, Nigeria can't solve the Boko

Haram problem, Europe can't solve the demographic problem, and Qatar, cheered on by al Jazeera, keeps on pouring money into Western economies from its right hand pocket and into the maw of the caliphate with its left hand moneybags.

The truth hangs by a thread, the lethal narrative was losing its wind, other stories came to the fore, evidence of journalistic malfeasance was piling up faster than the wounded at Shifa hospital, calls for an immediate ceasefire didn't make sense after Hamas violated the 8th, 9th, and 10th in the series. Granted, it was brushed over with a vague "neither side wants to stop fighting," but indignation had lost its sting. Here in France the government fell apart at the seams...again. Prime Minister Manuel Valls, appointed just 5 months ago, recomposed his government the other day, and the plight of the Palestinians vanished as if it had never existed. I don't know to what extent they were counting on moral support from the French ...

The Cheikh Yassine Brigade put together a pro-Hamas party at Place de la République. About 200 attendees and apparently they didn't even manage to throw a single firebomb but they did get across the essentialist message: "We don't say the Zionists are Nazis, we say they are worse than Nazis." The Brigade is known for its credible death threats against Hassen Chalghoumi, accused of being a friend of the Jews and a miscreant. Chalghoumi, who has been under police protection for several years, is the imam everyone turns to when they need to say Muslims in France disapprove of this or that savage act.

VICTORY CELEBRATION IN GAZA

The big chiefs crawled out of the tunnels, the triumphant population gathered in the public square to celebrate their victory. In a work of fiction, the Israeli Air Force would drop bombs and wipe them out in one fell swoop. The story would be over. The perpetrators of evil would be eliminated with the cheering crowd, the falsifiers would go up in smoke, truth would have the last word.

It didn't happen that way. The lethal narrative wasn't demolished by a happy ending. Hamas is celebrating in the rubble and Benjamin Netanyahu is getting a volley of rotten eggs.

Still I'd rather be defeated like Israel than victorious like Hamas.

Epilogue: A young Jewish couple was assaulted on the Upper East Side by men who rode off waving Palestinian flags. That is the victory Hamas is celebrating.

DISPATCH N°9

Thursday, 4 September 2014

Russians are stupid. They should send Hamas fighters into the Ukraine: they're undetectable.

Media attention has shifted from Gaza to the Ukraine where more than 2000 people have been killed since April. How many civilians, soldiers, children? No breakdown is deemed necessary. But the situation is troubling, Russia is accused of invading, economic sanctions are traded like gunfire, the image of pan-European peace is tarnished.

And then there is Daesh. The mother of kidnapped journalist Steven Sotloff appealed by video to the Caliph, begging for mercy, pleading with the Caliph not to punish her son for acts of a government over which he has no control. Declaring that she has learned much about Islam, she asks the Caliph to follow the example of the prophet Mohamed who protected the People of the Book. Similar appeals have been made in the past, many kept private, others made public. Is there a single example of one that was successful? Allow me to express my doubts. [September 2— Steven Sotloff was beheaded, as promised] What works is money, prisoner release, arms, safe passage. Not appeals for mercy, not misconceptions about Islam.

The Daily Mail reports that a guard from one of the prisons where James Foley had been held was executed the day after Foley was beheaded.[1] Was Abu Ubaida Almaghribi really guilty of giving information to British intelligence or was John-the-knife pissed off because the Brits identified him so quickly?

Meanwhile, some journalists were still foaming at the mouth in Gaza. A recent issue of *Libération*[2] fell into my hands the other day. After reading a human interest story from the ruins of Shujaiyeh, I had a fleeting thought of inviting the author, Luc Mathieu, to face me in an honest public debate. That's probably as hopeless as the heartfelt plea from Sotloff's mother. Mathieu's double-page spread of bitter complaints against a background of rubble is a variation on the theme of "Why did they destroy my house? I'm not Hamas..." No one is Hamas, no Hamas fighters were anywhere in reach, no rocket launch pads were on the rooftop and no tunnel entrances at ground level. Well, ok, maybe a little tunnel entrance, but it's no reason to bomb us to smithereens. The stink of putrefaction and the smell of raw hatred rise in crescendo, accusations mount skyward against the unfair air raids and land with disgusting details of desecration by Israeli soldiers bivouacked in the al Mghani home during the operation. They made a hole in the wall for their sniper, smashed up everything in the kitchen, left their excrements in the room with the birdcages... the cages are empty now. There is no attempt at verification, no other side of the story, no hard facts... it's not journalism. It's take my word for it because the victims are howling in pain. So what is it doing in a newspaper and what is its purpose? To fuel hatred of Israelis. And, since there aren't so many of them here in France, Jews will do. The article ends with an implicit justification for future attacks. "Saïd" (who requested his real name not be used) says he tried to enlist in Hamas but was rejected because he doesn't know how to shoot. The journalist asks Saïd's 17 year-old son if he'd join up. "I have just one thing to say: look around, look at our houses bombed to rubble. You'll understand what I'm going to do."

Echoes of another human interest story, *"Mohamad, simple enfant de Gaza,"* [Gilles Paris, *Le Monde*, October 11, 2000] a boy who loved birds, "killed by merciless Israeli soldiers in the Gaza Strip." Mohamed's brother Iyad, who wanted to be a doctor or an engineer, says "as long as the others [Israelis] are there, we don't have any future."

What's going on in Gaza these days? Nothing of interest for most media. Bitter quarrels between Hamas and Fatah? Not newsworthy. Fatah accuses Hamas of expropriating the humanitarian aid sent into Gaza throughout the operation and to this day. Well, you can't report that because you already reported that the Israeli blockade and bombardment deprived Gazans of everything. Too complicated to go back and rectify. No new damage, no new victims, no news. What changed? Why did the merciless Israeli child-killers stop shooting? Did they suddenly become merciful?

No. Hamas stopped firing rockets. That's all. None of the issues have been negotiated. Israel demanded an unconditional ceasefire and, after 50 days of combat, got it. Hamas can chatter about victory and the spoils, Abbas can boast about how the UN is going to give him what Israel selfishly withholds, the fact is the military operation was suspended. Calm replies to calm.

That doesn't stop the demonization of Israel from skipping down the garden path. Gaza is an open-air prison, withdrawal doesn't equal the end of the Occupation. The West Bank is Occupied. Hizbullah, too, justifies its warlike existence by an infinite combat against an indelible Occupation. Hamas is taking a pause and looking for ways to gear up for the next battle. As long as Israel is a Jewish state the conflict cannot end. Public opinion goes along with the narrative, Israel has to be accused of original sin: taking the land away from the "Palestinians." The solution is always the same. Kill the Jews and take back the land.

Ah! Israel announces it is classifying 988 acres near Bethlehem as national land that will be available for construction of the Gvaot neighborhood. This becomes, "Israel is grabbing Palestinian land." And the big guns fire up. Ban Ki Moon, Obama, the Europeans, opinion-makers, NGOs get back on their high horses, hollering that the bad guys are at it again. The U.S. is asking the Israeli government to back down. Never mind that the land never belonged to those that call themselves Palestinian today. Land for peace is the magical formula as long as Israel does the giving, but building homes for Israelis on land that will in any and all cases remain part of Israel is harmful to peace. Construction is the Israeli response to the kidnap murder of three yeshiva *bochers*, planned and executed by Hamas.

A friend visiting from NY walked in the door and said, "I'm a leftist but I agree with you on Israel," and went on to suggest that Israel take a chunk of land in response to every attack from Gaza and/or Judea-Samaria.

Isn't that land for peace?

What if Israel had given into international pressure to turn over the Golan Heights to Syria?

Relative quiet on the Gaza front and new threats on the Syrian border where the al Nusra Front has dislodged Assad's troops, captured more than 40 Fijian UN peacekeepers, and ordered a Filipino contingent to lay down their arms. Reportedly disobeying orders from UN headquarters, 75 Filipino soldiers fought for seven hours before finally escaping to...Israel. But you wouldn't know it from evasive reports that somehow manage to say they escaped without mentioning where they fled to. That's understandable if you're a media that had been hawking a Gaza ceasefire on Hamas terms, rattling off fake UN casualty figures, relaying dishonest UNWRA accusations against Israel, and giving credibility to cockeyed plans for replacing Israeli surveillance of the Strip with UN troops. And Ban Ki Moon? Having used up a year's supply of outrage (against Israel) during the Protective Border operation he apparently had no fingers left to point at al Nusra.

Benjamin Netanyahu advised Western powers to stop systematically condemning Israel and concentrate on the real problem: Daesh.

Months ago the approach in France was sociologically merciful, with much talk of preventing misguided youth from running off to fight the jihad in Syria. Today the emphasis has shifted to preventing brutalized soldiers of the Caliphate from returning to pursue their savagery here. The more pragmatic British are preparing emergency measures to keep jihadis from coming back to "wreak havoc" in the UK. Returning fighters will be tracked and nabbed, foreign nationals will be barred, dual citizens will be stripped of their British nationality, and passports will be temporarily confiscated from British citizens. Not so harsh after all, when you remember that, in a not so distant past, traitors in wartime went before the firing squad.

Illegal immigrants arrive by the tens of thousands on European shores, a large percentage of them with no ID documents so that they can't be deported to their native lands, but international law won't allow us to protect ourselves from sworn enemies who are so brutal that they scare the Saudis! Furthermore, sharia law does not recognize nationalities and passports. Everyone belongs to the umma. A world without borders, governed by sharia law.

If we are to credibly defend ourselves, it would help if our leaders stopped saying Daesh has nothing to do with Islam. The intrepid British Prime Minister is still striving to render his citizens clueless. "As I have said consistently over the last few weeks, [ISIS] terrorists speak for no religion...They threaten Syrians, Iraqis, Americans and British people alike and make no distinction between Muslims, Christians or any other faith." Barack Hussein Obama (at least he attended a madrassa) said "ISIL speaks for no religion. Their victims are overwhelmingly Muslim, and no faith teaches people to massacre innocents" (but I guess he didn't pay attention in class). What's the purpose of these cotton candy defini-tions of Islam? Though moderate Muslims might use them to burnish their creds in the West they could get into trouble in Muslim countries. Say it in the streets of the Caliphate and your head will be separated from its pedestal. In fact, "that's not Islam" has nothing to do with Islam; it's a question of brute force.

Our leaders, journalists and miscellaneous kibitzers did not, as far as I know, graduate from Al Azhar. If they had, they would not make such statements. The history of Islam is bloodied from the first generation to this day by warring concepts of what is Islam. Whatever the intentions, "that's not Islam" does not clarify the debate. The statement is inopera-tive, inappropriate, unsubstantiated, insincere, and dangerously mis-leading. When our leaders make such fatuous statements they deserve something more shut-your-mouth than proto-theological debate about radical and moderate Islam. How about, "Excuse me, sir, how are you qualified to say what is and isn't Islam?"

We are told that Western youths who run off to join the Caliphate don't even understand Islam, don't speak Arabic, don't follow the rules. They drink, fornicate, dress in track suits, and engage in criminal behav-ior. Right. Like the early followers of the "prophet." Once they get to the Caliphate, they straighten out, brotha'!

How did Daesh suddenly grow so powerful? Simple. It's because we didn't intervene immediately in Syria to help the good guys overthrow Assad. Because we did intervene in Libya, but it wasn't the right way (though the media loved every minute of it as it was happening.) Because of the illegal American invasion of Iraq followed by the stupid disband-ing of Saddam's army. Because we supported Iraq in its war against Iran. Because we funded the Taliban to defeat the Soviets in Afghanistan. Then there was Mosadegh, there was the Shah of Iran, and there is the discourse that goes back, back, back, like a man falling from a cliff and smashing on the rocks below. That's Islam....the rocks are Islam: we deserve to be punished because we did not recognize Mohamed as the ultimate prophet.

Details are emerging about the latest victim of "[ISIS] terrorists." Steven Sotloff, the grandson of Holocaust survivors, showed "deep love for the Islamic world."[3] He had lived in Yemen, spoke Arabic, went knowingly to report from dangerous areas. From 2002 to 2004 Sotloff studied journalism at the University of Central Florida, stamping grounds of the infamous Sami al-Arian.

And now we learn that Steven Sotloff made Aliyah in 2008. Comments published by friends and colleagues give the impression that, soured on Israel, he chose immersion in the Arab-Muslim world, where he prudently hid his Jewish identity, claiming to be a secular Muslim. Did he sour on that adventure too? It is reported that he was fed up with the Middle East and ready to go back to Miami to do graduate studies. But he went back to Syria for just one more Big Story. Now the family spokesman, Barak Barfi has addressed the Caliph Abu Bakr al-Baghdadi...in Arabic. "He said that as a brother of Islam, he was speaking in the name of Islam and did not agree with the Caliph's actions. 'Where is the mercy?' he asked the Caliph."[3]

In every gruesome story of violent death, time plays a tragic role. If she had only let that clando taxi go by, if he had not walked into the apartment just when, if they had left ten minutes earlier...Steven Sotloff wanted to get one more story. The three hitch-hiking yeshiva students got into that car and realized, one second later, they'd been kidnapped.

We seek solace. Like soldiers, they must not die in vain. The murder of Eyal Yifrah, Gilad Shaar, and Naftali Fraenkel led to discovery of the Hamas Rosh Hashanah massacre plan. Now the tunnel that went from Shujeiyah to a kindergarten in kibbutz Nahal Oz—one among more than 30 offensive tunnels—has been destroyed. Three teenagers were murdered, hundreds of children were saved. The slaughter of two American journalists, twelve years after the beheading of Daniel Pearl, is touching a nerve and, hopefully, awakening a healthy reaction of self-defense in the West.

DISPATCH N°10

Thursday, 18 September 2014

There is no word to accurately express the weight and scope of the Jewish Question

Anti-Semitism, Judeophobia, Jew-hatred, anti-Zionism, self-hating Jews...none of these terms captures the full range of negative relations to all that is Jewish. We use them for practical purposes, but they make it difficult to understand and confront a phenomenon of cosmic proportions that cannot be compared to commonplace prejudice based on color, nationality, tribe, social class, etc. The "Jewish Question" does not, as the above terms suggest, concern relations between two entities, Jews and Others. It is not about how Jews behave in general or in specific situations, it is not about how we are individually or collectively. It can't be influenced by any change in what Jews do or say. Both Jews and non-Jews are affected, in myriad ways, by the enormity of the Question posed by Judaism. Baffled by the impossibility to assimilate the sign "Jewish," otherwise normal people veer off into bizarre reactions.

The Jewish Question cannot be solved by an Answer. Anathema to totalitarian projects, Judaism inevitably provokes their murderous fury. When the destructive forces that periodically beset humanity reach cataclysmic proportions they always include the need to exterminate Jews and Judaism. This exterminationist fury ignites minor secondary conflagrations in different sectors of society that would never consciously support the extermination and, consequently, are terribly offended when accused of anti-Semitism. Today, Islam, which harbors genocidal hatred of Jews in its essential composition, has turned the very word "Israel" into a raw nerve that triggers blinding hostility, leading people to act against their own vital interests.

This explains the grotesque reactions to Israel's self-defensive "Protective Border" operation in Gaza. By any rational evaluation, Hamas would be seen as one of the countless tentacles of jihad conquest, and Israel would be admired or at least respected for its courage in facing up to the latest attempt by Hamas to annihilate the Jewish State. At the very moment when the free and not so free world is desperately seeking a strategy to deal with the Caliphate, Israel would serve as a model and precious ally. Instead, NATO, the UN, the EU are tossing and turning, abandoned by the superpower that once was the USA, timidly engaged in limited airstrikes and embroiled in confused rhetoric. The watchword is "no boots on the ground." Netanyahu is under fire at home for not achieving an overwhelming victory, while these big, rich, heavily armed purportedly allied countries promise defeat.

Can we take comfort in the planned 30 or 40-nation coalition, including the likes of Turkey, Saudi Arabia, Qatar, and Iran but not, of course,

Israel? French commentators are pouting this week about the exclusion of Iran, at American insistence, from the September 15th international conference in Paris. Qatar is apparently joining the coalition while continuing to finance the beheaders. Turkey might be skittish about anything that could encourage Kurdish sovereignty. Great Britain will do airstrikes over Iraq but not over Syria. Saudi Arabia and assorted Emirates will swish around in their long white robes and let the infidels do the fighting. The idea, according to the usual experts, is that it won't be the West killing Muslims, it will be a coalition led by moderate Arab-Muslim nations that will wipe out those caliphating renegades who don't know what Islam is.

Lethal narrative, my friends. Instead of facing the reality of jihad conquest and fighting like men, the West will fiddle with the truth and reinforce the lie behind which Islam creeps into and over our world. Skipping rapidly over the inevitable squabbles, pecking-order power struggles, underhanded tricks and untenable delays, allow me to predict the gem that will be fashioned deep in the bowels of this coalition: they will decree that there's no way to defeat the Caliphate unless and until Israel ends the Occupation by satisfying all demands imposed by the joint Fatah-Hamas government. In the meantime, the Caliphate will be increasing geometrically day by day.

THE BLINDING GLARE OF THE JEWISH QUESTION

There is no lack of concrete evidence to rectify erroneous reports made during the Gaza operation. Hamas intimidation of journalists, use of human shields, installation of rocket launchers in civilian buildings, tunnel entrances in mosques and hospitals... Corrected casualty figures show at least a thousand fighters among the 2,000 dead. The *Times of Israel* reported that, according to Israeli intelligence, none of the "collaborators" recently executed in Gaza were Israeli assets. They were in prison during the operation, couldn't have supplied information. The airstrikes that killed several Hamas top brass weren't based on human intel. The journalist who said on *i24 news* that Hamas had to shoot rockets from heavily populated areas because there are no open fields in Gaza has not, to my knowledge, retracted. But no single element of the lethal narrative is as important as the casualty figures that served as leitmotif to every broadcast everywhere: "2,000 killed, most of them civilians."

As soon as the unconditional cease fire was concluded, Hamas leaders came out of the tunnels where they had been hiding, and proclaimed victory. Their version of the conflict was confirmed by overwhelming support for Hamas in Gaza and Judea-Samaria. Khaled Mashal rightfully declared that world media had drawn their water from the Hamas well.[1] Indeed! They weren't interested in reliable information that contradicted the image fabricated in the heat of battle. But their ears perked up suddenly when 43 Israeli army reservists of the prestigious 8200 intelligence unit vociferously objected to "unjust practices against the Palestinian population in the West Bank." It was music to media ears, they couldn't get enough of it. The other side of the story, the other 99% proud members of the unit, the rebuttal from defense minister Ya'alon among others, the special circumstances in a time of war, the lives saved during the operation...could not drown out those luscious sounds of dissent.

Israel launches an investigation of 11 cases of possible misconduct during the operation, including the alleged hit on the school in Rafa, denounced by Thomas Victor as Pallywood staging.[2]

First, the investigations are reported as proof of misconduct. If it turns out there was no misconduct, they will be denounced as a whitewash. Hamas doesn't investigate anything; they run to Human Rights Watch and get guaranteed condemnation. No need for evidence, the complaint is enough.

The human interest stories churned out during the Gaza operation might be justified if the context were clearly defined. It never was. They were raised to a universal plane of human suffering where the only decent reaction must be compassion. In fact, on the human interest level, what's the difference between the family of a Hamas officer, the wife and children of a Daesh beheader, and a simple citizen caught in the middle? Same rubble, same dead relatives, same smashed furniture, same dismay, same denial: we had nothing to do with Hamas, Daesh, Hizbullah, the Taliban, AQMI...

Some of our best and brightest slip into mermaid discourse in the face of this stonewall. Israel, they say, has to learn how to get its message across. Stop infighting and bureaucratic inertia, use communications-savvy collaborators, stop apologizing, tell the world Hamas is Daesh and they're out to get all of us, don't forget to show what's happening to

Christians in the Middle East, occupy the media landscape, send articulate spokespersons... None of this advice should be necessary. The facts speak for themselves. But when they come from Israeli sources the blaring screech of the Jewish Question transforms them into white noise.

Talk about disproportion!

Flat-footed journalism, unable or unwilling to convey the enormous difference between Hamas and Israel, reduced the conflict to a match between two sides in the same category. Noble diplomats zipped back and forth trying to stop the massacre but "neither party wants to stop fighting." Chronology was reversed—rockets launched by Hamas become tat for the tit of Israeli bombings. Hamas statements of genocidal intent were ignored, Israeli explanations were dismissed.

And the Caliphate was spreading like wildfire. In its path, Christian and Yazidi women were raped, bought and sold, starved to death, slain for refusing to convert to Islam. Where were the feminists? A handful of Lilith activists, convinced that arms for Israel transited through the Liège airport, flooded a terminal with fake blood. On the outskirts of Paris, hysterical BDS harpies screamed themselves hoarse for hours in a Rosny-sous-bois shopping mall until they were dragged away by the police. Tragic irony—several days later in the same banlieue a modest 4-story apartment building collapsed, presumably by a gas explosion, leaving Gaza style rubble.

As French authorities shivered in their boots at the prospect of returning jihad veterans, the Jewish Question took a new twist: dual nationals who did their military service in Israel were equated with French jihadis who went to fight with the Caliphate. This grotesque equation was promoted by, among others, Argentine president Cristina Kirchner and French firebrand Jean-Luc Mélenchon of the Front de Gauche. Tawfik Tahani, president of France-Palestine Solidarité, outdid them: he claimed that one week before the start of the Gaza operation, an Israeli sergeant had come to recruit Jewish and non-Jewish French fighters. N.B. only Israeli citizens can serve in the Israel Defense Force.

This grotesque, and unchallenged, allegation was made during a broadcast— *Le Secret des Sources*—on the highbrow France Culture radio station; Tahani was there to balance Arno Klarsfeld, Esq., son of the famed Nazi-hunters Serge and Beate Klarsfeld. The idea of the weekly program is to re-examine the way journalists covered a big story. On

September 6th the focus was on Gaza. Instead of focus, we got sidestepping. One journalist explained that as they entered Gaza they were assigned a fixer who stayed with them the whole time. Did it influence their coverage? The question wasn't even raised. Another denied that it was forbidden to show Hamas fighters. "We didn't see any, that's all. It's normal. There was a war going on. They were hiding in the tunnels." Admitting that some images were falsified, a reporter chose a salient example: Israelis showed recycled footage of pompous funerals of soldiers dating back to earlier conflicts. Their notion of balanced coverage is simple: if you say something negative about one party to the conflict you have to say something negative about the other party.

Why would Tahani claim an Israeli recruiter was rounding up French fighters? In fact, the inclusion of one such damning—and patently false—accusation in hate-Israel barrages is recurrent: IDF soldiers' excrements in a home in Sheijaya, 45 minutes of gunfire aimed at Jamal and Mohamed al Dura, heartless Israeli soldiers kicking around a Palestinian baby like a football in Gaza... The latter from Hamas apologist Sara Roy's "Response to Elie Weisel" [*Counterpunch* September 9]. Lurid details that cannot be verified are dropped like a date-rape drug into the let-me-criticize-Israel cocktail. Their purpose is to hit the genocidal nerve of the Jewish Question. When this nerve is hit, rational reception is no longer possible, the message is raised to a lethal level of potency. The ingurgitation of a nerve shocking falsehood dissolved in a mix of misdemeanors that could be attributed to any government or society turns "Israel" into poison.

The tectonic shift in blame that makes Israel Public Enemy N°1 hinges on every sort of mental and moral perversion of which the human mind is capable.

Totalitarian movements periodically beset human history; they have never been perpetrated by Jews or fueled by Judaism. Not only does obsession with the Jewish Question undermine our only ally in the Middle East, it fosters mortal confusion about our real enemy. Daesh Productions Inc. has presented its third beheading film, with coming attractions for the fourth. AQMI chapters in Algeria and other Islamic fighters worldwide are swearing allegiance to the Caliphate, Boko Haram is taking over swaths of Nigeria, and our leaders are tongue-tied. Prime Minister David Cameron, standing upright and British after the September

12th beheading of aid worker Paul Haines, said "Islam is a religion of peace." Families or spokespersons for the decapitated journalists recite [abrogated] Koranic verses and insist "beheading has nothing to do with Islam." President Obama, like a doctor trying to get a kid to open his mouth and say aaaah, keeps promising "no boots on the ground." A retired French general commenting on air strikes against Daesh says reassuringly, "it won't be like Gaza." Coalition airstrikes, he says, will be aimed at military units out in the open, not in populated areas like Mosul. We should be able to handle this neatly, he adds, unless —as if it were the most outlandish possibility imaginable—the jihadis use human shields.

Conveniently forgetting atrocities committed under the reign of Saddam Hussein, commentators delight in latter day Bush-bashing. It's the 2003 illegal invasion of Iraq that brought us the Caliphate, they declare, not realizing there is something twisted about assuming a disbanded Iraqi officer would naturally turn into a Caliphate killer. Other causes are reeled off—it's because we intervened in Libya... and didn't in Syria, abandoned Afghanistan and let Maliki discriminate against Sunnis in Iraq. Isn't it time to realize it has nothing to do with our actions and mistakes? It's not the fault of the neo-cons, the Zionists, the Jews, the Christians, the Pope, the Tea Party. It is the dynamics of Islam, its history and its foundations. Unless opposed by overwhelming force Islam can only go in one direction, like a river into the sea.

In between two Caliphate beheadings, a woman was decapitated in her north London garden. Neither the victim nor the perpetrator had been publicly identified before the police declared the crime was "not terrorism." What did they mean? The killer wasn't Muslim? Then the killer was identified— a Nigerian, Nicholas Salvadore, and his victim—a loveable 82 year-old Londoner of Italian origin. But...it was subsequently revealed that the murderer is a convert to Islam. And some say he mistook the suntanned Mrs. Palmira Silva for a Jew. With that, the story slipped out of view.

It is a terrible portent.

Caliphators returning to Europe will not only attack Jews and other infidels they will tyrannize Muslims. Making use of local allies, they will take over neighborhoods the way they took over parts of Syria and Iraq, running roughshod over those moderate Muslims the progressives claim to love so much. They'll engage in bloody combat with rivals in the Muslim community, take over mosques and the drug trade, rob banks and munitions depots, take hostages for ransom, kill policemen, rape women...and who will stop them?

BOOTS ON THE GROUND

What should Israel do in the face of this unremitting sleaze that is slopped on its every word and act? Take care of business. That's what Israelis did this summer, in Gaza and at home. Do what had to be done. Resist Hamas rockets, destroy tunnels, bomb launch pads while alert citizens run into bomb shelters, bless the Iron Dome and the IDF, and let the commentators ruminate their curd.

5,000 French Jews made Aliyah this year. Instead of scolding them, like Christophe Barbier, for mistaken divestment, French people should be asking how they will manage without these upstanding citizens. French Jews should not be pleading and petitioning for greater protection and less media venom, they should be given concrete proof that their presence is desired. Not flowery words, not interfaith declarations, not shoah memorials, but courage, lucidity, a change of heart, and determined action.

I write these words with affectionate concern for the welfare of my adopted country.

Chapter 4/ Epilogue

DISPATCH N°11: GIFTED WITH JUDAISM
September 22, 2014 – June 3, 2015

Judaism is a rare and perplexing gift. In this world where human beings are counted by the billions, the chances of being born Jewish are so small. In the vast expanses of space and time, Jews should have long ago disappeared like a drop of color in the ocean, or be tucked away in the margins somewhere, visible only to experts of lost populations. On the contrary, Judaism is more vibrant than ever, drawing on inexhaustible resources, resilient, inventive, accomplished, distinguished, complex and brilliant.

Judaism is a gift that only a mother can confer. Conversion to Judaism is difficult and discouraged, drifting away from Judaism is frequent and apparently unstoppable; the combined effects of periodical genocides, forced conversions, and assimilation has kept the Jewish population at levels of 13.9 million, but Judaism still counts enormously. Judaism is not a gift like a free trip to the Bahamas or a case of champagne, it is a gift like a talent. The potential is boundless but only if one knows how to draw on it and develop it. You are born of your mother's womb, you are Jewish, it's like getting a jet plane for your first birthday. Maybe that's why our sense of humor is so highly developed.

We're born Jewish, we're in the cockpit, and all our life long we are trying to figure out how to fly that plane. And that's just one metaphor. Judaism is thrown into the category of religion and I don't deny that some Jews live it as a religion and Jews are influenced by the religious practices and styles of the societies in which they live as a tiny minority, but on a rigorous intellectual level, Judaism does not function as a religion. As long as you stay on the surface it might look like a you-go-to-church I-go-to-synagogue affair but as soon as you begin to study, you're embarked on a 120-year PhD program. There is so much to learn and most of us don't begin early enough; it dawns on us one day after so many courses of general studies and so many detours that we have neglected a treasure that was given to us with the gift of life.

It is easy to get discouraged by our patchy knowledge and myriad practical responsibilities. Where to begin? Sooner or later you realize that if you don't master Hebrew you'll remain lost in translation for the rest of your life. Impossible to catch up, impossible to give up. I gasp in admiration of children who know perfectly what I have half-forgotten: they will follow an ascending path that wasn't open to me at their age, precisely because we were taught a simplified Judaism that mimicked Sunday School Christianity. In those days, our intellectual appetite led us to university studies that ignored the particular contribution of Jewish thought to Western civilization. We espoused a falsified universalism. We mixed socially.

Judaism is a question without an answer. We are always running up and down the ladder, wrestling with the emissary. Running away from our Judaism, running back to it. Gathering together because that's the only way to practice it, slipping away because at heart we are not exclusive. Being Jewish is not only studying higher thought, it is living it in the everyday practice of every aspect of life in its concrete physical dimension. Some of these practices—*kashrut* [dietary rules] and respect for *shabat* [the Sabbath] for example—separate Jews from others. They also separate, within Judaism, the observant from the non-observant and everyone from the "ultra" observant. Rational people often dismiss the very idea of permitting certain foods and prohibiting others...in the name of what they consider to be nothing but a religion, that is, outmoded. And some currents of Judaism carry observance of these practices to a degree that the rest of us find extreme and often accompanied by hostility to us and even violence.

Our holidays are marvelous. In all my travels, in all my convivial sharing of feasts and festivals, in all my wholehearted acceptance of other people's sacred and secular festivities, I have never found anything close to Jewish holidays for their sense, their tastes, their style and content and coherence in cycles from day to week to month to year to sheathes of years, to eternity. But they don't yield their fullness unless they are cultivated, like works of art.

May 5 – June 3 2015

This text was created in an *élan*, a leap, a swoop upward and deep within. It was a defense and illustration of the love for Judaism that inspired my coverage of the Gaza-Israel conflict of the summer of 2014. I wrote the dispatches for the *New English Review* because I knew I could express myself fully and freely there. Because *NER* does not pinch my literary scope, I was able to go beyond journalistic coverage of events during that crucial summer without ignoring a commitment to getting the facts straight and in proportion. Hostility to Jews reached new depths in Paris in the summer of 2014; my writing was pushed to new heights from which I am compelled to imagine a different way of reacting to anti-Semitism, a 21st century strategy that could integrate all that we have learned since the very beginnings of Judaism...since the beginning of our world. In the past fifteen years, when my intellectual attention has been riveted on the question of preventing a disaster that could make the Shoah pale by comparison, I have come to understand that our aim cannot be to rid the world of anti-Semitism. On the contrary, we need to understand why it will never disappear. Then we will learn how not to be victims of something that is aimed at destroying the goodness that Judaism brings to humanity.

This is what led me to Dispatch N°11...that was interrupted by the *hagim*, the awesome month of Tishri, what's called the High Holidays in common parlance. My psalm in praise of Judaism was at its fullest at the end of Yom Kippur. But I wasn't able to put it in writing. I had to prepare a long-delayed trip to Israel. With intricate professional ramifications. In fact, it was—finally—the release of *Al Dura: Long Range Ballistic Myth*, which for personal reasons, had been published but not promoted months before. My connection to Yom Kippur has a special private link: My mother z"l invented my name, Nidra, because I was born *erev* Kippur, on the eve of Yom Kippur when the *chazn* chants the Kol Nidre.

In the coming days—I leave for Israel on the 10th of May to attend the Global Forum for the Combat against Antisemitism—I will develop the notes I jotted down last fall, trying my best to capture the context within which they were written at a time when, as always, we didn't quite know what was in store for us.

The world-famous activist philosopher Bernard-Henri Levy was put on the media chopping block like so many others that summer. I wanted to understand why the good faith explanation he gave doesn't work, why setting the facts straight doesn't help. You have to force the question back into the ulterior motives first, before granting anything whatsoever. You block the ball: Israel did what had to be done. That's the best answer to the insincere probing. They throw you dead Palestinian children. Duck the punch and lead with your right. What are you suggesting? That I am heartless? Partisan? That Israelis kill children for fun. Let me ask you first, how did they get into danger?

When one strain of Jew hatred reaches genocidal proportions it ignites minor forms that would have remained dormant, and creates a perilous maelstrom that endangers everyone, not only Jews. An imaginary enormous, threatening Jew spawned by that hatred obscures and attempts to annihilate the immense, beneficial message carried by Judaism.

Advice to humanitarians worldwide: Instead of masturbating with UNWRA-falsified death tolls in Gaza, compare the Jewish population in Iraq in the 1940s, about 135,000, and today, close to zero. Now calculate the radical decrease of Iraq's Christian population. Add the two subtractions and calculate what could happen to Christians in Europe.

K.M. is charming, intelligent, ambitious, skilled professionally and successful financially. The same can be said for her husband, and their children are well on the way to similar distinction. K.M.'s smile is luminous, her laughter is like bells. She told me she is so proud of how the Israelis handled themselves during the Gaza operation she's studying Hebrew... because she has decided to make Aliyah. This proud joyful Aliyah of bright dynamic Jews shouldn't be underestimated. If Jews were leaving France simply out of fear of bodily harm they wouldn't throw themselves into the middle of a conflict where rockets are launched from Gaza at all hours of the day and night, from one end to the other of Israel. Christophe Barbier relieves himself by scolding French Jews for "mistakenly" leaving France? He should be looking in the mirror and asking himself how he'll manage in an arid France leeched of its Jews.

The brother of the beheaded Haines comes on screen, reads a few Koranic verses, says this violence is alien to Islam, foreign to the people of the Middle East. At an international conference convened in Paris to deal with Daesh, everyone from the French president to distinguished editorialists can't be more emphatic: it has nothing to do with Islam. Radical Islam has nothing to do with Islam either. What's radical Islam? Dutifully following the Koranic injunction to strike off their heads. And radical Judaism? Performing the *mitzvoth*. The knife has nothing to do with the beheading that has nothing to do with the neck and none of it is Islam. If it were it would have a label and everyone would know.

Muslims know it has everything to do with Islam and the good news is that many are shocked to see it shape up in that strictly orthodox way

I'm searching for the neurological pathway that will demolish the lethal narrative and liberate normal defensive behavior in my fellow man. The cohesion of Israeli society across all lines during the recent operation was almost a chemical reaction to the rocket fire aimed at every corner of the tiny nation, including Tel Aviv. It was not mindless support of government and army, it was a clear apprehension of concrete reality. Step back and look at the widening concentric circles of the target. It includes all the West, all democracies, all freedom-loving people. What is the formula, what are the words that can connect the concrete reality of attacks against Israel with the widening circle that will encompass us all?

Of course, that's why genocidal Jew hatred and jihad attacks against the Jewish State are whisked out of sight. Let me say with a sardonic smile: fortunately they keep pushing themselves in our face.

We can't unlock the stranglehold of the Jewish Question unless we understand it. Understand it deeply and thoroughly, beyond anecdotal details.

There's no comfortable armchair to be Jewish in. No upward curve to follow assiduously all the way to the heights of Judaism. How do you grasp it for a lifetime, from generation to generation? Where exactly do we find it? In ourselves? In a collectivity? On the outside looking in, detractors imagine that Jews are strutting around like cocks in the barnyard, crowing their vainglorious pride. In fact, most of us are running away from it most of the time. It's too, as they say, awesome. You leave your mother's womb with a mission statement clutched in your tiny right hand: be Jewish. Above and beyond and within and around whatever else you are, be Jewish. You belong to a nation that counts for 0.2% of the world population ...and they all depend on you. Not for everything. That would be stupid. For something. Something too enormous to define. Without which all the rest would collapse.

Why, in my momentary Jewish observance and newfound Zionism, do I often feel like an impostor? Notice, as soon as I write about Judaism, the question marks spill onto the page. Other forms of wealth and success may or may not be given, but our supply of question marks is prodigious. Even Gertrude Stein, who was a model of assimilation, ended her life on that note. Or so the legend goes: on her deathbed Stein said to her beloved Alice B. Toklas, "What is the answer?" Did Toklas shrug her shoulders or shed a silent tear? Stein went to the core of her soul and asked, "What is the question?"

Why do I feel like an impostor? Because I knew, and then forgot, and now relearn in a sketchy last minute way. Because I was observant and now haphazardly do and don't. I was observant in the most harmonious, wholesome, fulfilling, comprehensive natural-as-breathing way. I suppose it was a first generation form of *yiddishkeit*. In my family, probably a mixture of Hasidism and Haskalah. Shtetl Judaism transposed to America at the dawn of the 20th century, lightened and brightened by its liberation from oppressive Europe. Yes. But sweetened and flavored and spiced with the Europe that never really left me as I became more or less but not really American. Judaism informed by my father's z"l solid yeshiva education, the only formal education he had, his perfect command of the texts, the Hebrew words that remained as if engraved in stone when congestive heart disease washed away the contents of his dashing handsome mind. The Judaism of my mother, the most savory ethics served with the highest culinary devotion, unpretentious wisdom, maternal, feminine, boundless love. Yes, I am true to the promise they transmitted. They who brought me whole Judaism led me out into the wider world. The first taste of shrimp. And other transgressions that never touched the core. Joyful freedom that doesn't deny the source. Yom Kippur. I reach back to them at the synagogue on rue Pavée. An art nouveau gem designed by Hervé Guimard, the architect of the famous floral bronze métro entrances. The synagogue is squeezed in between two nondescript buildings, its façade is grimy, the entrance a bit shabby, but the beauty shines through. A tree stands like a biblical figure visible through the frosted glass wall behind the ark. I am relegated to the mezzanine with the women whose constant chatter drowns out the words of the Lithuanian-born rabbi. The chairs are tasteless and uncomfortable. We lean our elbows on the chest-high carved wooden façade that needs some tender loving care, and look down on the men in *kippa* and *talit*, the chandeliers bursting with holy light, the yeshiva *bochers*, learned men, and officiants around the bima, little girls and boys running up and down the aisles, babies passed from the ground floor father to the mezzanine mother. I try to follow the text in Hebrew. The women next to me talk about their grandchildren, their health issues, births and deaths, recipes and dinner parties.

I frown, I groan, I wince, I put a finger of hush on my lips, nothing works. They are in another world. On the far right end of the mezzanine, the learned *frum* women dressed in white follow every word in the *siddur*, rocking gently in prayer. They, too, are in a different world from me. Sometimes I have a prayer book, sometimes not. Every year I promise myself to buy my own. Kol Nidre, all our vows. All our unkept vows.

"We used to live in this neighborhood," says my chatty neighbor. "This is where we get together." Used to...before or after the Shoah that decimated the Marais? I was far away then, in the United States. When we break the fast *chez moi* I have to leave the synagogue for an hour or two in the afternoon to make the kreplach. Everything else is prepared ahead of time, but the small squares of dough have to be filled and pinched and left to dry slightly but not too much. A young woman with a toddler and a babe in arms tries to follow the service. My socializing neighbor tells me the table she has set, the dishes she has prepared, the bounty of the feast that will break the fast. I can stand for hours, without eating or drinking, looking over the balustrade to capture the fervor of the chants that fill my heart and soul. The words are inscribed in me. In

Hebrew. I don't care if I "understand." I don't want any translation to interfere with my communion. The chants inhabit me, resonate for days afterward.

Strong voices rise up from the front of the men's section, row upon row of men that accompany the chants of the *chazn*, never weakening, growing stronger hour after hour, without food or drink, supplicating inscription in the book of life. It is not a choir, it is an alliance, a congregation within the loosely assembled attendance, a concentration of men whose eloquence intervenes on our behalf as we approach the fateful hour. The gates are open, the book is open, it is the eleventh hour and the women are still schmoozing as if they were at a café, men squirm and think about their emails, the minimum service crowd trickles in, just coming to hear the shofar that wraps it up. It's not a real book with pages and lists, it's a heart that beats to the miracle of life. Everlasting is not an option. Just give me one more year.

This year we break the fast chez E.G. One of the guests, an American, had chanted in the choir at the Reform service held in a Protestant Temple. She was uplifted. And I protested in silence. What ? Female voices ? A piano? A Protestant church?

The idea that everything should be subject to change seems just as bad as the idea that nothing should change. Marriage is a mother and a father for the children, it should be something solid that society can build on, not a whim to float with the breeze of fickle lifestyles. Annexes can be arranged for those who don't fit into the picture. Let Judaism be sturdy like the trunk of life, while branches, leaves, flowers and fruits delight in endless variations. Women don't need to be rabbis. This story of female emancipation and assertion is in a different dimension, it's part of a secular history we share with the whole world.

The voice, the body, the words, the music, the psalms, these come to us from our origins, from a different history, thousands of uninterrupted years, millions of repetitions without lassitude, a planetary wholeness that resonates in our hearts and minds as we repeat in unison in every corner of the earth the same service, the same sequence, releasing the same light and intelligence. We need to hear this music in its intact wholeness as it comes from the beginnings of human time, not in the name of narrow-minded purity but because we progress on an unbroken thread from generation to generation, *l'dor v'dor*, genetic material is handed from one to the next in an unbroken line that never produces an identical same.

This is why I come to the synagogue on rue Pavée for Yom Kippur. I walk past the ground floor offices that are strangers to me, where I don't imagine having a place or an exchange of ideas, though I might be wrong. I walk upstairs to the mezzanine, I endure the chatter of women, I greet with a silent smile familiar faces, a pharmacist, a shopkeeper, someone from the bookstore on rue des Rosiers, or strike up a brief whispered conversation with a fellow American. I am immersed in the meaning of this collective self-examination, ritualized in exquisite beauty. What does it mean to supplicate *hashem* to be inscribed in the Book of Life? We are not talking about a supersize grandfather with a long white beard and half moon glasses holding a leather-bound register. Our supplications are addressed to life itself. Keep me, let me live, despite my shortcomings and those of my fellow man, let life live and let me partake of it one more year. A lease on life, renewed once a year, but not forever. Yizkor. I release a torrent of tears for the loved ones spent and gone. The ache is reawakened to its first unbearable instant. How can a human being draw his last breath and disappear, leaving behind inert pounds of flesh?

I don't know who they are, the men seated in the rows between the bima and the ark where the torah scrolls are kept in their velvet livry and silver tasseled crowns. I am so happy to be Jewish because what we venerate is a book, *torah emet*, a book of truth. Not goods or gods or magical swishers. A book. I don't know who they are, these men whose voices fill my soul. They know every word, every note, every gesture. Who are they? Not a choir. I don't like synagogue choirs. It's not a performance. How do they achieve these heights of voice? They aren't professionals. They are what every Jewish man is supposed to be. Learned.

Despite our individual shortcomings we are collectively a force for goodness and a source of strength.We don't have to prove it, reality proves it. And the jealousy it provokes sustains the argument. We don't have to hoard this treasure, we don't have to selfishly keep it for ourselves, we can honor it without disparaging Others or spitting on their gods. Judaism doesn't damn other believers or non-believers. It isn't a contest for the World's Best in which we make the rules and no one else has a chance.

I think that Jews who proudly and somewhat defiantly declare themselves to be atheists are in the wrong pew. We don't have any god to not believe in. Our divinity is the striving for an unattainable excellence. It is "what shall be." And what shall be is our responsibility. It is, in the thought of Shmuel Trigano, an absent presence. Not out to lunch, a veritable withdrawal to a forever unattainable dimension.

My embrace of Judaism does not imply disdain for Others any more than my love for my family equals indifference to the fate of humanity. Love, in my Book, includes an ethical imperative.

I wear my magen David because defending my people makes me stronger, not partisan and not less humane. I hide my magen David when I circulate in hostile territory because I think I am more useful to defend our values if I remain alive and in good health than smashed up by a stray barbarian. The shame is not on me.

MISSING PERSONS
October 1, 2014

The beheading of journalists James Foley and Steven Sotloff followed by British aid worker David Haines has finally convinced European public opinion that we are at war. Unfortunately, this belated will to confront the enemy is taking shape around the alarming disappearance of the State of Israel, virtually evicted from the news cycle and Middle-East geography.

Last August a thousand correspondents were in Gaza sleuthing out the slightest Israeli faux pas and serving all-you-can-drink cocktails of Palestinian tragedy, a concoction of Hamas "information" bottled by the UN (= UNWRA). Images of ferocious combatants in keffieh facemasks (Daesh mujahidin lookalikes) were strictly prohibited; the face of Hamas was 100% civilian.

At the end of August the curtain fell abruptly on the Gaza-Israel show. Opinion-makers didn't bother to present the epilogue that would have corrected the false impressions cleverly maintained during the Protective Edge operation. The new production is called "all together against the Islamic State."

The savage headhunters are so terrifying that the whole world chokes on them, including their white-robed underwriters who don't of course cut off their funds before sweeping into the Paris Summit where exquisite strategists François Hollande and Barack Hussein Obama round up thirty countries ready and willing to smash, eviscerate, and eradicate Daesh.

Who ever saw such a performance? Bombardiers of all the Arabias side by side with the Yankees on a rescue mission for Civilization. How come? Because these nations, the whole region, the whole world is endangered by this unspeakable violence. Turkey, Qatar, Bahrain, the Emirates, Jordan, Egypt, Iraq of course, Pakistan, Saudi Arabia, all more or less neighbors of the gang of psychopaths that dare to call themselves "Islamic State."

Behold the moderates, our allies in the combat of good against evil. Hollande wanted to invite Iran too but Obama vetoed that, provoking the exasperation of a bunch of Iran-friendly specialists. Marine Le Pen and her lieutenant Florian Philippot, for example, denounced the submission to American diktats that keeps us from establishing good relations with an indispensable Iran. And Israel in all that? A neighbor targeted by the jihadis? A strong reliable ally? No. Israel disappears from the configuration.

Commentators and actors alike nibble on petits fours and dabble in geopolitics as if they were playing mah jong. They rediscover the pleasure of badmouthing G. W. Bush's America. It's all the fault, they declare with gleeful certitude, of the illegal invasion of Iraq in 2003 and glory to France for abstaining. Some add Libya to the demotion chart, with a kick in the pants for Bernard-Henri Levy and Nicolas Sarkozy.

Isn't it simply lovely to a wage a humanistic war? The nations threatened by Daesh are tenderly named and taken under our wing. All except for Israel. The Arab-Muslim aviators are celebrated, the good guys congratulate themselves for knowing how to work together harmoniously, proof that it is not a war of the West against Islam. *We say Daesh, you see, because it's not a State and it's not Islamic.* [In fact it's a caliphate but hush! that touches a raw nerve.]

One after the other, Western governments decide to join in the airstrikes but promise, like slick seducers of virgins, they won't go any further. Is it possible to wipe out those fanatics without a ground invasion, a real dirty war? Where are the journalists who just came out of Gaza?

Can't they remember the dilemma that faced the Netanyahu government? Ambush, young soldiers killed, public discontent with Tsahal, diabolical tunnels, the miraculously averted Rosh Hashanah massacre, imported rockets, embezzled funds, the uncompromising leader plushing it out in 5-star Qatar...

Do they know what it was, that Gaza thing? It was a branch of the global jihad movement on the warpath, again, as ever determined to eliminate the State of Israel once and for all! Israel, the only country in the region that can defend itself. The only Western nation that courageously shoulders the burden of war as the price of its freedom and survival.

Israel, the only reliable ally in the region, is kept out of the family portrait to accommodate a pot pourri of cynical manipulative dictatorships. What's the use of this phony coalition? It's a chorus line dancing to the popular tune: without Israel we'd all get along famously in the Middle East.

It's not Islam, it's barbarian!

The French were more horrified by the beheading of mountain guide Hervé Gourdel in Algeria than the mass murder of Christians and Yazidis in the burgeoning caliphate. It's cultural. The land of human rights is shaken by the death of one man, a star, a backpacker. Earlier victims dragged around in flimsy orange outfits were worn down by years of cruel captivity. Hervé Gourdel went in the space of 24 hours from the heights of the virile alpinist to the abyss of the beheaded.

Flags at half mast, silent marches, the nation traumatized ...and they tell the good folks that it's not Islam. Like an army of murderers frantically scrubbing floors and walls to wipe out every trace of blood, our media swear that it's not Islam. Stylish journalists in high-heels, specialists-apologists of Islam, philosophers, sociologists, criminologists, and politicians turn into halfpenny theologians of an imaginary Islam. Slitting the throat of a brave mountaineer who loved the Maghreb? That's not Islam. They're criminals, terrorists.

It's not Islam, it's barbarian! Read *l'Exil au Maghreb* by the late David Littman and Paul Fenton. North Africa was called "Barbary." And one of the punishments imposed on the Jews of Barbary was salting down severed heads. It's not lslam? Read *The Legacy of Jihad* by Andrew Bostom MD, a documented account of Islamic conquest, from its origins to modern times. Tamerlane, in the 14th century, ordered his men to pile up skyscrapers of severed heads. Mohamed, the prophet venerated by Muslims, lent his hand to the decapitation of a thousand men of the Jewish Bani Quraizah tribe, signing in blood the enduring ethical model for the faithful. Muslims who claim today that beheading is not Islamic are themselves descendants of survivors—or perpetrators—of Islamic conquest massacres.

This summer in London, a Nigerian by the name of Nick Salvadore beheaded a British-Italian grandmother, Palmira Silva, in her garden. Salvadore is an Islamic convert. The other day, Alton Nolen / Yah'keem Yisrael, a Black American Islamic convert, beheaded a fellow worker in a food processing plant in Moore Oklahoma. In 2009, Muzzamil Hassan, who founded *Bridges TV* to give a positive image of true Islam, decapitated his wife Aasiya on the station's premises.

Dalil Boubaker, rector of the Central Mosque of Paris, addressed a small beheading-is-not-Islam demonstration. *Pas d'amalgame*, he pleaded, no backlash please. Avoid backlash at all costs. Muslims gathered to publicly share the sorrow of d'Hervé Gourdel's family were primarily concerned with warning French society: *pas d'amalgame*. We have nothing to do with this. The rector read Koranic verses, some of which are lifted from Jewish scripture but let's not make an issue. He convinced the coquettish *BFM TV* anchor, who dutifully deplored the highjacking of the religion of peace by lawless faithless criminals.

It just happens to be false. Anyway, it isn't presented as a rational argument it's delivered as an unquestionable fact. No debate. Intellects that are more discerning on any other subject drop dead at the feet of this doxa: it's not Islam, it's the very negation of Islam. What are those Koranic chants of peace and tolerance worth? They are abrogated by verses of murderous hatred and, moreover, contradicted by historical and contemporary reality. Circumstantial statements by European Muslims who are sincerely shocked by the brutality of jihadis are music to Western ears; they have no value as a challenge to sharia.

Casting out the Jews is the tradeoff for a *vivre ensemble* [getting along together] built around the negation of the genocidal hatred of kuffars taught by Islam. To wit—the Emir of Qatar, great ally of the coalition, accuses Israel of crimes against humanity in Gaza. What's a couple hundred people standing in front of the Central Mosque to deplore beheading compared to the tens of thousands that disturbed the peace with pro-Hamas stampedes last summer?

Islam is whitewashed of its connection with the "terrorists" and airbrushed out of the picture of endless Muslim assaults against Jews over the past fifteen years, punctuated by several murders of horrifying cruelty. To keep us from falling into the trap of a "war against the Muslims," the lethal narrative of an ecumenical coalition is fed to the endangered population, weakening our defense against jihad, fueling hostility against the State of Israel, jeopardizing the security of Jews in Europe and betraying the small minority of freedom-loving Muslims who still do not dare to revolt against tyrannical Islam.

— *Times of Israel (français)*

PALESTINIAN STATE:
THE GREEN LINE OF JIHAD

24 November 2014

And now they want us to believe that the creation of a Palestinian State is the answer! What's to be done about those attacks against Israel, beginning with the kidnap murder of three yeshiva *bochers* and culminating—at least for now—in the slaughter of Jews praying in a Har Nof synagogue? A Palestinian State

Don't think the "Palestinian State" they're talking about has anything to do with a political entity located in a geographic space. "Palestinian State" is a catch-phrase, a password, a weapon. The idea of creating that State lies on the other side of the green line of jihad, along with the atrocities committed since June. The innocent façade of the word "State" masks a genocidal project.

Fervent defenders of Israel, too, are upholding the two-state solution as proof of goodwill.

Why now? That's what we have to understand. Why are they digging up this "solution" again today, when the Palestinian "peace partners" are outdoing each other in savage attacks?

Fatah joined forces with Hamas that shamelessly proclaims it will exterminate the Jews, then picked up the relay and started the battle of Jerusalem the day after the ceasefire in Gaza. After the rockets and tunnels, came killer automobiles, knife murders, and the campaign for by-pass recognition by the UN and European governments with the sneaky complicity of the American president.

18 November 2014, Kehilat Bnei Torah, Har Nof, Jerusalem: two Muslims armed with axes, knives, and a handgun, shouting *allahu akbar*, massacre Jews as they pray.

Four were killed instantly, others are critically wounded or maimed for life. A new level of horror. Some media were so destabilized, they fell into abject incompetence. *CNN* gave us "2 Palestinians killed by a terrorist attack in a mosque."

On *BFM TV*, the well-named Emmanuel Faux [*faux* = false], son of Gisèle Halimi, babbled about the Judaization of Jerusalem and the provocations of Jewish extremists. If a conflict that is in reality territorial and political has become religious, he says, it started when Jews insisted on the right to pray on the "*esplanade des mosquées*" [Temple Mount =mosque compound].

Alain Gresh (*Monde diplomatique*) adds colonization, Occupation, injustice, and illegal unification of Jerusalem for good measure.

Know-it-all commentators locate Har Nof in East Jerusalem or include in the death toll of victims of terrorism the assassins—cousins Ghassan and Uday Abu-Jamal that hacked heads, chopped off arms wrapped in *tfilin*, and made blood gush over prayer books.

Over at *Sky News* and the *BBC*, they wonder how destroying the homes of criminals—especially when they're dead—could lead to reconciliation. For some reason, mainstream media weren't inspired by the exploit of the heroic young Druze policeman, Zidan Saif; he and a fellow patrolman were the first to arrive at the Har Nof scene.[1] Saif shot at the killers, one of them came running out of the synagogue and shot him point blank. He died of his wounds.

While fans are offering sweets in honor of the Abu-Jamal shahids from Jabel Mukaber, genteel well-wishers in the civilized world serve the plat du jour: peace process, two-state solution, stop colonization, divide Jerusalem.

Only two days before the synagogue killing, a Daesh video hit the screens, starring two proud bare-faced Europeans, brandishing a butcher knife in one hand and, with the other, clenching the neck that would soon be separated from the victim's head.

One of the butchers, identified as Maxime Hauchard, a 22 year-old French convert who abandoned his Normandy cows for the sands of the Caliphate, shouts *allahu akbar* in unison with his comrades.

In Jerusalem, Jews who had made aliya from Canada, Great Britain and the United States were slaughtered because they were praying in a synagogue; in the Caliphate, European and American beheaders invite their buddies to follow suit in the West.

They too work on a two-state solution—*dar al harb* and *dar al islam*—with the ultimate aim of creating one total Caliphate ruled by Allah and his sharia law.

Earnest folks who want to stand on the good side of the green line of atrocities swear that lopping off heads has nothing to do with Islam. Same goes for the Israeli-Palestinian conflict. It is not religious or at least it wouldn't be if Jewish extremists didn't harass Muslims on the "*esplanade des mosquées.*"

As they see it, Jews on the Temple Mount are extremists and Muslims that massacre Jews as they pray are victims "slaughtered" by the police. Jews who live in Jerusalem neighborhoods stamped "Arab" by international opinion are criminals. A government that builds housing for Jewish residents in neighborhoods labelled "colonies" by do-gooders is Far Right. Israel, with a 20% non- Jewish population, is an "apartheid" state but the curiously noble intention of Mahmoud Abbas to build a 100% Jew-free Palestinian State deserves the support of European parliaments. It's genocidal logic!

Gérard Marx [B'nai B'rith hatikvah lodge] wonders why the *Times of Israel* doesn't give some background on Green Party Senator Esther Bonbassa,[2] notorious for her diatribes against Jews with "complexes," and boastfully proud of presenting the motion for recognition of the State of Palestine: "Recognizing the State of Palestine is a clear way of saying no to the messianic-expansionist ideology supported by Benyamin Netanyahu's coalition and a significant portion of the Israeli population." More than a hundred members of Parliament say they'll vote against the resolution but remind us of their undying commitment to the two-state solution that they believe must be reached by negotiation.

How can we resist batting at the howlers broadcast over the past few days? Take, for example, "*On ne va pas se mentir*" [we're not going to lie to ourselves] (*i-Télé*, November 19th). Under the direction of Audrey Pulvar, four stunningly ignorant-arrogant "experts"— Philippe Bilger, Anne Giudicelli, Claude Guibal, and Myriam Benraad— construct a Middle Eastern mockup in which each brick of Muslim aggression is gleefully thrown at the head of a guilty Israel.

Some gems: The Israeli government has been radicalizing ever since the assassination of the three teenagers in June. The Palestinian population sees terror attacks as a normal reaction to the crimes of the *colons*. We are witnessing a return to fundamentalism on both sides: the terror attacks/ the siege of Gaza; Palestinians seduced by the question of the Islamic State / Israelis by the question of a Jewish State. The best way to prevent [these attacks] is to avoid provocation. Israel exploits these isolated incidents to get a pass on its unacceptable policies...

Followed to its endpoint, the logic of these *jusqu'au bout* specialists would prove that the blood bath at the Har Nof synagogue is the fault of the Jews: they shouldn't have bled.

What is the end game of this discourse? What element in and of itself justifies this constant punishment of Israel? It's the failure of the peace process that was supposed to culminate in the two-state solution. A solution that is totally, absolutely, resolutely divorced from all factual reality. In fact, it's not about a process or a State, it's a smoke screen to hide the horrors committed in front of our eyes while at the same time blaming them on the Jewish State, guilty of the original sin... of not being the Islamic State...not submitting.

Like the Temple Mount travestied in "*esplanade des mosques,*" the State of Israel should be transformed, by way of a jihad strategy disguised as a peace process, into a sharia-submissive State.

Coffee in Paris with Zvi Mazel. He hands me a short piece in *le Figaro* where it says that Israeli authorities, for the first time in a very long time, have authorized access to the *esplanade des mosquées* without age limits. "Our embassy does nothing," says Zvi. "They should tell the *Figaro* that it's the Temple Mount." A few days later, embassy spokeswoman Michal Philosoph doesn't raise a peep when the *i-Télé* anchor refers to the "*esplanade des mosquées.*" On the contrary, she reassures the journalist and the world: the Israeli government is firmly committed to the status quo.

"A tiny little 600 square-meter mosque in the corner of an expanse of 14.5 hectares," sputtered Zvi, "and there's no room for Jews? And now they've named the whole thing the Al Aqsa Temple Mount."

The conflict isn't religious? What about the al-Aqsa Intifada triggered in September 2000 by Ariel Sharon's "provocative" visit to the Temple Mount and the staged "death" of the shahid Mohamed al Dura? It's not religious, they insist, it's political, it's territorial. And Islam? Isn't it political, territorial, jihadist?

It's exhausting to keep ringing the alarm on the willful blindness of specialists, political leaders, and journalists, and trying to show them the harm they do. Do they have the slightest idea of the harm they do? They bow their heads before the beheader, embrace the jihad strategy that dooms them, place the knife in the hands of the ungrateful compatriot, barely adult and already proud to be an executioner. Our commentators radicalize themselves! They're self-radicalized.

No parliamentary recognition of Palestine will change the reality of rivers of blood, the hand that wields the knife, the mastermind that drives it. No discourse will deflect the Har Nof butchers coming for them...too.

— *Times of Israel (franças)*

NOW LOOK WHAT THEY'VE DONE
25 November 2014

"Now look what they've done!" That sums up the reaction, in certain quarters, to the November 18th slaughter at Kehilat B'nei Torah. They who? Palestinians? Israeli Arabs? Terrorists? Mujahidin? Activists? Résistants? No. The Jews. Israel = the Jews, look at what they've done now. Will they never learn?

The massacre is condemned, that's the first step. Then the condemnation makes a U-turn and aims at Israel. like one of those killer cars unleashed since... when? Since the Protective Border operation pushed back the all-out attack from Gaza, leaving Hamas with phony victory celebrations in the rubble and Israelis with a hollow feeling in the pit of the stomach. The cease fire in Gaza was directly followed by a new double-pronged phase of the ongoing assault on Jews in their State: random assassinations and a "diplomatic" campaign to create a fake Palestinian State that can be used as a real weapon.

But that isn't enough. Because there is something so atrocious about attacking men in prayer with a meat cleaver, knives, and a gun, there is something so unbearably eloquent in the sight of thick red blood on prayer books and tallit, there is something so barbaric about smashing into a synagogue to butcher pious rabbis, that certain commentators feel a need to defend themselves from accusations of bias. The campaign to create a cardboard Palestinian State is buffered by a communications offensive. Media coverage? It's faultless, they say, and we are tired of your complaints. The creation of a Palestinian State by European parliamentary fiat is the appropriate response to "lone wolf" attacks by hopeless Palestinians, they opine, in unison with lawmakers, leaders, and anointed specialists. Extremists on both sides are spinning this political & territorial conflict into a religious war, they warn, and that must be nipped in the bud.

Daniel Haïk, political commentator on *i24 news* in French, faces a Belgian correspondent. With a little help from anchorman Jean-Charles Banoun, Haïk politely suggests that there is something twisted about coverage of the latest attack. *"Mais non mais non,"* responds the Belgian correspondent. "We condemned it. We all condemned it." Fifteen minutes of "yes, buts" did not suffice to squeeze out a single drop of self-criticism. They condemned it, that's the ticket to paradise. And they "contextualize" it. That's the part that makes us wince. Contextualizing means it's the fault of the far-right Netanyahu government, the pursuit of colonization, the failure of peace talks, the intrusion of Jews in Arab Jerusalem and fanatic Jewish prayer mongers on *l 'esplanade des mosquées* (French for Temple Mount).

Wouldn't you rather write for *Haaretz* and be invited to lunch by your French colleagues than get kicked in the pants like a tramp begging for a crust of bread?

You're choking on an overdose of factual errors, misinterpretations, grotesque analyses, lopsided round tables, cockeyed interviews, and indecent tongue lashing of anyone who even vaguely suggests that the Har Nof attack and others before it are not the fault of Israel... and they don't even want you to make a squeak.

Are they right? Am I some kind of hypersensitive, partisan, paranoid, kvetching Jew? Am I so uncouth that I don't know how journalism works, how experts analyze, how European parliaments legislate (in Israel's stead)? Shouldn't I be ashamed of making a big stink just because *CNN* broke the news on the Har Nof massacre with "Deadly attack on Jerusalem mosque"? Don't you know that news travels at the speed of light? And you're claiming a simple mistake is evidence of bias?

"*Le Secret des Sources*" is a weekly program on state-owned high-brow France Culture radio. Journalists give a peek into the backroom, tell how they milk sources, navigate in government circles, circumnavigate obstacles, face dangers, and get the story. The story on Saturday November 22nd was the Mideast conflict.

The lineup tells half the story: Charles Enderlin, *France 2*; Philippe Agret, *Agence France Presse*; Olivier Ravanello, *i- Télé*; Gideon Kouts, *Maariv* and *Kol Israel*, and no one to challenge their self-satisfied hypocrisy. Except, briefly, Kouts who dared to make two remarks that perturbed the unanimity. I guess they hung up on him. He was never heard from again. Charles Enderlin, father of the Mohamed al Dura blood libel, dominated the chit chat.

Talk about kvetching! Where's the justice for journalists who report with good faith on a grinding conflict that has worn international nerves to a fray? They swap persecution anecdotes. During the "Gaza offensive" Ravanello didn't even look at his Facebook account. How about you, Charles? Yes, in fact, there were all kinds of threats after my report of the death of a Palestinian child, he replies. No one pronounces the name "al Dura," Enderlin is urbane: it still comes up now and then, insults and whatnot, but it's over for me. (My *i24 news* interview centered on the release of *Al Dura: Long Range Ballistic Myth*, aired on November 20th.)

Later in the program Enderlin threw a dart at *i24 news*, "a pro-Netanyahu radio network [it's television] that forces journalists to use the term 'disputed' territories." This is obviously bad journalism. As an example of good journalism, Enderlin's colleagues explain that terminology guidelines are issued by their media. Ravanello gets hot under the collar about the terms "terrorist" and "*résistant*": an act can be labeled "terrorist" but not an organization!!! Got it, fellows? Hamas = *la résistance*.

The overall impression was that journalists impartially covering the Mideast conflict are in mortal danger from disgruntled Jews. Gideon Levy, says Enderlin, needs bodyguards. Somehow they made this danger more eloquent than the hatchet massacre in a Jerusalem synagogue and the celebrations it earned in Muslim circles. The real gore was on their Facebook pages.

Inviting Charles Enderlin as an example of integrity is equivalent to reporting the Har Nof massacre as an attack on a mosque: it's a dishonest mistake. If his colleagues had read my book, they would know that a French court, having viewed raw footage shot by his cameraman Talal Abu Rahmeh at Netzarim Junction on September 30, 2000, included staged scenes. Some of which were aired in *France 2* newscasts. This obvious falsification justified, in the eyes of the court, Philippe Karsenty's right to publicly express his opinion that the al Dura "death scene" is a hoax. If I'm not mistaken, none of these journalists attended court hearings on the controversy. They probably applauded Charles Enderlin's book *Un Enfant est mort* [a child is dead] without reading it or my critical analysis of same.

This is just one example of an international media onslaught. Anchormen and women jump out of their skin when faced with a defender of Israel. Journalists and specialists spill out sewers of defeatism about contemporary Israeli society, wealth disparities, tent protests, inaudible Leftist peaceniks & intellectuals, far right government, inexcusable pursuit of colonization, refusal to negotiate with the eminently moderate Mahmoud Abbas. A guest on *"Moi président,"* a program hosted by the very Ravanello who hobnobbed with Enderlin on *Secret des Sources*, said Israel is reduced to a mixture of Tel Aviv hedonists and Jerusalem religious fanatics; the disillusioned army was defeated by Hezbollah in 2006. [Or was it Ravanello himself? I came in at the end of the program and can't find it on the *i-Télé* site to confirm this detail.] At the end of the program all four of his guests and 67% of viewers vote yes for French recognition of a Palestinian State. The real debate will take place in the French Parliament on Friday November 28th with the vote scheduled for December 2nd.

The esteemed philosopher Alain Finkielkraut, distinguished member of l'Académie Française and loyal supporter of JCall, will not join the European version of JStreet in calling for recognition of a Palestinian

State at this stage.[1] Finkielkraut is profoundly aware of the horrifying significance of the synagogue massacre. A symbolic threshold has been crossed: These men were not killed as colonists, not as Israelis, they were slaughtered because they are Jews. Finkielkraut recognizes that the "occupation" that supposedly justifies such crimes applies to the whole of Israel. He acknowledges incitement. Mahmoud Abbas threatens war if "al Aqsa is contaminated by Jews." That being said, he goes on to pummel Binyamin Netanyahu and Nafthali Bennet. He's disgusted by their "jubilation." They pounced on the occasion to dig in their heels and refuse to negotiate with Mahmoud Abbas. And the rest follows like rocks thrown by *shababs*: colonization, Temple Mount fanatics, extreme right coalition, refusal to negotiate, to make concessions. Netanyahu's policies are dangerous and ineffective. They're going to lead to Diasporism!

What is going on? What explains the sudden intensification of criticism of Israel and the urgent need to fabricate a Palestinian State? An unremitting offensive that began with the kidnap and murder of three yeshiva *bochers* and has been carried through several stages including rocket attacks, tunnel infiltrations, pro-Hamas stampedes in Western countries, assassinations by car ramming, slaughters with knives and hatchets, culminates in a campaign for recognition of a Palestinian State. Opinion assaults against Israel rise in rhythm with physical attacks from Hamas, applauded by the Palestinian Authority and global Islamist forces.

This is what I call the lethal narrative strategy. Physical violence aimed at harming and demoralizing Israelis—making them suffer at home and look bad abroad—culminates in political and rhetorical offensives to destabilize the State, with the ultimate aim of toppling it. We witness a perverse logic in media and government circles that replaces the sense of horror, when praying Jews are hacked apart, with outrage at the State that allows itself to be persecuted. The obvious comparison between the Har Nof blood bath and Daesh decapitation orgies is stubbornly denied. The fanatics are not the demons that wield butcher knives but Jews who think there is room for them to pray on the Temple Mount. The source of conflict, the element that blocks any and all negotiated solutions is not the forked PLO tongue it is the refusal of a "far right" Israeli government to make the necessary concessions and create the Palestinian State. And, finally, the origin of a wave of aggression that has continued from June to date is, retroactively, the failure of a 9-month stint of peace processing driven by US Secretary of State John Kerry.

All of these causes can be more or less examined. Except for one: the failed peace process. It is the First Cause. What issues were discussed last summer? What were the stumbling blocks? In what way did those negotiations resemble previous efforts? These and all other verifiable details are locked in an unbreakable safe. The First Cause cannot be examined. And Israel is guilty.

What explains the failures of previous rounds of peace talks? In September 2000, after walking out on the Camp David negotiations, Yasser Arafat organized "spontaneous" demonstrations that blossomed into the "al Aqsa Intifada." Last week Israeli forces intercepted a shipment from China labelled "Christmas decorations." It contained 5,200 knives, 1,000 swords, 18,000 firecrackers, 4,300 Taser-flashlight devices, and 5,000 electric shock devices destined, obviously, for "spontaneous"demonstrators.[2] This explains the ebb and flow of shabab operations in "Arab" Jerusalem. The same forces that purchase street weapons from China decide when and where to spontaneously uprise. Punitive measures against perpetrators and their families—house demolitions, withdrawal of residence permits and welfare payments, transfer out of Israel—might not be effective if the lone wolves were really alone. They aren't. Their paymasters and dispatchers will have to factor the new measures into their calculations.

But we still need to understand why the "international community" feels the urgent need for a Palestinian State. The conflict, they say, has gone on for too long. Nothing has worked so far. Now it is getting more violent and, worse, it is turning religious. If Daesh is not Islamic and the Palestinian ambitions are strictly political and territorial, who are the religious troublemakers?

The Jews.

If an outside observer—the EU, the UN, or your corner journalist—presumes to impose a solution to a conflict that stubbornly persists, he should be expected to think the issue through in all its dimensions. Otherwise, it is quite unrealistic to imagine that the outsider knows better than the concerned parties. When it comes to thinking through the "Israel-Palestine" conflict, one element is locked tight and unavailable for analysis: the two-state solution. It is the touchstone, the holy grail, the silver bullet.

Why is The Solution not forthcoming?

It's the fault of the Jews. That's why they are attacked with rockets, tunnels, cars, cleavers, and parliamentary resolutions. Like misers, they withhold The Solution. The good folks looking on from their high places are not without pity. They condemn the bloodshed. And impose the remedy. The State of Palestine...

...that will punish the Jews for refusing to submit.

— *Midah (Hebrew translation)*

Chapter 5/ Jihad attacks in Europe

HEAD-ON COLLISION AT *CHARLIE HEBDO*

Friday, 9 January 2015

12 dead, 20 wounded

Clash of civilizations, star wars, the big bang... a certain idea of France was murdered in cold blood on January 7th. An *allahu akbar* commando stormed into the offices of *Charlie Hebdo*, executed twelve people, wounded another twenty, four of them critically. It is painfully difficult to sort out nuggets of accurate information from the sound and fury that fills the airwaves and the streets of Paris. [12 noon, the government has decreed one minute of silence ...outside my window I hear car horns furious at someone blocking the street, rumbling machines working on a nearby building almost drowning out the dirge sounded by the church bell on the corner, icy rain pelts hurried passersby...].

An infinitesimal minority of the 5 or 6 million Muslims living in France—two brothers identified as Sherif and Said Kouachi—wiped out the staff of an in-your-face magazine that has been offending everyone for 45 years. A mixture of pornography and scatology was served up weekly in a hallmark sloppy cartoon style with brief texts that lashed out like a not yet emancipated adolescent at chosen targets. The sweet smiling faces of yesterday's victims—Charb, Cabu, Cayat, Tignous, Wolinski, Honoré, Maris—convey the abiding innocence that was brutally assassinated. They made good-natured grotesque fun of everyone including themselves...in a heretofore protected world.

In 2006, *Charlie* published the Mohamed cartoons with the same insolence as it habitually employed on priests, rabbis and other benighted believers. Courageous, yes...but also blinded by their own enlightened tolerance. On this and subsequent occasions the Charlies reiterated their faith in humanity, Muslims included; mocking fanatics was a gesture of affection for fellow citizens of the Muslim faith. The mockery was inclusive, not aggressive. It was a way of saying "you belong to our wonderful culture."

Today, Phlippe Val, who directed the magazine when the Mohamed cartoons were published, cannot hold back his tears. "I've lost all my friends." Val gives credit to French governments Left and Right that have protected him and his staff since that fateful day. "Without police protection we would not have been able to carry on." Though *Charlie Hebdo* was acquitted of defamation in 2006, the court established de facto anti-blasphemy by granting the magazine a limited right to offend Islam in the context of the worldwide controversy surrounding the Mohamed cartoons. Dalil Boubaker, rector of the Central Mosque of Paris, one of the plaintiffs in that case, was represented by Francis Szpiner, who also represented *France 2* in its lawsuit against Philippe Karsenty and, subsequently, the family of Ilan Halimi against the Gang of Barbarians.

Boubaker had voiced disapproval of the violence ripping through the Muslim world over the cartoons, while pleading for respect for Islam and the prophet. Yesterday he rushed to the site of the killings and voiced his disapproval of an act that "sullies Islam and betrays its sacred respect for human life." If the *Charlie Hebdo* massacre is France's 9/11 as many suggest, the *religion of peace* message that so quickly replaced *don't tread on me* in the US is even more insistent here in France.

The usual array of experts, specialists, authors, former secret service agents and well-trained journalists is making the distinction between Islam and these *allahu akbar* fanatics. The bodies of the victims were still lying in pools of blood in their boardroom while the concern had already shifted to the innocent Muslims who might be fingered because of this aberrant misuse of their beautiful religion.

Spontaneous demonstrations formed all over France, 100,000 in all, with 35,000 at Place de la République. The *Je suis Charlie* [I am Charlie] slogan caught on instantly worldwide. Sincerely moved, often to tears, honest citizens stood in the frosty cold, holding up pencils as a sign of *résistance*. We Are Not Afraid they declared in a little light show at Place de la République. Memorial candle burners occupied the field that had been conquered last summer by flag burners, the black mournful mockup of a *Charlie Hebdo* front page replaced the black flag of jihad flown last August, yesterday's tribute to two policemen killed in the line of duty, was made in the place where the caliphators had attacked police with rocks and bags of broken glass last summer.

[2:30 PM—it is reported that the two suspects robbed a gas station, abandoned the car they had hijacked on the run yesterday, and are somewhere in a zone between Villers-Cotterêts and Crépy-en-Valois. Commandos in Puma helicopters are circling the area, under the watchful eye of TV cameras. The bucolic place names have all the perfumes of an eternal France that is slashed today by the intrusion of another world it still refuses to see.]

In 2008 a different sort of scandal targeted *Charlie Hebdo*: editorial director Philippe Val was accused in some quarters of "censorship" for kicking out the unashamed anti-Semite Siné. In my coverage of that story—"Tempest in a Trashcan"[1] — I noticed an element that had escaped other commentators: an article in that issue by Charb making fun of those who claim the al Dura video is a hoax, and relaying the bit about Israelis killing Palestinian children wholesale.

The firebombing of Charlie's offices in 2011 raised a first ripple of public indignation. Defiant, the staff brought out a *Charia Hebdo* issue, under the direction of editor in chief Mohammed. A full-page interview with David Chemla, president of the French branch of Peace Now and European secretary of the JStreet lookalike JCall, was prominently featured in that issue chock full of scandalous acts, positions, and nudity on the theme of sharia. Chemla says the release of 1,000 prisoners in exchange for Gilad Shalit, including 280 responsible for the death of 600 civilians shows that Israel can erase its red lines for a good cause. They will have to do some more erasing, he advises, in order to make peace with the Palestinians. In a video filmed before a mountain of charred documents, Charb admitted that he might need police protection from now on. But he said he had more chance of getting run over by a Vel-lib (municipal rental bike) than to be killed by an Islamist... "there are so few in France." [2]

"Love is stronger than hatred," proclaims the cover of the November 9th issue that followed *Charia Hebdo*— a cute little *Charlie* kid hungrily swallows a drooling kiss from a sweet bearded guy in Salafist dress. The pages are filled with testimonials from all over the world. The spirit is "we will not be cowed." In his personal account of the aftermath of the fire, Charb has "a thought for Muslims, who are the first victims of this fire." It's going to be exploited by the Far Right to discredit all Muslims, he regrets. In fact, wrote Charb, we can't be sure the attack did come from Islamists. Maybe it was fascist provocateurs! Anyway, the hacking and death threats come from foreign Islamists.

But the Kouachi brothers, of Algerian origin, were born in Paris!

In January 2013 *Charlie Hebdo* brought out the first volume of an irreverent apologetic Life of Mohammed comic book [*La Vie de Mahomet*] illustrated by Charb. The prophet is portrayed with comical awkwardness but his message and life story are told with orthodox respect.

The philo-Muslim theme is endlessly repeated over the past 24 hours. Imams that swear allegiance to the values of the Republic are featured on TV. Those who preach jihad are not mentioned even in a whisper. The Muslim in the street is spotlighted, a caring citizen like any other. A woman in hijab places flowers on the altar in front of the *Charlie Hebdo* offices. In reply to a journalist who asks "Are you concerned?" she offers a little homily: "The prophet never attacked unless he was attacked. Then he responded with kind words and only if they were ignored did he fight. When he fought, he really fought!"

The younger brother, Sherif Kouachi, was briefly imprisoned for his activity in the 19th arrondissement terror cell that recruited jihadis for Iraq. At the time, journalist Mohamed Sifaoui, himself a refugee from the Algerian terror wave of the 90s, declared that it was the American invasion of Iraq, not Islam, that provoked the Buttes Chaumont terror cell. Today Sifaoui claims that rising xenophobia in France fuels Islamic radicalization, and we have to deal with both. The *BBC* outdid everyone, bringing in the sly wily Muslim Brother Tariq Ramadan to tell us infidels how we should behave to avoid this kind of attack.

I24 news commentator Ali Waked candidly admitted that he had been in the midst of a "group" not far from the station's Jaffa studio Monday night: "The majority said *Charlie Hebdo* had insulted the prophet and got what was coming to them."

Worldwide media are showing an unprecedented mobilization in France. Undeniably, a nerve has been hit. There has been nothing like it since the first Islamic attacks going back to the 80s and increasing exponentially since October 2000. There was no public outcry last month when the *i-Télé* channel dropped the popular debater Eric Zemmour, after publication of *Le Suicide Français*, in which he expands on the Islamic problem facing France.

Of course the issue of press freedom takes on immense significance when the staff of a magazine is decimated by two men with Kalashnikovs. The reaction to the *Charlie Hebdo* massacre is neither artificial nor hypocritical. But the question of Islam is an abyss. Unless it is faced honestly, fearlessly, without false reassurance, the masses of enlightened citizens standing up for their freedom today will slide into that chasm.

— *NER / Iconoclast*

MORE THAN A MILLION MARCH IN PARIS

Sunday, 11 January 2015

The latest estimate is 1.5 million marching in Paris today. We have never seen anything like it. It's 5:20 PM as I start to write and the Place de la République is still filled with an overflow crowd that will probably never get to follow the route to the official destination at Place de la Nation, but that's not what matters.

So far there have been no reports of incidents. I didn't expect the punk jihadis to turn up and face what looks like the entire population united against them. This is probably the safest day since September 30, 2000 when a different crowd massed in Place de la République with posters of Mohamed al Dura and shouted "Death to the Jews." I was concerned about crowd control. The French are notoriously undisciplined, they mill around, don't queue up, park on the sidewalk and cross against the light.

But today is different. The crowd applauds the police, applauds each other and itself. There is no rush or crush. The police control the flow, there is no pushing from behind. I've never seen anything like it since I settled here in 1972. And I have seen hundreds of demonstrations of every sort. This is not a demonstration, it is an affirmation. Je suis Charlie could translate into the long awaited awakening of the democracies. Or it might be one more ocean of illusion to drown in.

I walked around for hours in the Marais, up and down the side streets, up and down the boulevards, between la République and la Bastille. People were pouring in from all directions, walking north, south, east and west. Nothing else seemed to matter. The winter sales— a national sport—began on the fateful Wednesday January 7th. By noon that day the fervor for bargains was replaced with the horror of the *Charlie Hebdo* massacre. Sunday, always a big shopping day in the Marais, is double triple during the sales. Hardly anyone in the shops today. No line at l'As du Falafel where fans wait patiently for an hour or more to get a table on Sunday. Every street was filled with I am Charlies on their way to Place de la République. The mood was calm, respectful, quietly determined. Like people at work, not like rowdy demonstrators defending special interests.

There was hardly an in or out of the march. Everyone was in and it was everywhere. As if a leader had finally arose and convoked the population to stand up and defend itself. Is François Hollande that leader? I doubt it, but he stood in the leader's stead today. Were the heads of state—about 60 in all, that flowed into Paris like the Parisians flowed into the Place de la République— the united front of democracies that will truly face up to and defeat jihad conquest? Hardly, but they stood in their place today.

The immense spillover crowd that could not march down the designated routes on Boulevard Voltaire and Avenue de la République filled the boulevard du Temple / Filles de Calvaire /Beaumarchais wall to wall. Night is falling. What light will dawn?

Benjamin Netanyahu and Mahmoud Abbas marched a few meters away from each other to the right and left of François Hollande. That doesn't bring anyone closer to peace, it blurs distinctions, but the idea was to have open house in Paris today. With all its contradictions. The sinister ex-comic Dieudonné tweeted his intention to join the march.

Reporters without Borders did not appreciate the presence of certain heads of state that are notorious for suppressing press freedom. True, but unless I am mistaken, neither Erdogan nor Rohani was present. Much is made of the shining diversity of the crowd—"an authentic cross section of French society," according to enthusiastic journalists on the ground. I don't think that was the demographic today. It's not a question of ethnic nitpicking but a necessary search for the truth. What I saw today, as I deliberately walked against the flow of the crowd, the better to see its composition, was something more like the silent majority.

I have repeatedly ended my reports on the distressing situation in France in particular and the free world in general with words of hope. Democracies, I wrote, don't commit suicide. Even if today's "we are all Charlie" message was rather primary, it can mature. Democracy is not the happily ever after of societies composed of all the same, it is the non-violent way of negotiating differences.

At least we can say that a million and a half people in Paris and hundreds of thousands all over the world offered a rousing show of hands...and feet to the aspiring caliphators in our midst. It won't be enough to send them slinking away like cowed dogs, but it is a start.

Ceremonies for all the victims are scheduled tonight at the Central Synagogue, rue des Victoires, and in front of the kosher grocery store at Porte de Vincennes this evening. I will be on *Voice of Israel* radio at 7 PM Paris time and on the *Lisa Benson Show* at 9.

The four victims savagely assassinated by Amedy Coulibaly in the Hyper Cacher market at Porte de Vincennes will all be buried this Tuesday in Israel.

— NER / Iconoclast
— Photos by Jiro Mochizuki

PROLOGUE: TRUE & FALSE NOTES
January 20, 2015
[messages to close friends in response to hasty conclusions ...]

MESSAGE N°1 JANUARY 12

I am certainly not gushing.

The Arab "spring" showed its face immediately. There was no mystery, just mystification. The unprecedented show of hands and feet in Paris yesterday shows a face that has not been visible over the past fourteen years.

When you witness an event like this, an expression of collective opinion and determination on a scale never seen in the nation's history, you can't simply dismiss it. Of course you can, you are free to dismiss it. But I don't. And that's based on what I saw and heard.

The *Je Suis Charlie* slogan is not a simple trendy message. It's the slogan around which the movement coalesced, so people expressed it in those terms. If they held up posters saying *"Je suis contre le jihad"* it might have been closer to the truth of what sent them into the streets. For 14 years I have been puzzling over what seemed like passive or willing acceptance of Islamization. For 14 years I have been wondering how a nation could resist if there were no open media, no honest debate, so little reliable reporting.

The answer was given yesterday. There would be a tipping point.

Now the cards are on the table.

In the early hours of the *Charlie* massacre, journalists and commentators were saying that Marine Le Pen would reap the benefits. As it turns out, she didn't. The dreadfully unpopular François Hollande pulled off something that switched attention from a major security failure to a spectacular popular demonstration of force.

It can go either way. But it can't go the same way it has been going.

I'm following it in detail, in all its nuance. I'll report as always honestly and carefully.

MESSAGE N°2

This is the novelist speaking. I don't try to guess what will happen next, I try to penetrate the mystery of what I just saw. A quick overview in either direction is altogether justified: it's a show, nothing will change, they'll go back to their bad habits OR what a magnificent display of citizens standing up for their rights and values, nothing will ever be the same.

That doesn't interest me. It is journalistic. You skip over the concrete realty, do a quick review of the facts, come up with a conclusion, and go on to the next subject.

What explains the mobilization of 3.7 million people in France? It is not, it cannot be the same thing that inspires demonstrations by all sorts of particular interests defending or protesting something. That's not the same mechanism, it doesn't give the same results.

You can't think it through in 24 hours, you can't grasp it properly from a distance. If my work has any value it is because of my way of assimilating tons of information over long periods of time, organizing it, using it where others have forgotten or never noticed. So it is with this march.

What I think, at this point, is that all the characters in this drama are now on stage. The first act was September-October 2000—al Dura, the jihad intifada. I won't go back over it all in this short message, only to say that different factions came on stage and played their roles, including the leftist pro-Palestinians, the pro-jihad Muslims, the punk jihad troublemakers, the savage killers, the inept governments, the slightly effective governments and, how could we forget, the media. Sunday, the other population finally came on stage.

As I said to someone close to me today, "If they sang my slogans and carried my ideas, it might have been perfect but there would have been 37 not 3.7 million out in the streets." The millions who marched do not analyze the *matsav* the same way we do, they didn't march for us all these years when we needed them, they don't read the same books we read, they might flake out as quickly as they arose, but on that day in that place something different happened.

Media discourse has changed, government discourse has changed, measures are being taken. Why? In response to the will of the people. The Hollande government did not create this collective movement, it is trying to keep pace with it. Hollande didn't want Bibi? He was hissy? Obama doesn't like Bibi? Hollande made Bibi wait for the bus, put him in the second row where he was fished up by the president of Mali and placed finally in the front row? Abbas was there, frowning as if he were making a speech at the UN? Obama left Bibi in the waiting room some years ago while he had supper with his family?

Not very nice. But it has had absolutely no influence on the balance of power. Israel is strong. Bibi speaks eloquently. Israel resists. French Jews resist. And 3.7 million people who wouldn't have marched if the killers had only aimed at Jews were out in the streets. They knew Bibi was there. They didn't pull out. And the pro-Palestinians? They knew Abbas was there. They didn't show up.

I wouldn't contradict any French Jew who says "I'm out of here. It's time to go." I wouldn't argue with any Israeli who already left France and says, "Don't wait another minute, come home."

But I still care what happens to France. And I know that there are enough decent people in this country to make a difference. They don't have to agree with me about everything or anything but one thing: reverse the slide into ignominy, show their strength, stand up to the forces of destruction.

PS: in reply to the question from C. I:

"Dear R., could you please ask Nidra if the show of solidarity might not be due to the fact that this time the target was the Left? Or a left-oriented magazine that mocked religion? That they didn't do it for bombings and killings in London, Madrid, Brussels, Canada, etc., or in defense of Hirsi-Ali or Mark Steyn, etc."

3.7 million people is too many to fit into any category! Though people in their fifties and beyond may have been *Charlie* fans since their teens, many thousands or hundreds of thousands of Sunday's marchers never read it and don't know anything about their politics. Others have no taste for *Charlie's* vulgarity. How many Jewish marchers know about *Charlie's* garden variety anti-Zionism? It didn't keep them from marching. French people are usually quite snooty about the police and mistrustful of the CRS riot police, not to mention the military. They applauded them with heartfelt sincerity on Sunday. How many hundreds of thousands had never made the connection between jihadis who attack Jews and those who ram shoppers at a Christmas market, attack the London tube, or plot to blow up la Tour Eiffel? The Kouachi brothers and Amedy Coulibaly made the connection for them.

When rivulets turn into an ocean they overflow their particularities.

MESSAGE N°3 JANUARY 19

Marine Le Pen? Are you kidding? What's the cause of this disconnect?

First of all, let me tell you how it went here in France. Yes, here, where the jihad attacks occurred and the reactions reacted. In the minutes after news of the *Charlie Hebdo* massacre slashed into our lives and before we even knew the names of the victims, the media were saying this would fall to the advantage of Marine Le Pen. Hmm? So they were admitting they knew all along that the dangers of Islamization denounced by the Front National were real and not the emanation of some kind of irrational hatred. Not Islamophobia, not xenophobia, just a mirror of reality and the coming attractions of a horror movie that would be real.

There wasn't even a moment of grace in which to suggest that the killers might be Far Right thugs or disgruntled cartoonists. The killers shouted *allahu akbar* we have avenged the prophet we killed Charlie Hebdo.

Superwoman Marine to the rescue? I guess you didn't read my articles about the dark side of the Front National, its Syrian connection and plans to woo banlieue youths to its ranks?[1] I've been telling you for years, the day the two parliamentary parties, right and left, start to take action against Islamization, Marine Le Pen will deflate.

And that's what happened. She didn't join the million and a half in Paris, supposedly because she wasn't properly invited. She did a little march of her own in a small town in the south of France, and the media didn't cover it. She banned the circulation in her ranks of a video by her foreign policy advisor Aymeric Chauprade in which he declares that we are at war with Muslims...not all Muslims... some Muslims...that are at war with us. Madame Le Pen told the media that Chauprade was nothing special, just one of dozens of FN Eurodeputies. Not true. They were verrrry close, he was her chief Eurodeputy and most trusted advisor.

When I saw the huge anti-*Charlie Hebdo* demonstration in Grozny complete with Disneyland style cutesy "I love the prophet" badges, I wondered if the FN's Russian connection might have anything to do with her marching out of step on January 11th. Or did she sincerely feel she was not welcome? Either way, it was a strategic error.

I am still wondering how you can scoff at the millions of French people who stood up to be counted that day (the latest estimate is a total of 4.5 million), and look on Marine Le Pen with such benevolent respect.

We know what the perversions of antiracism have wrought. Is antijihad going to play the same tricks?

Björn Söder of the Sweden Democrats, defending his party's parliamentary motion to ban circumcision of males under 18, implicitly equated it with female genital mutilation:

"Boys should have the same right to avoid both complications of reduced sensitivity in the genitals, painful erections, increased risk of kidney damage and psychological distress by permanent removal, and the tremendous violation of privacy that circumcision actually means."[2]

TRUE & FALSE NOTES

February 2015

ADDING INSIGHT TO INJURY

Glued to the television, the computer, the radio from morning to night, out in the streets, in a state of high alert for three days without pause and then, bound to the aftermath, debates, investigations, declarations, piles of flowers, candles, handwritten messages, and Je Suis Charlie stickers and posters. Soldiers stationed in front of synagogues and Jewish day schools. Tens of thousands of Je Suis Kouachi tweets. Sullen rebellion in certain schools, where some refuse the minute of silence and others articulate alien values: "They insulted the prophet, they got what they deserved." Picking through the flotsam and jetsam, straining to understand fully and in detail what happened to France and how it spread worldwide.

In French, the bright orange flight data and cockpit voice recorders are called *boîtes noires* [black boxes]. The other night I dreamed I saw dozens of small black wooden boxes floating in the waves. I kept saying "The information is in the *boîtes noires*, I mean the real black boxes, not those orange things…"

What really happened between the starting gun, when the Kouachi brothers arrived in front of *Charlie Hebdo* headquarters, and the finish line, when French RAID and GIGN commandos simultaneously killed the *Charlie Hebdo* mujahidin at a provincial print shop 42 kilometers from Paris, and their brother in arms Amedy Coulibaly at the Hyper Cacher grocery store at Porte de Vincennes on the edge of the city? What exactly happened at Montrouge, 10 minutes from Montparnasse? Coulibaly, not yet publicly identified, fatally shot a policewoman in the back and critically wounded a municipal employee who reportedly tried to intervene. We've never heard another word about that hero. Why? It was the day after the *Charlie Hebdo* massacre. Authorities repeatedly insisted that the Montrouge incident had nothing to do with the "terrorist attack" at *Charlie Hebdo.*

The next day— Jewish hostages were already in the savage grips of Amedy Coulibaly, four were dead— the Hyper Cacher murderer was identified as the Montrouge killer. Furthermore, he was a buddy of the Kouachi brothers. They had called each other at least 500 times this year, using cell phones registered in the names of their wives. Infuriating! Not only for the bereaved victims and traumatized survivors, but also for law enforcement. Handcuffed by outdated legislation and a lax judicial system that releases jihad recruiters halfway through feather light prison terms. Blinded by a combination of inappropriate obstacles and antiquated IT systems that impede the rapid communication of crucial data.

Motorcycle police that stopped Coulibaly and his Islamically wedded wife Hayat Boumedienne on December 30th in a "random check" consulted a data base and saw he was under surveillance for terrorist connections. They informed higher levels, got no response, and let him go. He subsequently drove Hayat to Spain along with the Belhoucine brothers. From there they flew to Istanbul and are believed to be in Syria. How do we reconcile the enormity of snuffed out lives with the mediocrity of bureaucratic slip ups?

Multiple examples come to mind, and it is not just a question of hindsight. Failure to correctly assess the nature of jihad attacks combined with inadequate data processing and sharing has tragic results. Mohamed Merah's killing spree stretched from the 11th to the 19th of March 2012. The brutal murder of Jews at the Ozar Hatorah school might have been prevented if investigation of the first execution, in Montauban, had been more intelligent. And this time? Why did authorities repeatedly deny that the murder of a police rookie on January 8th was an act of "terrorism"? It is now believed that Coulibaly, blocked on his way to commit a massacre in a Jewish day school at Montrouge, took out his rage on the policewoman.

Some call it fate, others explain by divine intervention, luck, or random probability that crucial instant when the thread of a life is snipped...or spared. The imbalance between cause and effect is unbearable. Luz was late for the *Charlie Hebdo* staff meeting. He was bringing a cake. It was his birthday. François-Michel Saada, who had already bought an apartment in Israel in preparation for retirement and Aliyah, absolutely wanted to buy a *chala* for shabat. He pleaded his way into the Hyper Cacher as the shutter was closing. And was gunned down by Coulibaly.

What did the hostages see and feel in those interminable hours? What did the victims think in the flash of a second as they saw their colleagues picked off and knew they were next? What is the strategy of special forces? How much do they know about what is going on inside? How do they manage the risks? Why did it take so long to liberate the hostages at the kosher grocery store? There were babies and children and four dead bodies. Most survivors are not talking. Isn't it, on a very small scale, something like those who returned from the death camps? The horror and the shame. The humiliation. The answer, I dreamed, is in the black boxes. I am not searching for information out of sick curiosity. In fact, I don't want to know. But I must plow through the mass of repetitions and see what we missed.

Bits and scraps of information were thrown out, picked up, circulated, and uncritically inscribed. The role of the 24/7 news media is appreciated and deplored. Even as we watched events unfold in real time, the question was itching the back of my mind: we're watching but so are the Kouachi brothers and Coulibaly. Isn't it dangerous for them to know everything? We can't see what's going on inside the print shop, the kosher grocery store, but they can see what's going on outside. How do you outsmart these guys who are so skilled at the trigger and so bumbling about everything else? They leave tracks everywhere like a dumb dog who runs in from a muddy field and climbs all over the white sofa with his filthy paws, dirties the tile floors, the beds, the doorknobs. The problem is not so much finding their accomplices, jihad networks, and international ramifications; the problem is there are so many of them, so many like them, and not enough investigators to follow them, not enough police to rake them in and maximum security prisons to hold them.

It all happened so fast at the *Charlie Hebdo* editorial meeting. And it was interminable at the kosher grocery. The Charlie cartoonists and writers, aware of the dangers, had chosen to defend their rights and principles. Customers and employees at the Hyper Cacher might have known they were vaguely in danger in a Jewish store in France but didn't think they were risking their lives as they shopped for the Sabbath. *Charlie Hebdo* was "protected." Editor-in-chief Charb had a full time body guard. Outgunned in a second. Perhaps the protection was flimsy because the threat was underestimated? Jewish sites such as the Centre Rachi and the Jewish museum are protected by fully manned bulletproof double door security entrances.

HEROES

Everyone, both heroes and passive victims on flight 93 that crashed in a cornfield in Shanksville Pennsylvania on 9/11, is dead. There are at least 16 surviving Hyper Cacher hostages, and very few accounts so far. A gentleman in his sixties, a civil servant who had spent much of his career in Arab-Muslim countries, told his story to journalist Ruth Elkrief (*BFM TV*)...with his back turned to the camera. He had dropped into the kosher grocery to buy humus on that fatal Friday. Due to his professional experience, he immediately recognized the sound of a military weapon as Coulibaly burst into the store, guns blazing. This gentleman, let's call him X, was in the group of customers that ran to the back of the store, rushed down a winding staircase to the cellar, and hid in a cold storage room.

Shortly afterward, someone was sent down by Coulibaly to tell them they had to come upstairs or he would kill everyone. Some obeyed, others stayed where they were. X went upstairs. Three bodies were lying in pools of blood and a fourth man who had just been shot was agonizing. X learned subsequently that the young man had tried to grab Coulibaly's weapon.

X's description of Coulibaly's chilling mixture of savage brutality and something resembling politeness is displayed in the killer's two-bit shahid film. He resembles a certain type of mujahid featured in Daesh videos—soft punks that grew up in the easy lap of developed democracies, pumped up with poisonous Islamic hatred, and turned into ruthless killers. That combination of soft cheeks and knife sharp eyes is the hallmark of mujahidin of the Western world.

We would call him a *crâneur* in French, a nobody who thinks he's hot stuff. Except that Coulibaly had assault weapons and had already killed four men. "He told us his name," says X, "and explained why he was a fighter." X adds, "I'm interested in Islam, the true Islam of Avicenna and Averroes." Coulibaly asked each hostage to declare his name, age, profession, and origin. When X gave his origin as "French" Coulibaly corrected: "Catholic." And X, who had never before been asked to define himself as Catholic, understood that he might be killed as such. "I felt what it is like to be Jewish."

X did not mention Lassana Bathily, a young man from Mali—like Coulibaly—who worked at the Hyper Cacher and, reportedly, saved hostages by taking them down to the cellar, showing them into the cold storage rooms, and turning off the refrigeration before slipping out of the building on the freight elevator. None of the hostages followed him out, the story goes, because they thought it was too dangerous. Bathily, who had almost been deported as an illegal immigrant a few years ago, was unanimously hailed as a hero and given French nationality in a solemn state ceremony.

Some sources questioned Bathily's version of his role. I have no inside information. There are so many nasty rumors and conspiracy theories circulating; I wouldn't want to accredit anything I can't verify. However, if two young men died trying to disarm the killer, we should at least be talking about three heroes. The most detailed account of survivors has now been published by *Israel Hayom*:[1]

Zari Siboni and Andrea Shamak, two Hyper Cacher cashiers, tell the sequence of events in great detail. Zari is the person sent to order the people in the cellar to come upstairs. They do not mention Bathily, at least not in the published account of an extensive interview. I can't stop wondering why no one else chose to escape via the freight elevator. Another way of saying, "What would I have done?"

The question nagged me. As if I could retrospectively save the hostages by developing a strategy. We have fire drills, the Japanese have earthquake drills, the Thais improved their tsunami alert system, weather forecasters help us reduce risk and damage of exceptional storms...

don't we need to be trained in hostage defense? All I could come up with was an image, a sort of wishful thinking cartoon image of the hostages slipping into one aisle of the Hyper Cacher, silently and simultaneously picking up heavy cans and jars, throwing them at Coulibaly, knocking him senseless.

Then came a knife attack in a Tel Aviv bus. A 14 year-old boy boards the bus, sees the driver fighting back after being stabbed in the chest, and alerts the passengers. They all run to the back of the bus, the killer pursues them, the boy throws his back pack at the stabber and the bus driver slams on the brakes. The assailant falls, the passengers rush out of the bus, run for their lives, the stabber runs after them, stabbing wherever he can.

There's a difference between a knife and an assault weapon. But there is something universal about the delicate balance between submitting, in hopes of surviving, and fighting back with desperate courage.

SWEETHEARTS

Jeanette Bugrab, an outspoken critic of radical Islam and former minister in the Sarkozy government, suddenly emerged in the media as the grieving companion of Charb. The love story — brutally terminated by the Kouachi brothers — between the gorgeous sophisticated highly educated Algerian-origin Conservative and the far Left boyish Charb who was a cartoon of himself was a poignant surprise to the uninitiated.

A few days later Charb's brother tersely denied any sentimental relationship between Charb and Bougrab, and asked her to never mention it again. *Paris Match* published romantic photos of the couple, she continued to give interviews but agreed to stay away from the rousing funeral ceremony complete with jokes and song. What explains the slap in the face? Is it Leftist political orthodoxy that bridges no romantic exceptions? [Months later a reliable source gives me the reason for this rebuff: Charb had a legitimate partner, Jeanette Bougrab was what used to be called a mistress. In short, a French triangle.]

MARINE LE PEN

I'm trying to figure out the American infatuation with Marine Le Pen that flared up immediately after the jihad attacks in Paris. Mainstream media profiled her, the *WSJ* interviewed her, my own knowledgeable friends and colleagues wrote flattering articles about her. Some were so impressed by occasional truths uttered by the president of the Front National that they want her to be president of France! Others scolded me for insisting on her dubious entourage, unsavory electorate (recent polls show they rank third, after the Far Left and Muslims, for anti-Semitic attitudes), questionable alliances, and zigzagging judgments. Besides, she doesn't have a party ready to govern. Is this a time for amateurs? This American crush on Marine Le Pen reminds me of the French love affair with Obama in 2008!

Does it matter? It matters to me. How can it be so easy to convince intelligent people that you are France's best hope for countering Islamic aggression, when your close collaborators have connections with Nasrallah, do PR for Bashir al Assad, or dine at the table of Mustapha Tlass? Where is the Front National coming from and where is it going? Marine Le Pen has publicly disowned Aymeric Chauprade, her foreign policy advisor and head of the party's European parliament delegation, after he circulated a video in which he says we are at war with Muslims, not all Muslims but some Muslims who want to destroy us. This week she is snuggling up to our Far Left/ Greenies coalition and celebrating Szipras' victory in Greece. If Syriza can make an alliance with the Far Right, join Gaza flotillas and pro-Hamas demonstrations, why couldn't the Front National hook up with our Chavez wannabe who'd like to unite France with the Maghreb?

I'm just about to wrap up this article when two items hit the press: first, a poll shows Marine Le Pen with a large lead in the hypothetical first round of the 2017 presidential elections and, second, her close collaborator Frédéric Chatillon[2] is under investigation for a variety of financial irregularities connected with the Front National's 2011 and 2012 campaigns. He's the one who met with Nasrallah in 2002. Let the polls sing, I predict an implosion of the Front National in the coming year.

JE SUIS CHARLIE, CHARLIE IS ISRAEL

שארלי Charlie Israel ישראל

Charlie, written in Hebrew, is an anagram of Israel. Isn't there some truth to the paradox? Je suis Charlie, meaning I am Israel, targeted for elimination. I am Israel, I have a choice, I can defend myself. I am Israel even if I have been told since the dawn of this century that Israel "got what's coming to it." That Israel is the cause of the hatred aimed at it. As if to prove the anagram, calls to boycott French goods are heard in the Islamic world — new opportunities for BDS. If that weren't enough, our own prime minister accused us of apartheid in an over the top breast-beating confession of society's responsibility for the disaffection that breeds homegrown jihadis.

Je suis Charlie doesn't mean I'm a martyr. It doesn't mean I necessarily want to draw spoofs of Mohammed, missionaries, nuns, and politicians. It means I want to be free, free to live and breathe without fearing that someone I offend will shoot me instead of shouting at me. Granted, the je suis Charlies weren't Je suis Ilan Halimi. Does it mean they don't give a damn about Jews getting killed because they went to buy groceries? And when they see soldiers guarding Jewish schools aren't they afraid the jihadis might attack public schools? Je suis Charlie means I'm not going to accept the death penalty meted out by freelancers after it was so proudly abolished in the French constitution. Je suis Charlie means I suddenly realize what happens when you get shot with a Kalashnikov. I don't want Kalashnikovs in the hands of thousands of wild men with French passports who think we deserve to die.

It's about something more than freedom of speech.

THE WILL OF THE PEOPLE

The will of the people was not expressed with unmistakable clarity. The government did not instantly straighten up and march with utmost determination in the right direction. But we have witnessed a turning point in contemporary history. This is the way societies are transformed and the course of events is irreversibly altered. This mixture of lucidity and deliberate retreat back into confusion is authentic. Our days are filled with hope and exasperation. Purveyors of taqqiya have a field day. But honest Muslim voices that had been stifled are given a hearing. Jihad cells that had been under desultory observation for years are cracked and hauled off to jail. The broken record plays "It has nothing to do with Islam." And Islam is on everyone's mind. Attention is focused on the schools, the banlieue, the projects, the unintegrated, unqualified, unemployed pools of potential jihad killers, while studiously ignoring the wide range of profiles, including teenage girls from good families, converts, promising young men with college degrees. Little attention was given to the case of the law trainee in one of England's topmost firms who did a 20-minute YouTube diatribe in defense of jihad.[3]

But the most poignantly ironic thread, especially but not only for French Jews, is undoubtedly this bit about apartheid. The idea is that certain ethnic populations are not given the opportunity to become decent law-abiding integrated citizens of the République because they are artificially concentrated in virtual ghettos. The solution, then, is *mixité*. Mixing. If nobody stops them, this government will use busing and other tricks to keep people from running away from troubled schools and neighborhoods.

Only one third of Jewish children still attend public schools in France. A bit more *mixité* and it will go down to one tenth. More than half of the Jewish population in France today is Sephardic, essentially refugees from the Maghreb. In the past fifteen years they have been fleeing Muslim-dominated neighborhoods in French cities. And some are fleeing all the way to Israel, the US, and other destinations.

FLIGHT OR FIGHT

French Aliyah doubled this year and may triple next year. Or become an exodus. It depends.

The French government is a bit scared. "France without the Jews would not be France." In more ways than one, *mon vieux*. Remove the lightning rod and your house might go up in flames.

The manager of the Hyper Cacher, who had taken over only four days before the murderous attack, says he's leaving for Israel. Other hostages or bereaved family members of victims are staying. There is no argument with personal decisions. My grandparents left Europe before the First World War. I left the United States to live somewhere in Africa and ended up in Paris. Staying and leaving both make sense to me personally. I do not think we are in a 1930s configuration where the danger was concentrated in Europe; Jews with foresight escaped to safety. Today the same threat hangs over us, Jews and non-Jews, everywhere. The question that faces us collectively is how to defend ourselves wherever we are.

The *Charlie Hebdo* lesson is that no matter how much is done to dissuade the citizens of the still free world from defending their precious values, reality prevails. One or two or two hundred big and small incidents can be ignored or misinterpreted but finally reality will prevail.

Cockeyed schemes will be concocted to delay the reckoning but reality will knock them over like bowling pins.

The personal answer to the question of staying in France or leaving is by definition correct. The choice that isn't offered — as long as we are alive — is leaving or staying in the world. However we name the destructive force that is on the march, it is everywhere, it has to be confronted everywhere.

EPILOGUE

January 27, 2015: I followed the entire 70th anniversary ceremony at Auschwitz-Birkenau and then watched hours of debate on a variety of outlets. No, it's not a hypocritical commemoration exercise organized by a cynical world. It's a moment of crushing reality.

The ceremony and debates were marked this year by the Paris jihad attacks and the January 11th reaction. How can that momentary flicker be conserved, and fanned to a life-giving flame? You cannot reverse the tide of confusion that unwittingly feeds genocidal hatred unless you can speak to the heart of your fellow citizens. Unless you believe the person you reach out to has a heart.

— New English Review

JIHAD ATTACKS IN DENMARK: DATELINE PARIS

Thursday, 19 February 2015

French Interior Minister Bernard Cazeneuve was on official business in Morocco when informed of the jihad attack against a free speech meeting in Copenhagen. He immediately flew to Denmark where he joined his personal friend François Zimeray, French ambassador to Denmark. Zimeray, who attended the "Art, Blasphemy, Freedom of Speech" event at the Krudttønden Café organized in reaction to the *Charlie Hebdo* massacre in Paris, put it succinctly: "I went to the meeting by bicycle and left in an armored car."

All-news channels *BFM TV* and *i-Télé* went into Special Edition, reporting on the attack non-stop from Saturday afternoon to Sunday night, and then some. Frequent zaps to other available stations—*CNN, Sky News, BBC, France24*—yielded low to negligible interest in the story...aside from the *BBC* recording of Inna Shevchenko's speech at the event. The Ukrainian Femen, commenting on the current state of press freedom in the West, asked "Why do we say we have freedom of speech, but...?" As she repeated for emphasis the "freedom but" her words were brutally punctuated by the sharp crackle of gunfire.

French-Danish solidarity goes back to *Charlie Hebdo*'s publication of the original *Jyllands Posten* Mohammed cartoons in 2006. Few imagined, even one month ago, that this solidarity would turn into a ping pong of posters, bouquets, and memorial candles. We suspect the ceremonies will eventually wear thin from repetition. But, unless you followed the story on French media, you wouldn't know the extent of this fraternity: vigils and presidential visits at the Danish embassy in Paris, the Paris mayor in Copenhagen, the Chief Rabbi of France, the president of the CRIF, leaders of political parties, special correspondents here and there, countless media debates ...

When the story broke Saturday afternoon (Valentine's Day no less!) the gunman was already on the run, one man— misreported as a passerby—was dead, and two policemen were wounded. Tight-lipped Danish authorities gave the media little to chew on. The hunger for images had to be satisfied with the café's plate glass window pocked with bullet holes.

We, the gawkers, knew that the assailant had not been able to get inside. The suspense came later in a sort of playback when participants told how it felt in real time. They thought they were going to die. The gunman and the potential victims—there were 30 to 40 people in the room— were following the same *Charlie Hebdo* scenario. "Copycat," surmised a few French commentators, proudly sporting the trendy English term. No, *mes amis*, it's something worse than copycat.

And the something, this time, was immediately identified as jihad. Yes, the linguistic tricks are still fluttering like coquettish fans — Islamism, radical Islam, hijacked Islam—but there is no taboo against "jihadi" or "jihadist." And there was no beating around the bush on *BFM TV* and *i-Télé* last weekend. Journalists and invited commentators recognized another three-pronged attack against liberty, law enforcement, and Jews...by a jihadi.

Suddenly, there he was, the killer, described by police as looking "North African," wearing dark clothes and a stylish bordeau ski mask, captured by CCTV in all his punknificence. A bit of a surprise for us here in France, where authorities are notoriously skittish about letting the public know who is out there armed to kill. This led to tragic consequences in the case of Ilan Halimi (see the Alexandre Arcady film *24 Days*, available in DVD). The police withheld the identikit image of one of the young women who had been trolling for Jews to kidnap. Ilan was already dead when they finally released it, immediately leading to the arrest of Fofana and his accomplices.

Some of the more knowledgeable anchors were absent when the Copenhagen story broke at the start of a two-week winter break. Was *Agence France Presse* slow in processing information from Danish sources? For this and other newscast reasons, journalists weren't reading heat & serve press releases. There was a lot of improvisation and, consequently, less double talk and more wide-eyed ignorance. It reminded me of earnest five year-olds discussing serious issues with a mixture of childish honesty and an immature world view.

But the story was big, bigger in France than anywhere else but Denmark itself. As the hours went by, commentators streamed in and out of TV studios. The usual Islam-apologists were not among them. Are their words no longer comforting or convincing? No imams to tell us this brutal act has nothing to do with Islam. A simple consensus emerged: the jihadis are at war with us, they want to destroy our society, deprive us of our liberty, make our lives desperately miserable... And we aren't going to let them get away with it. We won't go overboard like the Americans—the Patriot Act is poison to French ears—but we have to change our strategy and face this challenge squarely. We are at war, this war is global, and our response has to be global—increased security cooperation with our European neighbors, the United States and, for example, Turkey. Granted, no one had the courage to mention Israel as a light unto the nations when it comes to fighting enemies within, without, and all about. But secretly they know it's true.

I went off screen Saturday night wondering why the policemen assigned to guard that obviously sensitive meeting were wounded, while the gunman was able to shoot up the façade, jump into his car, and ride off to an unknown destination. Why didn't they shoot him? For wont of that notorious American police "brutality" a dangerous killer was on the loose. Isn't this a big part of the European problem? The late Charb had bodyguards, Lars Vilks, prime target at the Copenhagen event, has one or several bodyguards, but they seem to be guarding against bows and arrows, not assault weapons, not jihadis.

First thing Sunday morning I switched on the TV to see if they had found him. Yes. He was already dead. But not before he had killed a Jew. *Mission accomplie.* 37 year-old Don Uzan was on duty, protecting a bat mitzvah party in the synagogue annex. Two policemen were slightly wounded, the Jewish man was killed, and the gunman was on the loose again until dawn when, in a now familiar confrontation with SWAT-type forces, he was shot dead.

Was it foolhardy to go ahead with a bat mitzvah party when a jihad killer was on the loose? Then again, isn't that what we do? Live our lives. Go to our places. Show our faces. *Charlie Hebdo* brought out an issue two weeks after most of the staff had been brutally gunned down. The Hyper Cacher at Porte de Vincennes is closed and deathly silent but Jews go to kosher delis, kosher restaurants, kosher synagogues. Policemen and policewomen direct traffic, answer domestic violence calls, arrest drug dealers. Dozens of jihadis have been detained this month in France.

A few days later the parents of the bat mitzvah girl, interviewed by the *Algemeiner,*[1] say they felt safe under the protection of the late Dan Uzan. The rabbi wonders how the killer got through when the whole city was under police control. An unverifiable report claims the killer, now officially identified as Omar Hamid el-Hussein, got through the first line of police protection by pretending to be a drunken guest at the party, and reached the inner courtyard where he shot Uzan in the head.

If you remember, one of the Kouachi brothers left his ID card in the getaway car they abandoned shortly after killing 12 people at the *Charlie Hebdo* offices. Well, our Danish specimen abandoned his (stolen) getaway car and called a taxi! I repeat, he had just killed one man, wounded two policemen, shot up a café in an attempt to massacre a free speech meeting, and he calls a taxi and has the taxi drop him off at the door of a safe house...or maybe it was his home address. Add this to the profile of the soft-cheeked jihad killer of the Western world and you've earned your degree in criminology. The taxi driver recognized Omar from the CCTV photo and notified the police but the killer was gone by the time they got there. Where did he spend the next five or six hours before executing a Jew? At the movies?

Documentary film maker Finn Noergaard—the man killed at the free speech event—had posted on Facebook last month the photo of a victim carried out on a stretcher from the *Charlie Hebdo* offices, with a comment on the horror of being killed for expressing oneself. Why was Noergaard in the line of fire when everyone else was behind closed doors? Had he arrived late for the meeting...stepped out of the room for a minute? What sealed his fate?

Special Editions on the second day focused on anti-Semitism without forgetting blasphemy. No journalist, no commentator, no invited guest, no public official underplayed or cast doubt on the Jew hatred that motivated the second attack. CRIF president Roger Cukierman took a slap at President Obama for tossing off the victims of the Hyper Cacher massacre as random targets.

It took fifteen years, but the lesson has been learned: anti-Semitism doesn't only endanger Jews, it destroys a nation. Now there is a desperate last ditch effort to convince French Jews to stay. Sometimes it takes the form of perverse disdain for the Israeli prime minister's outstretched hand. Repeating the welcome extended after last month's jihad attacks in Paris, Netanyahu told European Jews that Israel is our home. And the invitation is still making waves and provoking pretzel dialogues. Jews in France and now in Copenhagen are asked if it was right for the prime minister to tell them to leave. Should European Jews move to Israel, will they really be better off, isn't it more dangerous there, can they adapt to a "foreign" country ...? Most often the sample Jew dragged into one of these baroque interrogations replies that one should make Aliyah for positive reasons... Jews shouldn't flee in fear.

If you ask me, this is no time to judge whether Jews should stay and tough it out, leave on a spiritual cloud, or run for their lives! And what about European non-Jews? Where will they go if this relentless attack on our lives and liberty continues unabated?

One thing is sure. For all the talk about backlash against Muslims we haven't seen them fleeing Europe to enjoy a better life in a country that beckons them to come home.

Round about midnight that Sunday, *BFM* editorialist Christophe Hondelatte is getting down with Frédéric Encel. The political scientist explains that the Mohamed caricatures are a pretext. Hondelatte: So...

even if we stopped doing them, it wouldn't change anything? FE: Right. Encel sketches out the nature and scope of this murderous hatred aimed at us no matter what we do. Hondelatte follows the logic: an army could rise against us in the banlieue? FE: Right ... so... Suddenly the light dims. The moment of truth falls into the sociological trap, something about how we better start doing what's necessary to make them feel wanted, give them the chance to succeed...

Like they do in Denmark, my friends? Journalists visiting the tidy housing project where Omar el-Hussein reportedly lived off and on with his Jordanian Palestinian father, encounter like-minded buddies who say he was a great guy. His stint in prison for savagely stabbing a young man on an urban train obviously doesn't faze them. Fellow students in adult education classes noted his passionate defense of the Palestinian cause. And, of course, it is generally admitted that he was "radicalized" in prison. Did he have to go that far to find fuel to stoke his rage?

The inimitable, invaluable MEMRI brings us a video of a sermon delivered in a Copenhagen mosque on the eve of Omar Hamid el-Hussein's jihad performance.[2] The message is implacable: shun the Christians, kill the Jews, keep to yourselves and your Muslim ways— the whole world must submit to the will of Allah.

How ironical it is to even think of accepting the myth of exquisite religious sensitivity that moves Muslims to kill when their prophet is not respected and should consequently move us to at least partially accommodate them on the grounds of "respect for religion." These exquisitely sensitive Muslims, after they kill free speechers and shoot at police, kill Jews.

Monday morning, Prime Minister Valls named the enemy as Islamofascism.

The debate ebbs and flows. At its worst it paddles in the shallow waters of socio-economic determinism. Underprivileged youths suffering from unemployment and racism stumble into crime and then, misguidedly seeking elevation, grab at undigested Islamism to give meaning to their lives. What do they know about the noble religion of Islam that has nothing to do with their sleazy lives and abject crimes?

What does the foot soldier know about military strategy? Did he graduate from St. Cyr?

Denmark is—or was?— something of a model in the business of de-radicalization. According to the *Daily Mail* the approach includes "dialogue with a mosque regarded as a hotbed of extremism, after authorities found 22 of the young radicals who went to Syria had worshipped there. But those who return are not expected to renounce their support for radical Islamic goals."

Hundreds of bouquets in front of the Krudttønden café, hundreds at the synagogue, and more than enough at the spot where el-Hussein died. *Le Figaro* reports, citing *Agence France Presse*, that one bouquet was offered by an elderly Danish woman who said the boy didn't realize what he was doing.[3] But the accompanying video shows immigrant youths paying floral tribute to the Copenhagen shahid. Another layer of meaning is added after nightfall. A dozen guardians of the faith toss the bouquets in the garbage because it's against Islam to lay flowers where someone died. One of the brothers declares, "He wasn't a terrorist. The terrorists are Denmark, the United States, Israel." And they march off with a defiant *allahu akbar*.

Radicalized? Moderate? Or simple garden variety Danish youths?

— *NER/Iconoclast*

Chapter 6/ Acquiescence

P5 + 1 & THE POPE SUBMIT

May-July 2015

And now the Western world is offering its neck to a two-state solution with a nuclear armed Iran. The principle is the same: a force that unashamedly declares its intention to annihilate you builds a military machine before your eyes, engages in subversive activities and proxy wars to surround and weaken you, demands or accepts negotiations aimed at ending the conflict, refuses to compromise on any issue, and proudly reiterates its genocidal declarations. And the answer is a two-state solution? Why would well-armed freedom-loving democracies accept such a dirty deal with Iran? Is it because they have been relentlessly trying to force the same one down the throat of Israel?

The mechanism set in motion with the 1993 Oslo Accords has been grinding away ever since. It spits out two-state solution rhetoric and stocks a wide array of attack weapons: Occupation, apartheid, genocide, open-air prison, war crimes, crimes against humanity, militaristic theocracy... Failure to implement the two-state solution is attributed solely to Israel, paving the way for an uninterrupted barrage of warnings, condemnation, and threats of an internationally imposed solution. A shadow Palestinian State creeps from European parliaments to the EU and the UN, and nestles in the ineluctable public opinion that has replaced Western thought.

The Western mind is softened and remodeled. The courage to defend liberty has been choked up with adulterated human rights grease, and dissolved in crocodile tears. Undercurrents of old-fashioned Jew hatred swept up by torrents from the Islamic source have rendered the West incapable of defending its interests. Essential values are reduced to flotsam and jetsam. The connection between antisemitism and Western surrender to Islamic jihad is not circumstantial; Judaism is the origin of our civilization.

And so, after chasing the Jews out of the Muslim world, Islam is going after the Christians. It didn't begin with Daesh. No sooner relieved of Saddam Hussein and the Taliban, Iraq and Afghanistan started to persecute Christians. What explains the lackluster response? Is it because so many of the world's two billion nominal Christians are not observant? Then why is international opinion mobilized in the defense of tiny remnants of Amerindians here or large numbers of Tibetans there? The secular West should be moved by the plight of Eastern Christians on humanitarian grounds. On the contrary, in the name of *laïcité* the Parisian transportation authority wanted to censor the words "for the benefit of Eastern Christians" on a métro station poster for a concert by singing priests. The courts finally ruled in the priests' favor but the dhimmitude mentality was laid bare in the process.

Acquiescence. Lethal narratives are gobbled up and spit out in mindless media. Acquiescence in the myth of a territorial Israeli-Palestinian conflict, acquiescence in the ploy of legitimate criticism of Israel, acquiescence in the proliferation of Islamic Jew hatred in Europe, spinning excuses for violence against Israelis/Jews... all of these seemingly minor indulgences have emasculated Christendom.

Christians are beaten to death, burned alive, beheaded, crucified in the Muslim Middle East. Does the Pope finally join hands with the Jews to stand up to this all-purpose hatred? No. The Vatican recognizes the State of Palestine, beatifies two "Palestinian" [Ottoman] nuns, and receives Mahmoud Abbas with open arms and ambiguous grammar. Global media parroting major press agencies reported that the Pope called

Abbas "an angel of peace." By the time the record was corrected[1]–the Pope said Abbas could be an angel of peace—the media had lost interest, though the *NY Times* did link to an article by Tom Gross. The same professionals that swallowed the al Dura hoax with dull eyes and ideological stubbornness copied and pasted the angel of peace absurdity without an ounce of skepticism. In the last analysis, the conditional is still too far from the truth.

Charles Enderlin, producer of the al Dura blood libel, quietly retired from state-owned France 2 TV this spring. Absurdly touted as a renowned Middle East expert, the pretentious hack slinked away to near-unanimous indifference, with the exception of some Jewish media. The French journalists' union [SNJ], chastised for inviting Daniel Leconte to a *Charlie Hebdo* tribute event, jumped at the chance to reiterate unflinching support for Enderlin, victim of a "hate campaign and unfounded accusations" of falsifying the report of the killing of a Palestinian youth by Israeli soldiers.[2]

In the aftermath of the January jihad attacks, the French government has been surprisingly forthright and proactive. Soldiers stand guard in front of Jewish schools, community centers, and synagogues. Harsh light is focused on jihad fighters that join Daesh and come back to haunt us on the home front. Extremists are deported, jihad cells are dismantled, Islamofascism is denounced. But the (barely) foiled plan to shoot up Christians at Sunday mass in Villejuif was met with embarrassed silence. Granted, the mass murder did not take place. But the fact that it was an inch away from happening should have been enough to provoke deep and broad coverage. Algerian-born Sid Ahmed Glam was repeatedly described as an IT student, even after it was revealed that he had lied on his application, didn't attend classes, while benefiting from a scholarship and first-class student housing. Granted a French residency permit under the family reunification plan— his father was a legal resident—Glam was soon flagged as a potential security risk, which didn't keep him from procuring Kalashnikovs, handguns, bullet-proof vests, flashing police lights, and other gadgets, much of it stored in his dorm room. He communicated with accomplices in France as well as a dispatcher in Syria that instructed him to attack churches. DNA and other reliable evidence reportedly identify Glam as the killer of Aurelie Châtelain, a lovely young unemployed dancer from the North who had come to Paris for a workshop. It is speculated that he wanted to steal her car, but no further information about his motives or method has been provided.

Apparently, after fatally shooting the young woman, Glam was on his way to pick up more weapons and join three accomplices but he accidentally shot himself in the leg (perhaps in a struggle with his victim). Bleeding profusely, he called for an ambulance. The police came along with the first responders. They followed the trail of blood back to Glam's car, loaded with weapons, and then went up to his room where they found more arms, €2,000 in cash, and the usual incriminating computers, cell phones, and documents.

Though the French are notoriously secular, there were at least 300 people celebrating mass in one of the targeted churches. The fact that the attack was planned in Villejuif [Jewtown] adds a touch of irony to the plot: even when jihadis target Catholics they can't leave the Jews out of it. In fact, French churches are vandalized on a regular basis without arousing particular interest.

Twice-burned media didn't even try to put a lone wolf figleaf on Glam. In fact, alleged accomplices were rapidly sought, detained, or identified. The *Canard Enchaîné* claims Glam was close to the Kouachi brothers who wiped out the staff of *Charlie Hebdo*; they were together in the "Buttes Chaumont" jihad recruiting cell and were neighbors in Reims. Glam gave the Reims address on a demand for naturalization filed shortly before the planned church attack. The Glam story broke on April 23rd and disappeared five days later...except for a small item that just popped up: Glam's nine year-old brother reportedly warned authorities of his radicalization. The boy's voice wasn't heard a month ago, when the suspect's mother and aunt monopolized the media, swearing he was innocent. Misled perhaps, but innocent. The proof? He couldn't have shot himself in the leg! And he wouldn't have murdered that young woman.

And here's another item that has been soft pedaled: The story broke without fanfare early in May: three French soldiers serving under a UN mandate in the Central African Republic are suspected of sexually abusing boys at a refugee shelter in exchange for food rations. Subsequently the figure was raised to seven soldiers and eventually to fourteen. The abuse was reported to UN officials that supposedly launched an investigation but one year after the alleged crimes no results had been revealed.

Finally, a UN staff member blew the whistle and was immediately dismissed (and subsequently reinstated according to recent reports). The Minister of Defense displayed shock and awe as if he had just discovered the scandal but it seems that he had been informed a year ago. French investigating magistrates have been dispatched, local authorities have stepped in, promises of stern punishment are made though doubt is cast on the testimony of the boys.

When was all of this taking place? The widespread sexual abuse was allegedly committed from December 2013 to June or July 2014. While the UN, global media, French authorities, and worldwide commentators were accusing Israel of war crimes in Gaza, including the unjustified bombardment of UN operated schools, African boys were allegedly indulging the lust of French soldiers under UN auspices. Breaking the Silence for an Israeli army fighting a genocidal Hamas; polite silence for French pedophile soldiers.

Which brings us to the question of "legitimate criticism of Israel." And why I don't countenance it. "Legitimate criticism of Israel" is the underground spring of Jew hatred in a configuration where jihad masterminds man the upper spheres of an international strategy of conquest. What do you hear on any day of the week? Israel=the peace process, 2-state solution, Occupation, checkpoints, mistreatment of Palestinians, discrimination against Israeli Arabs. A new government is formed and everyone from Barack to Ban twitters about hopes for peace negotiations leading rapidly to a 2-state solution. Cabinet appointments are judged by the gold standard of prospects for negotiations with the Palestinians.

And when the Palestinians or assorted Iranian proxies launch military attacks against Israel, legitimate criticism switches to: excessive force, killing children, destroying property, starving civilians, committing war crimes and crimes against humanity. Take away these endlessly repeated barbs and what's left to say about Israel? Nothing. It doesn't exist in the popular imagination. Look squarely at this so-called legitimate criticism and it boils down to one thing: submit. Surrender to jihad. It's not legitimate criticism it is the confluence of the underground spring and the over-arching jihad masterminds. It is an injunction aimed at leaving Israel as defenseless as a village in northern Nigeria or a Yazidi town in Syria.

THE SINGLE CELL ILLUSION

You cannot judge a human being by examining one cell under a microscope, you cannot evaluate a statement by reading a single line, a thread is not a garment, a thread is interwoven, a fabric is shaped, cut, sewn, worn. It is impossible to combat antisemitism today without recognizing the generalized state of war within which it operates, both as a primary goal and a way of getting traction for the pursuit of broader objectives. Mistaken as civil conflict that can be treated by criminal law, or recognized as war without acknowledging its jihad specificity, this destructive force is allowed to advance as if we were helpless to thwart and ultimately defeat it. For the West in general this results in a military inhibition timidly overcome on a case by case basis—the French in Mali and Central African Republic, drone strikes on Daesh, a helping hand against Boko Haram.

For Jews in particular this leads to the misconception that democratic nations, primarily in Europe where antisemitism is raging, can treat it as a domestic problem with an arsenal of measures including strong statements against antisemitism, increased Shoah sensitivity, tracking and tallying antisemitic crimes, repression of internet hate speech. Though the link between anti-Zionism and antisemitism is now admitted, a clear distinction between Jews and Israelis is proposed as a salutary measure. In fact the sovereign Jewish state is the bulwark against genocide. Instead of striving relentlessly to undermine that sovereignty, France and other European countries could stand together with Israeli authorities to effectively protect the Jewish population. An Israeli soldier side by side with his French ally in front of a synagogue in Sarcelles, for example. Unthinkable? Every summer, joint controls are organized with policemen from a wide variety of foreign countries including China, to protect tourists from predators. Behind the scenes, Jewish communities and French government authorities call on private Israeli security companies for protection. The advantage of having Israeli soldiers stationed in front of Jewish community centers, schools, and synagogues is that it would make the protective role of the State of Israel visible and would give the lie to the notion that European Jews will no longer be targets if they detach themselves from Zionism.

The problem is not exacerbated by the "importation of the Middle East conflict" that disrupts good relations between Jewish and Muslim "communities" in France. The antagonism is imported along with Muslim immigration and perpetuated by ingrained attitudes in their culture. Orthodox Islamic Jew hatred is preached by foreign imams in foreign-funded mosques. If Salafist preachers can be brought to France to foment antisemitism, why couldn't Israeli soldiers be invited to combat it? A foreign invasion? Wouldn't Eastern Christians welcome protection from the soldiers of nominally Christian countries?

TRIPWIRES, TUNNEL VISION, TAQQIYA, TIKKUN OLAM

In an interminable interview with the *Atlantic*'s Jeffrey Goldberg, the president of the United States gives the prototype "father knows best" argument that passes for legitimate criticism of Israel.[3] Arab and Jewish leaders are skeptical about his nuclear deal with Iran? He'll convince them that the deal will "enhance their security." Take one step outside the Goldberg-Obama tête-à-tête and this neat little reassurance disappears in a puff of smoke. Here in France, President Obama's Middle East policy inspires zero confidence. But, strange as it might seem, his assessment of Israel's best interests is widely shared. Motivated by "his love for the Jewish state" Obama warns that it must live up to its Jewish values, make the "stark choices" he imposes...or else. And he won't let the "Jewish right, and the Republican Party" label criticism of the Netanyahu government as anti-Israel or anti-Semitic. Skipping lithely from Israel's obligations to its Arab citizens and Palestinian kids, the American president traces a direct link between the right of the Jewish people to a homeland and the civil rights of African Americans.

Goldberg hears the music of *tikkun olam* in the president's heartfelt riff against "some political forces" that accuse you of being anti-Jewish because you refuse to "rubber stamp" the current Israeli government, or question settlement policy and express sympathy for Palestinians blocked at checkpoints... Goldberg thinks the president sounds like a rabbi striving to bolster support for "Israel's ... sometimes unpalatable reality." Securely confident of his love for the Jewish people, President Obama is confident that he knows what is best for Israel's security: a two-state solution.

Why, if the same argument has been presented for decades, has the solution never been implemented? Obviously, they imply, it's because Israel will not accept the conditions imposed by the "peace partner."

Which is why it is legitimate to criticize Israel and why the legitimate critics never apply their reasoning to any other situation. For example, in the name of African American values the American president should be concerned about the welfare of Christian kids in Pakistan, Yazidi women in Syria, schoolgirls in Nigeria, and Palestinians in Yarmouk... Hashtagging is not enough. The concern has to be translated into robust policy that gets results. If not, how could one expect Israel, Saudi Arabia, Egypt and the others to entrust their security to President Obama solely on the basis of his sincerity and love of humanity?

By what logic should a democratically elected Israeli government surrender responsibility for the security of Israeli citizens and, by extension, of Jews worldwide to the "first black president of the United States?" Barack Hussein Obama knows more about Jewish values than Binyamin son of Benzion Netanyahu, and the Israelis that elected him? He loves Israel and the Jews better than we love ourselves? A few smoochy kisses are enough to convince American Jews that he is sincere, trustworthy, honorable, and brilliant? What could be less brilliant than regurgitating outworn peace process rhetoric? It is all so dismal.

Yes, as David Bernstein claims, Obama's nostalgia for the good old days of Kibbutzim and socialist fervor might be understood as a preference for a "white Ashkenazi" Israel but that's not the point.[4] The president likes a pre-1967 Israel, vulnerable as a little bird to an enemy that would break its neck.

It didn't happen. So the "legitimate critics" want to give jihad another chance by forcing Israel to shrink down to the shape of a vulnerable bird that can be destroyed with a twist of the neck. It's called the "2-state solution." In fact, the territory that would be left behind the 1949 armistice lines misrepresented as a border does not leave Israel with a narrow waist... it's a fragile neck!

And it's not going to happen. Even Israeli Leftists won't accept it.

In his opening address to the 5th Global Forum for Combatting Antisemitism (GFCA), Prime Minister Netanyahu expressed his Jewish values.[5] Obsession with the Jewish State, he said, is antisemitism. It does not just bubble up from below, it percolates from the top. The difference is, we are no longer a stateless people seeking haven. We have a sovereign state. What has changed is not antisemitism, it is our capacity to defend ourselves.

There is no concept of legitimate criticism of Islam. It is qualified as Islamophobia and perniciously mixed into the antisemitism/ racism / xenophobia cocktail where it functions as a tripwire to prevent examination of the Islamic roots of contemporary genocidal Jew hatred. The issue of "anti-Muslimism" was raised by a wide array of speakers at the GFCA, giving the impression that Jewish indifference to the plight of Muslims was as much a matter for concern as the violence against Jews perpetrated by a "small minority of misguided Muslims who don't understand their religion." Interfaith activists at the Forum nourished comforting notions of shared Jewish and Islamic traditions, fueled vain hopes of stemming antisemitism by improved Shoah awareness, and entertained confusion between murderous Jew hatred and a vague mutual rejection of the Other. Rabbi Michael Melchior offered a reassuring interpretation of the Islamic curse on Jews as "sons of apes and pigs": it only refers to Jews that didn't live up to Jewish values. Muslim apostates that tell the truth about Islam are considered extremists in the West, and exposed to mortal danger. Goodhearted outreach Muslims come to us with a discourse that amounts to *taqqiya*, quoting sweet Koranic verses about the Jews while hiding the fact that they are abrogated, and vowing solemn respect for "our" prophets without admitting that they have been converted to Islam in the texts.

Tripwires separate the documented historical evidence of Islamic persecution of Jews from the scriptural basis for this hatred. A tripwire of respect for religion protects mosque sermons from prosecution as hate speech. Another tripwire imposes the generic term "terrorism" in place of the accurate word "jihad," allowing for sterile debate on relativist definitions: one man's terrorist is another man's freedom fighter.

Antisemitism is often compared to a virus, particularly for its ability to mutate and adapt to changing circumstances. Unfortunately this contributes to the misunderstanding that antisemitism is a vague component floating in the air along with all sorts of other particles. People who catch it say bad things about Israel and the Jews. The weaker "victims" go so far as to physically attack or even kill Jews. The masterminds of jihad disappear behind this metaphor. They are not absent-mindedly sprinkling antisemitism dust over towns and fields! The masterminds, the prime movers, are busy manipulating the masses and carrying out step by step their publicly declared intentions.

Western governments that cannot protect their own interests cannot deal effectively with antisemitism because they treat the symptom while participating in the cause. Motivated by what it mistakes as noble humanitarian values the same French government that sends soldiers to guard Jewish places from lowdown thugs promotes a UN resolution for a two-state solution at its worst. Sincerely determined to staunch the flow of antisemitic filth and jihad recruitment in social media, the French government is unable to own up to its responsibility in the production and dissemination of the single most virulent incitement to violence against Jews since the Shoah: the al Dura blood libel.

To combat the full-fledged assault on civilization we must rethink the problematics of antisemitism, anti-Zionism, and the two-state solution. Antisemitism pedals along on a two-wheel configuration: a naughty, recalcitrant, or misguided Israeli government—no matter which one is elected—that refuses to make peace with the Palestinians is balanced against a beleaguered Jewish Diaspora worthy of commiseration in memory of the Shoah. This shaky contraption is hitched to the juggernaut of jihad conquest, a codified form of warfare aimed at uprooting the Jews from Israel, Christians and other minorities from the Middle East and, ultimately, *kuffars* everywhere.

No effective military or political strategy is possible in the Middle East without a radical conceptual shift that will deflate the fallacy of "legitimate criticism of Israel," disarm the tripwires, and deactivate international bodies, beginning with the United Nations, that have been perverted into jihad facilitators.

There is apparently no way to stop the well-meaning friends of Israel from mouthing the two-state solution as an expression of concern for Israel's survival. Whatever the naïve expectations that once inspired it, the two-state solution has no resemblance to a geopolitical project that can be sketched out and modified in response to concrete realities. This inexhaustible source of Jew hatred is an article of faith upheld solely by hollow repetition.

The time has come to detach the "Palestinian" issue from unjustifiable claims on Israeli territory and to recognize its rightful place within the reality of internecine Islamic war. The fate of "Palestinian" Muslims living in Gaza, Judea & Samaria and elsewhere in Israel, or scattered in a self-styled Diaspora, will be determined within the oumma, side by side with the PLO, Hamas, and Hezbollah, straight in the path of Daesh and Iran.

The prospect is terrifying? How cozy for the "Palestinian cause" to confront Israel, when the Daddy of international opinion is always ready to pay for another turn on the peace process merry go round, rather than to go naked into the Islamic inferno. Gaza-Israel in the summer of 2014 was like tossing pillows at a pajama party compared to fighting it out with the decapitators or begging for mercy from a nuclear-armed Iran. At this writing, Daesh is threatening to attack Gaza while Hamas stands ready to pounce on Fatah and Hezbollah vows to destroy Israel but can't achieve a decisive victory for Assad in Syria.

The free world is cramped in a defensive cringe. Domestic surrender to Islamic intimidation weakens resolve to confront the enemy on the international battlefield. The United States of America slips into ambiguous isolationism, washing its hands of responsibility but strutting and jiving about a so-called deal with Iran. John Kerry's broken femur is emblematic. Supposedly negotiating the terms of a life and death issue, the 71 year-old American Secretary of State in full cyclist rig takes a break to run a mountainous stretch of the Tour de France. He bumps into a credibility gap. And misses the Paris summit on defeating Daesh.

France, abandoned by the superpower, its military capacity stretched to the limits, calls in vain for help from its pacifist European partners. Diplomatic war against Israel inflates instead of receding when one troubled state after the other collapses, creating power bases for jihad fighters and multiplying the number of refugees and victims of barbarian slaughter.

What will become of the Muslim majority that, we are assured, asks nothing more than to live decently? It will have to find a way to prevail on its own ground against the tyranny generated by its own heritage. Western-trained and armed soldiers collapse like toothpicks in the face of swashbuckling Daesh. Rich petromonarchies tremble in the shadow of wily Persians. Heads roll, antique treasures are reduced to rubble, refugees run hither and thither with sunken eyes and parched mouths. Daesh keeps its promise of sending them by the tens of thousands across the Mediterranean to flood Europe; the threat is deliberately forgotten, the misery is embraced like the kiss of death, humanitarians plead for mercy and act as accomplices for the enslavers that pocket the refugees' life savings and push them off the plank. Like the Arab slave traders of old, they siphon up Africans. This time around they are used as arms against Europe rather than muscles to do the dirty work.

STRENGTH IS NOT IN NUMBERS

Strength is in resolve, and resolve demands lucidity. This war of jihad conquest operates through a conceptual attack on the rational mind by a strategy of lethal narratives. Small Jewish populations in Europe and the Americas do not weigh heavily when the votes are counted but intelligent minds can achieve the change in perspective that is the collective hope of the free world. There is no place for the retrograde image of Jewish victimhood in the Diaspora and surrender to diplomatic warfare in Israel. The disgusting violence against Jews that has been flourishing for the past fifteen years at record levels in Europe while spreading worldwide and not sparing the United States can be effectively confronted and forced to retreat. Will the West move from self-righteous cowardice to courageous offensive action?

Palmyra (Tadmur) stands as an eloquent illustration of all that has been said here. The capture of the antique city was met with consternation, but nothing compared to the indignation over an Israeli strike against the home of a Hamas chief in Gaza. The civilized world looks on, horrified, as Daesh makes its way through Syria and Iraq, smashing idols and selling antiquities on the black market. Instead of mumbling "that's not Islam" it would be appropriate to recall the ongoing destruction of first temple artefacts by the Waqf, the Jordanian desecration of synagogues and tombs during its illegal occupation of Judea-Samaria, and all the way back to the construction of a mosque on the ruins of the Temple of Jerusalem.

Media that not so long ago were ecstatic about the "Arab Spring" are still playing the silly game. *Sky News*, for example, ran footage of some men in Palmyra—described as "the population"— welcoming Daesh with *allahu akbars*. One had to consult alternative sites to see photos of beheaded corpses lined up in the street and reports that four to five hundred, mainly women and children, were murdered in the first days.

Tadmur, the bustling crossroads of ancient times, where the caravans of King Solomon traded with merchants from all corners of a magnificent Middle Eastern civilization; silks and spices, gold and precious gems, beautifully crafted objects, delicacies, and necessities came and went across those fertile routes. All that is left of Tadmur is the ruins of Palmyra. The ruins of that ancient civilization of which Israel was one small component.

Palmyra stands in ruins and even those ruins could be smashed from one day to the next.

And Israel stands firm on the edge of an immense expanse of chaos, rubble, and blood-soaked victims of atrocities.

PEACE PROCESSING IRAN

August 2015

The principle is similar: faced with an enemy that repeatedly declares its genocidal hatred, acts on it wherever possible, constantly strives to improve its ways and means, you peace process. Why was it successful with Iran and not with the "Palestinians"? Perhaps because, in the case of Iran, the comical P5 + 1 applied the pressure to itself, leaving no one to resist. The same pressure applied to Israel since 1993 has failed to produce total surrender. Drastic concessions were proposed but the enemy insisted on the right of return of "refugees" down to the third, fourth, and forever generations that would spell the elimination of the Jewish State. There were no significant limits to the concessions made by the P5+1 and no expectation that the deal will yield anything other than itself. The deal is that there's a deal.

The devil is not in the details it is in the evil, the collusion with evil. Antisemitism in its modern form of antizionism is the ultimate perversion: choosing death over life, it reverses good and evil. The perverse subject embraces evil while proclaiming his goodness. The Iran "deal" is not the result of American government naiveté, faulty negotiating skills, or realpolitik. It has nothing to do with slowing Iran's nuclear arms development. It is an international seal of approval for Iran's genocidal project. A wink of complicity.

What better proof than the hasty visit of German Vice Chancellor Sigmar Gabriel accompanied by a regiment of businessmen? Germany of all nations, still heavy with the weight of the Shoah, had to demonstrate immediately that the deal is a practical matter of trade and polite relations. But the truth bled through the window dressing and, as befits

THE BLACK FLAG OF JIHAD

perversion, was expressed in an outright lie: Gabriel reminded his Iranian counterparts that they must not question Israel's right to exist. "That is unacceptable," he declared, accepting it as if it were a second helping of ham hocks. Italy's molto simpatico PM Matteo Renzi reassured his amico grandissimo that his country would always be there to defend Israel. With what? French MFA Laurent Fabius who distinguished himself by taking a strong position during negotiations —before caving in to pressure—waited an extra week for his sober visit, *sans* traveling salesmen but bearing a missive from President Hollande inviting President Rohani to visit him in November. What could be more grotesque, more obscene than these frantic gestures laced with hollow excuses?

Obama&Kerry are trying to force, cajole, intimidate, manipulate Congress and public opinion to approve the phony agreement that will, they claim, slow down Iran's nuclear arms project while giving the Islamic Republic (as they prefer not to designate it) time to become the friendly partner they deserve. All the concrete evidence proves the contrary. So what have they really accomplished?

While talking up the deal domestically, with special emphasis on Jewish organizations, they sent Defense Secretary Ashton Carter to dangle yummy defensive military goodies in front of the Israeli government as a consolation prize. What have they wrought? Kerry, grilled by the Senate Foreign Relations committee, is scolded for being duped. If his only fault was a failure to get better terms from those crafty Persians, then the honor of America's chief negotiator and aspiring Tour de France cyclist would be intact. Now, fearing the slick sale pitches will not do the trick, the Secretary of State has moved on to sinister threats. Invited by the Council for Foreign Relations to defend the deal, he warned that if Congress should vote against it, "Israel will be more isolated and more blamed [sic]."

So that's the win-win? If the agreement is approved, Israel will be in greater danger, if it is rejected, Israel will be blamed. In fact, it doesn't matter. The collusion agreement with Iran has nothing to do with foreign policy or non-proliferation of nuclear arms. It is a call to ratify the genocidal equation: Iran is deserving of trust, Israel can be thrown to the dogs. Good and evil are reversed. The damage is already done.

While Europeans were creeping to Iran like worker ants, each with a few crumbs to sell, the EU parliament was mulling over a measure that would stigmatize products from the Israeli "colonies." Grotesque perversion. Iran, by virtue of the deal, instantly becomes a suitable trading partner while Israel, an apartheid state guilty of Occupation, is unfit for human consumption. Gays swinging from the hangman's rope, political prisoners tortured to death, arms and treasure flowing to jihad forces that wreak havoc throughout the Middle East and sow subversion in the rest of the world... all disappear with the lethal narrative fed to global media by the wire services: After months of negotiation...a historic agreement...Iran forgoes nuclear arms development in exchange for removal of sanctions and the dawn of normal relations with the well-behaved world. Unprecedented inspections regime. Money-back guarantee. Snap-back sanctions. Diplomacy trumps war.

Death to America, Death to Israel. Our plan to erase Israel from the face of the earth is not negotiable. We will never abandon our right to develop nuclear arms and advanced delivery systems, we will arm our allies, no American will be included in the inspection teams, our military sites are forever off limits, *allahu akhbar*, flag burnings and raucous bloodthirsty cries... Secretary of State Kerry proves he's a good sport by briefly admitting that if Death to Israel Death to America were actually a statement of policy, it would be worrisome. But it's just rhetoric.

The once-free world, draped in virtue to exclude Israel from the concert of nations, mired in perversity to welcome Iran with open arms, dives into the abyss. And a significant percentage of American Jews, apparently, buy into this perversion. Out of the goodness of their hearts they become deaf, dumb, and blind to Iran's words and deeds, and reserve their severity for an Israel they could accommodate if it would stop throwing monkey wrenches into the global jamboree.

Vainglorious President Barack Hussein Obama, displaying his major diplomatic exploit—bouncing up and down the stairs of Air Force One—makes his victory lap in Kenya, where he lectures the locals on, of all things, clean government, democracy, and homosexual rights. Tell it to yer mulla', brotha'!

Though the personal responsibility of Obama, Kerry, Mogherini, and other grinning negotiators is enormous, it won't help to blame them, because they are upheld by populations that are themselves captive. People who sincerely believe in their own decency and wish to do no harm recoil at the very sound of the name "Israel." Americans, who win

147

all the polls for loving Israel, dumbly follow their twice-elected president though he made his intentions clear from the first step of the primaries. How many American Zionists repeat the absurd fairy tale about how Iran will be contained, mollified, and magically turned over to the freedom-loving youth they see on *BBC* news? British Prime Minister David Cameron interjects "Islam is a religion of peace" into a forceful defense of the nation against Islamist ideology. France, still reeling from the latest beheading/impalement incident, sails into a new plot to behead a naval officer. The denial machine tries to photoshop the Chattanooga jihad attack against a military base. The body count in Syria rises inexorably, Bashir al Assad thanks Iran and Hezbollah for their invaluable support, the Middle East, with the exception of Israel, is being ethnically cleansed of Christians, and the good news is that Iran signed something? With disappearing ink.

"It starts with the Jews but it doesn't end with the Jews." This isn't an incidental geopolitical fatality. It starts with the Jews because it is the triumph of evil and death over goodness and life. Judaism is the source of the ethics on which our civilization is founded. Antizionism, the contemporary variety of antisemitism, is a lethal perversion. When the genocidal hatred of the Islamic Republic is validated by an international agreement piloted by the United States of America, when every single concrete detail is clearly available for public information, when every public statement by governments that defend the deal is patently false, when the "alternative to war" is a virtual onslaught against Israel's existence, when the immoral United Nations is invested with powers stolen from democratically elected governments, we have reached the catastrophic level of perversion.

Rational arguments will be useless unless this perversion is understood, exposed, and confronted.

— *New English Review*

HUMANITARIAN JIHAD
September-October 2015

After the Arab Spring comes the refugee crisis. Once again our media and complicit opinion-makers dance to the beat of the Islamic street. Moved to ecstasy by compact masses of Muslim men leavened with a sprinkling of women and children trampling the ground we stand on, they incite the citizens of Europe to abject surrender in humanitarian guise.

The photo of a child victim triggered a massive onslaught on the West. The doll-like body of Aylan Shenu (aka Al Kurdi), face down at the water's edge, looking like a peaceful toddler sleeping the dreams of innocence, has produced the al Dura effect: a white flash of emotion, hasty judgment, swift punishment of the guilty, total impunity for the aggrieved party.

Why in fact was this child washed up on the beach? His parents embarked with their two boys on troubled seas in an overloaded inflated boat that would supposedly carry them from the Turkish beach of Bodrum to the Greek island of Kos and from there to A New Life. The father survived, his wife and two sons drowned.

Apparently none of them had life jackets, though I have no way of judging the veracity of various contradictory accounts of the incident. The father, Abdullah, says the boat capsized because the passengers stood up. He was holding on to his wife and children, lost them one by one. Five year-old Galip died, the father had to let go of him; he saw Aylan's eyes fill with blood, and bid him farewell; his wife was afloat, puffed up like a balloon, unrecognizable. Zeinab Abbas, an Iraqi who lost two of her three children in the shipwreck, claims that Abdullah is a people-smuggler who was piloting the overloaded boat. She says he went too fast, causing the accident. There weren't enough life jackets to go around. Survivors of similar crossings testify that the smugglers are never aboard. They choose one of the passengers to act as captain. What, then, justifies the payment of thousands of euros for the perilous crossing? Why wouldn't people buy their own boats and life jackets, and increase their chances of survival by traveling in small groups? Obviously they don't, as can be seen by the constant stream of overloaded dinghies arriving on Greek shores. Often it is the children who don't have life jackets.

But practical questions of this nature were strictly verboten as the lethal refugee crisis narrative triggered by the iconic figure of Aylan unfolded. No *pas d'amalgame* for the dead child. When a Muslim commits an attack, the chorus chants *pas d'amalgame*, don't blame Muslims collectively and besides, it has nothing to do with Islam. When I first saw

THE BLACK FLAG OF JIHAD

the photo I thought it was taken on a Greek or Italian beach. The addition of the word "touristic" gave the Turkish beach of Bodrum extraterritoriality, like a foreign embassy. The poor child was crossing the waters in an inflatable boat instead of taking a plane like overpriveleged tourists. What about the 38 Europeans gunned down on a beach in Sousse last summer? They weren't icons of Tunisian indifference. Tunisia was the victim of "a small minority of extremists who pervert Islam."

The photo of Aylan Shenu produced the al Dura effect: Guilty of his death, we are fair game for anything anyone wants to do to punish us. The only acceptable reaction was to blame Europe for criminal negligence. The campaign was kicked off with hashtags, graffiti in the sand, heart-rending reiteration, and self-satisfied indignation. All the oceans of the world could not contain the tears that Europe should shed. No gesture of atonement-hospitality was deep and broad enough to save us from eternal damnation. The punishment was rapid and severe. Europe was deprived of its sovereignty, its borders, and the right to enjoy its just deserts.

Even as the Finnish prime minister offered his summer home to two families (how would they be chosen out of the hundreds of thousands marching as to war?) and a French woman created a free-of-charge "Airbnb" to lodge all comers, Europe was beating its breast, covering its head with ashes, and accusing itself of heartless indifference to the plight of the victims. First identified as migrants to avoid the shameful accuracy of "illegal immigrants," the masses arriving by land, sea, and air were anointed as refugees and the default emotion was uncritical compassion. No, it was more like infatuation, adoration...swooning submission.

At least that is how mass media framed the story in Phase One. Government officials, with notable exceptions, were tearing their hearts out of their breast pockets to demonstrate compassion. It will take time to determine the degree of sincerity on each level of their discourse and action—follow-the-media emotion, desperate EU attempts to impose quotas for resettlement of asylum seekers, promises of swift deportation for economic migrants ineligible for asylum, and the frantic restoration of border controls within the Schengen free-circulation region and on its frontiers. On intellectual territory, the slightest deviation from the party line by analysts, specialists, or philosophers provoked a virtual lynch mob.

The publication of the photo of the drowned child on September 2nd was immediately followed by a massive increase in the number of illegal immigrants arriving in Europe. Day after day the refugee crisis dominated the news stream. Zapping from one channel to another, one online media to the next, we were faced with the irresistible flow of refugees and the ongoing lethal narrative of their inalienable right to come, to see, and to conquer the good life. Excited journalists, some of whom had starred in the Arab Spring show, ran through Serbian fields, pushed up against Hungary's security barrier, crammed into trains and buses, camped in the Munich train station, shouted with the mob, cuddled wide-eyed babies, filling the screen with outpourings that drowned rational thought in the capsized dinghy of an orchestrated craze.

And yet there has been no popular refugee-welcome enthusiasm in France. Hopes of rousing another *Je Suis Charlie* movement fell flat. At least one "*Je Suis Syrien*" sign was raised when an estimated 8,000 people gathered one evening at Place de la République. A few days later a solidarity concert attracted a few hundred in the City Hall square, nothing to compare with Germany's open arms. The pernicious effect of the operation is to be found elsewhere, in a sort of quiet resignation to the violation of the basic attributes of sovereignty. The current unprecedented stampede is simplistically equated with previous waves of immigration, deliberately or unwittingly ignoring the difference in scope, context, attitude, and circumstances. One commentator compared it to the "immigration" of *pieds noirs* from the Maghreb. Never mind that the *pieds noirs* were French, forced to flee a newly independent Algeria, and the Maghrebi Jews that fled with them were not only French but also indigenous to the region where they had settled long before the 7th century Islamic conquest. A small Muslim minority with no roots in the region muscled in and offered the death-conversion-or-dhimmitude option. Their barbaric cruelty was slightly restrained during the period of European colonization. Heady with the joys of independence, they chased the Jews. And Christians. Then followed them to France and are chasing them again. While their brethren are trying to chase them from the Middle East.

As could be expected, European Jews are caught in the crossfire. Again. Future victims of these Muslims that will add their share of genocidal anti-Zionism to the current overdose, Jews may well turn into the refugee's refugees. At least we will be welcome in Israel! On the heels of major atrocities committed by the likes of Mohamed Merah, Mehdi Nemmouche, and Amhadou Coulibaly, Prime Minister Netanyahu has invited European Jews to make aliyah. This provoked an outcry from the same people who are melting with bounty today as they invite essentially Muslim refugees to come up (= make aliyah) to Europe, their promised land. The Jews, defined by the Shoah, are enjoined to hand over their refugee costumes to the no less deserving newcomers. Shocked by the wishes of certain French local officials to give preference to Christian over Muslim refugees, the speaker of the Parliament Claude Bartalone exhaled: "After the yellow star the green crescent."

Why is this stampede into Europe different from all previous immigrations? Jewish refugees from Central Europe and Germany did not enter France illegally, were not received with open arms and bundles of goodies, and made a life for themselves despite the cold shoulder. When the Nazis marched into France, these foreign Jews were stuffed into cattle cars and sent to their death. Today, Jews who have been living peacefully in France, contributing to the economy, society, culture, and politics, causing no problems for anyone, are getting boxed in and in some cases squeezed out by an ever-increasing Muslim population grown from earlier waves of immigration. Is it indecent to mention it? Did refugees from Chile, Argentina or China turn around and persecute Jews or citizens of the host country?

Christian solidarity is not only lacking, it is taboo. Officials of municipalities or nations that franklly express a preference for Christian refugees are treated with contempt. Earlier this year the Parisian transportation authority tried to censor a poster advertising a benefit concert for Oriental Christians. No sooner had military operations liberated Iraq from Saddam Hussein and Afghanistan from the Taliban, than the new governments started persecuting Christians. Did we hear any objections from the United States and its allies? It should come as no surprise that the "Arab Spring" –in fact a jihad uprising–sprouted poisonous berries for Christians in the region. Churches are destroyed, Christians are enslaved, hacked to death, burned alive, crucified... These victims elicit less manifest support in Europe than Hamas rocket-shooters.

It happened more than once that Muslims crossing the Mediterranean on smuggler boats threw *kuffars* overboard. This didn't provoke any lessons on decent/indecent. The old rules of chivalry that taught men to save women and children first don't apply. Boats capsize, women and children drown, men survive. And don't die of shame. Prime Minister Manuel Valls took the opportunity, when expressing his Rosh Hashanah greetings to the Jewish community in a Parisian synagogue, to give a human rights sermon: "We don't sort out refugees based on religion!"

No, this human battering ram against Europe's doors has nothing to do with the influx of Jewish refugees in the 19th century, and even less with Jewish refugees fleeing Nazi extermination in the 1930s and 40s— refused entry in Europe and barred from immigrating to Palestine. But there is a valid comparison with Zionism and its antis. The masterminds of jihad are applying to Europe the same "solution" that Europe has been trying to impose on Israel: Right of return of Palestinian refugees, indefensible borders, and then no borders at all. The Caliphate.

YOU ARE EXAGGERATING, THE MODERATES WILL SAY

We have seen how the lethal narrative strategy operates a constant assault on the West by parasiting the very values its adversary is determined to destroy. Civil rights in the United States, decolonization in Europe, Palestinian self- determination in the Middle East, the Arab Spring, women's rights to wrap themselves in hijab, respect for religious beliefs, diversity, equality, freedom of speech, peaceful coexistence...the list of values that can be turned against us like a knife in the back is endless.

But no lethal narrative is more forceful than blood libel. The ongoing paroxysm of genocidal Jew hatred was triggered on September 30, 2000 by the al Dura hoax. The unfounded accusation that Israeli soldiers shot a Palestinian "child" in cold blood, ingurgitated without a shred of evidence, has been stubbornly perpetuated despite exhaustive evidence that the "news report" was a clumsily staged scene.

What better proof than this exchange with the producer of the al Dura broadcast, France 2 journalist Charles Enderlin, interviewed on the occasion of his retirement from the state-owned news channel:[1]

Michaël Bloch: Don't you regret saying that the gunfire [aimed at the Al Duras] definitely came from the Israeli position?

Charles Enderlin: Absolutely not. A campaign was mounted against me in 2001 to convince Jews to ignore my reports, books, and documentaries that contradict the official Israeli version that the Palestinians refused a generous offer at Camp David, started the Intifada, and want to destroy Israel by flooding it with millions of refugees. It's false!

This is precisely the explanation I gave for the refusal to admit that the al Dura scene was falsified: it would undermine the broader hoax of a Mideast conflict based on legitimate Palestinian aspirations to statehood, blocked by Israeli intransigence. The al Dura blood libel that served to justify atrocious attacks against Jews in Israel, Europe, and beyond, paved the way for subsequent attacks against Christians in the Middle East, civilians in Europe and the United States, *kuffars* anywhere and everywhere.

Aylan washed up on a Turkish beach is our fault. Any attempt to retrace the chain of circumstances that led to his death by drowning is met with righteous indignation. Heartless, indecent, obscene. Details emerged, some troubling, some confusing, but the innocent victim had immediately become an idol to worship. Nonbelievers were excommunicated, while the bereaved father was absolved from all responsibility in the death of his wife and children. Subsequently this absolution was extended to any and all of the hundreds of thousands of refugees marching into Europe with nothing but the clothes on their backs, demanding by their very empty-handedness to be immediately rescued and given the basic necessities. Guilty of fatal indifference to the innocent child, we the spoiled and pampered brats of Europe had to restore our dignity and respect our noble values. A rosy media spotlight was reserved for the noble souls that rushed to the rescue, bearing gifts and signs of welcome, radiating the celestial light of goodness.

The German chancellor was the highest bidder. We will take 800,000, declared Angela Merkel, putting fellow European leaders to shame. The warm-hearted folk of Munich stood in the train station applauding their newfound friends. No words were too glittering for El Dorado Germany and Mama Merkel, beloved all the way down the line, as tens of thousands massed in train stations along the route, pushing upwards to their cherished destination, wrapped in the media's enveloping narrative. Europe's woes disappeared. The Greek financial crisis, widespread unemployment and sluggish economies, domestic jihadis coming back to haunt and kill us, disgruntled dairy farmers and livestock raisers, a beleaguered middle class, deteriorating schools and universities, explosive banlieues...all our troubles were magically carried away on the wings of our angelic generosity.

Even in Israel the humanitarian blackmail reared its head. Opposition leader Isaac Herzog took to the moral high ground, asking how Israel can be deaf to the pleas of these refugees when we were once in their shoes. Prime Minister Netanyahu dared to respond with his feet on the ground: We don't have the demographic or geographic depth to take in masses of needy people. We must maintain a strong Jewish majority. Besides, these refugees come from Syria, a country that has been at war with us for 60 years. We can't take in our enemies. Herzog says Bibi doesn't know what it means to be Jewish.

For the past four years, without fanfare, Israeli medical facilities have been indiscriminately treating wounded Syrian civilians and fighters of all factions who come across the northern border. Healed of their wounds and often astounded by their discovery of the real Israel, the patients go back to Syria; they can't tell they were in Israel because they will be persecuted, assaulted, maybe killed. The Palestinian Authority wouldn't take in Palestinian refugees from the Yarmouk camp in Syria when it was besieged by Daesh. Their place was not in the "Palestinian territories" but in the refugee camp where they can fight for the right of return [to Israel].

Israel has never stopped resettling and integrating "refugees," more exactly "homecomers." The Jewish State takes care of its own! It is a haven for Jewish refugees that would not be welcome anywhere else if times got tougher. Israel is a model for resettlement. The same public opinion that is mobilized today for the alleged Syrians fleeing war is periodically mobilized in virulent hostility to Israel, its right to self-defense, to its very existence. It cannot be repeated often enough: Israel is pronounced guilty for defending its citizens from physical and diplomatic violence, which is exactly the protection that Syrian and other refugees wanted from their governments. Israel is criminalized for being a strong state, not a failed state that sends its citizens running to developed countries for succor.

Western nations flail blindly in their own confusion, desperately trying to put together military operations with imaginary coalitions to stop the creeping expansion of a brutal caliphate. Israel acts boldly and is damned for the use of "excessive force."

A Kuwaiti official explained that his country could not take in these refugees that torment the conscience of civilized people. The refugees couldn't afford the high cost of living in Kuwait, and besides, they are not like us, they wouldn't fit in. Saudi Arabia can't take them in, but offers to fund the construction of 200 mosques in Germany to accommodate the new population. The Emirates have no use for Syrians, Kosovars, Eritreans, Senegalese and other lost souls.

Taking care of your own is not selfish, it is healthy. The first building block of society is the family, within which goods and services are equitably shared by members that cherish and protect each other. Society functions in concentric circles of responsibility, reaching from the core of the family to the outer limits of the nation and, far less reliably, to international bodies. Citizens are protected by physical borders— locked doors, fences, gates, and guards—and by rules and regulations in neighborhoods, on roads, in public places. This is why the massive entry of people who do not respect borders, rules, or procedures is an assault on the sovereignty of European nations and a violation of the social contract. Governments don't create wealth, they collect the wealth created by citizens and use it to maintain services essential for civilized life. Generosity with taxpayers' money cannot be justified by an asylum policy that was conceived in the aftermath of the Shoah. All the parameters have been modified.

Parks and beaches on small Greek islands turn into nightmares of filth. Central European train stations, parks, river banks fill up with garbage and human waste. The Mediterranean is a watery grave. Not a day goes by in France without reports of another makeshift "refugee" camp that has to be dismantled because it is a health and security hazard.

This summer, 100 illegal immigrants shepherded by an ad hoc association commandeered an abandoned school in Paris. Instead of ordering their immediate removal, the deputy mayor Bruno Juillard approved the fait accompli and promised, with the approval of Mayor Anne Hidalgo, to renovate the school and make it an official shelter. (Juillard had defended the controversial "Tel Aviv on the Seine" operation by contrasting the open-minded, secular, modern residents of Tel Aviv with the brutal Israeli government.)[2] By late October, when authorities decided to evacuate the school, the population had increased seven fold. In fact 1300 illegal immigrants were living there in deplorable conditions.

PHASE 2, THE DISAPPEARING ACT

About a week or ten days into the crisis, the refugees abruptly disappeared from the mass media. The story wasn't concluded, it was amputated. From Greece to Hungary to Austria, one country after the other, abandoning all hope of law and order, washed its hands of the problem by shunting the refugees up to Germany. Somewhere in Austria the mass media lost interest. From one day to the next, the columns of men trudging through fields and along railroad tracks, forcing their way into overcrowded trains and buses, triumphantly zipping across borders, vanished from TV screens. Shocking behavior had occasionally been filmed but was brushed off by commentators or blamed on police brutality. The reality show was over, reality reared its head, but the media that had enchanted us with the beautiful story of asylum didn't bother to mention the troublesome, disturbing, frightening, harrowing, disgusting reports that began to emerge off screen, from readily available reliable sources. Male refugees raping women and children in German centers, fake Syrians boasting and real Syrians deploring the indiscriminate reception of unidentifiable masses, *allahu akhbar* contempt for infidel hosts, human traffickers gleefully awaiting approval of their asylum requests, ethnic strife among refugees, the staggering cost of providing for hundreds of thousands of unemployable refugees plus the inevitable multiplication of dependents when they exercise their right to family reunification. Big stocks of counterfeit Syrian passports were discovered. A Lebanese official told visiting PM David Cameron that the exodus was organized It became obvious that no one could give reliable figures on the number and nature of those who were flowing into Europe hour by hour. Attempts by the EU to impose quotas looked increasingly ridiculous: nations that do not want to take refugees will not comply. Refugees don't want to live in former Eastern bloc countries that are not culturally, linguistically or economically able to absorb them, and the number of refugees to be theoretically redistributed was rapidly overcome by reality.

"These are refugees from war torn Syria, we cannot turn them away" How did televised images undermine the "ineluctable modality of the visible"? The al Dura "death scene" is a sterling example of the method, which must be understood in depth and in detail if it is to be countered. It is interesting to note that the daily *Libération* is the only French media that used the al Dura photo in its repertoire of iconic images, like the

157

picture of Aylan, that change the world. Why did the other media eschew this obvious choice? I think they know it is a fake. Again, today, ample visual evidence contradicts the edifying tale that would justify preposterous surrender to a stampede of well fed, strong, healthy young men dressed in fashionable sports clothes, with trendy haircuts and neatly trimmed beards. For many years already, boatloads of visibly sub-Saharan Africans coughed up by the Mediterranean and deposited on Europe's shores have been described as refugees from war torn Syria and Iraq.

Journalists, constantly repeating "these are Syrians fleeing war," had focused whenever possible on the tiny contingent of women (almost always in hijab) and children. Who wouldn't want to flee the horrors perpetrated by the Syrian regime, Daesh, and various rebel combatants, with no end in sight? And yet, compared to Yazidi captives these migrants are over-privileged. When they are not from Kosovo, Nigeria, Pakistan, Albania, Bangladesh or Senegal, most were living in camps or private homes in Turkey. This is the case of the Shenu family whose personal loss has become an international *cause célèbre*. The destitution of the hundreds of thousands pouring into Europe this fall is self-imposed. Large sums of money were spent on air fare, train tickets, bribes, and smartphones. The intruders count on the swift steed of public opinion to carry them in a few days from Turkey to the good life in Germany. Why are they so often arrogant, disdainful of the countries through which they pass, so quick to anger and turn violent if their demands are not met?

Is it heartless to reflect on this unprecedented movement of large masses of human beings? Or is it mindless to cover it with borrowed images and fabricated emotion? The flood of "refugees" is accompanied by a perilous flood of hogwash. Standing on the soapbox of Europe's highest values, the open-hearted intoxicate themselves with unjustifiable metaphors. The current parade of (essentially Muslim) asylum seekers is compared with Jewish refugees from the Nazis, conveniently forgetting the Evian summit that sealed a collective decision to refuse entry to Jews fleeing extermination. In the space of four years, 6 million Jews—two thirds of the European Jewish population, half of the world's Jews—were exterminated. These Jews had lived peaceably in their respective countries. They had no collective conflict with the society or nation. They had no country of their own, no army, no donation of weapons and funds to organize their resistance. Compare this to the horrifying Syrian death toll in a comparable four-year period: over 250,000. Jews were persecuted in every European country, with the rarest exceptions. Syria is surrounded by a vast territory of Arab-Muslim nations, some of them extraordinarily wealthy, all of them above starvation level. Millions of refugees have been taken in by Turkey, Lebanon, and Jordan, with substantial financial help from Europe.

The fledgling nation that would become the State of Israel accommodated and integrated a many as 179,000 survivors of the Shoah and, shortly afterward, 900,000 Jews that fled Islamic lands, including Syria. None of these hard facts enter into the picture today when the simple words "train" or "numbers" or "selection" trigger acute Shoah-itis. Hungarian police herd intruders into a train, promising it will take them to the Austrian border; it stops inside Hungary where they are told to go into a retention center, called a "camp," for processing. And it's the trains to Auschwitz. Czechs put numbers on the intruders' arms with magic marker. Auschwitz again. A participant in a serious French TV debate flushes red and chokes on his Adam's apple at the thought that agents somewhere somehow will have to separate asylum seekers from economic migrants. Selection.

An open heart with no discernment is like an undifferentiated blob of muscle and blood disconnected from any nervous or circulatory system. If it is indecent to question the refugee narrative, how much more indecent to drag in the Jewish refugee metaphor, when Europe's Jews are currently destabilized by earlier waves of Muslim immigration? *Times of Israel* reporters who interviewed Syrian refugees in centers in Milan and Berlin found the same virulent anti-Zionist attitudes that have created a hostile environment for Jews in Europe since September 2000.

Our societies are accused of Islamophobia whenever they act to protect freedom of speech, women's rights, national identity, mutual respect, law and order. Why do hundreds of thousands, millions, tens of millions of Muslims want to come to our Islamophobic countries? They have lost faith, we are told, in their own homelands. They want a better life. How can we deny their fervent hopes? Germany, in particular, needs workers to fuel its healthy economy, and child-bearing women to beef up its declining population. Former Soviet bloc countries now integrated into the EU are severely reprimanded for refusing to follow the German example of generosity. EU leaders meet in Brussels in desperate attempts to impose quotas, while refugees go on the rampage if authorities try to follow the rules and process them at their point of entry into the Schengen free-circulation zone. In Hungary, Serbia, Croatia, Slovenia they hold up crude cardboard signs proclaiming "We not want stay here." They attacked the police and broke through the security barrier on the Serbian border with Hungary. Familiar images of shebabs masked with scarves or keffiehs slinging rocks and firebombs give an eloquent hint that this wave of refugees is different from those that fled the Spanish civil war, the Armenian genocide, the fall of Saigon, Pol Pot in Cambodia, the colonels in Greece, Pinochet in Chile.

The question is threefold: where do they come from, what do they bring with them, and what forces are organizing this spontaneous exodus? European rail traffic is periodically disrupted, social services and government budgets are stretched beyond limits, and Daesh flourishes on the heap of misery. Smugglers charge exorbitant sums for overloading dinghies and unseaworthy boats. Hundreds drown, feeding the humanitarian narrative, sucking up aid and surrender from the West. Hundreds of thousands are rescued, dissolving Europe's southern Schengen borders, wiping out rules and regulations. Illegals have preference over asylum seekers that go through legal channels, sometimes waiting two years for a decision in France. Suddenly the prize goes to the ones with the sharpest elbows. No time for ID or background checks, no way to verify claims, authorities are overwhelmed by the sheer flow.

In France, where thousands of security threateners are flagged, and dozens have already planned or perpetrated brutal killings, we are now told that it is appropriate, advisable, mandatory to accept people who have disposed of their passports and provide no verifiable information about themselves. Innocents have been murdered because overburdened intelligence services cannot keep up with the comings and goings of Daesh operatives or the devious schemes of "radicalized" Muslims whose families and neighbors always swear they are normal young men, not fundamentalist fanatics. Sub-Saharan African illegals set up tent camps in Paris, causing severe problems of hygiene and security. The police evacuate them, leaving the occupants to wander aimlessly, or housing them—temporarily and expensively—at public cost. The Calais "jungle" festers, periodically interrupting tunnel traffic, preying on truck drivers in attempts to cross illegally into the UK, spoiling life for the resident population. In Paris, the rue de Rivoli looks like Kolkata with a clump of homeless bedded down on every block from the City Hall to Place de la Bastille. None of these problems are tackled let alone solved, and now the government wants to force municipalities to take their share of the new *misérables*, irregardless of particularities on both sides of the equation.

NUMBERS GAME

Numbers are tossed around like rose petals. There are only x thousands. Only 0.x % of the total European population. A feather in our cap, not a weight on our back. Properly shared out, they will be hardly noticeable. Anyway, we need their skills. These are college graduates, doctors, engineers, refined middle class people who will enrich our diversified societies. A few French mayors who dared to announce publicly that they only wanted to take Christian refugees whipped up a firestorm. It is already forbidden to mention that another influx of Muslims will bring more of the same problems currently facing European nations, and now it is uncouth to point out that Christian refugees are not welcome in the refugee camps of Syria's Muslim neighbors. Thousands of Yazidi women are held in brutal captivity by Daesh. Christians are tortured, churches are destroyed. What makes the masses stampeding into Europe in the wake of publication of the iconic drowned toddler photo more deserving of humanitarian largesse than other victims?

At the height of the crisis, new cohorts were piling up on Turkey's border with Greece. The land route is less perilous than the sea. They are establishing a new criterion for entry into Europe: the stampede. Why is it acceptable for Turkey, a Muslim country, the last legitimate Caliphate and rightful rulers of the oumma, to fail to take care of its own? Four years into the war, Syrian refugees are still living in tent camps. If Turkey, Lebanon, and Jordan cannot provide these refugees with basic necessities, integrate them into society, the work force, the educational system, allow them to make their precious contribution to the host countries, why should European nations be expected to provide seamless integration into far higher living standards while magically whisking away linguistic and cultural barriers and problems of professional equivalency?

In the first phase of what has been entitled the "Refugee Crisis," the story line was sharp and clear. These are refugees fleeing horrific war in Syria and Iraq. References to comparable situations in the past were used, not to clarify the situation and bring out the best in potential host countries but to replace the visible reality with an edifying fiction. It didn't take statistics to recognize that the overwhelming majority of the arriving masses were strong healthy young men fit for military service. How could flight be a gauge of their virtue? The irony was compounded when President Hollande announced a more vigorous military offensive, with the extension to Syria of bombing raids previously limited to Iraq. Further, he admitted that Daesh cannot be defeated without boots on the ground. Whose boots? Local troops, he suggested, knowing full well that soldiers armed and trained by American and European forces have been a disgraceful failure. Would it be thinkable to send French soldiers to defeat the enemy while these able-bodied Syrians enjoy a safe haven in Europe?

We are faced, once more, with the Israel paradox. A tiny land in the midst of a virulently hostile expanse of Islamic nations, Israel survives precisely because of its strong self-defense, equally powerful high-tech economy, intellectual and strategic acumen, and vibrant democracy. The Jewish State, which exerts a strong attractive ingathering force, is the object of an international campaign of vilification—accused of war crimes, crimes against humanity, apartheid, colonization—and held responsible for the absence of a solution to the conflict with the Palestinians. For the sake of accusing Israel of destabilizing the Middle East, Daesh atrocities, Iranian nuclear ambitions, Libyan disintegration, Muslim Brotherhood subversion, and other exacerbated tribal clashes are deftly underplayed.

What is driving the successive waves of immigration into the West, culminating in the current massive overflow? As former European colonies in Africa, the Middle East, and the Indian subcontinent successfully fought for independence, most ended up with dictators, corruption, poverty, and oppression. The liberated fled in great numbers into the former colonial countries. Some were able to enjoy freedom and build successful lives and careers. Too many brought with them the very culture that causes the ills they fled. If you believe, as I used to, that Europe is responsible for this failure and flight, it only intensifies the Zionist paradox. Extermination is at least as crippling as colonization! Europe's guilt on that score is unambiguous. Yet Jews have never dropped the burden of their existence on the former persecutors.

Assuming that at least half of the men pouring into Europe are Syrian, what earns them the tabula rasa flashed in the face of public opinion? They are presented as helpless victims fleeing persecution, cleanly detached from the recent history of their own country, where Nazi criminals found refuge after their defeat in WW2, Jews were ethnically cleansed, Lebanon was colonized, attacks against Israel were hatched and genocidal terrorists were harbored in unconditional defense of the cause of the Palestinians (who, at the time of the creation of the Jewish State, considered themselves Syrians).

At the turn of this century we got 9/11. When the United States under the leadership of George W. Bush hit back, as other nations do (e.g. Jordan after the pilots were burned alive, Saudi Arabia in Yemen, Turkey against the PKK) we were the bad guys again, punished by an uninterrupted string of smaller scale jihad attacks, ultimately leading to the choice of Barak Hussein Obama as the president of reconciliation with the Muslim world. Then came the Arab Spring, with the bitter fruits of jihad— sharia, internecine warfare, rubble, casualties, Daesh, and refugees. Again, we're supposed to pick up the broken pieces.

Every political, diplomatic, military and/or coalition solution that was attempted has failed miserably. That doesn't keep commentators and officials from repeating outworn phrases: We must bolster the economies in countries that are pushing migrants our way. As if decades of development plans for Africa have been able to overcome corruption, dictatorship, and assorted endemic failures. It is urgent to call (another) international conference to bring an end to the Syrian war that is provoking the massive flow of refugees. Time to get serious about defeating Daesh ...without boosting Assad and his allies Iran, Hizbullah, Russia, and writing off hundreds of thousands of deaths and atrocities. We need to strengthen the moderate opposition, we should have done it from the start. Already tried that. They turned out to be Al Nosra, or useless, or allied with Daesh. Instead of aiming at the head of the snake, Western leaders are including Iran in all their pseudo-solutions.

We are not the problem. The West does not hold the keys to the solution. Europe is not at fault, Israel is not guilty. We intervened there, stayed out of it here, allied ourselves with this or that group, trained others, gave weapons or withheld all support, it doesn't matter. We are not the cause of the upheaval in the Islamic world. It has its own logic, its own momentum, its own ideological and historical sources. It is like a huge machine full of gears and pistons that runs on its own mechanical principles for its own reasons. We duck in, get knocked around, scram out. It doesn't change the machine's operation. The crusades, the combat against the Barbary pirates, colonization, the defeat of the Ottoman Empire were attempts to deal with the problem in the past. But it's back again and it can't be ignored because it cannot, by definition, keep to itself. It is a machine of conquest. It crushes its own and reaches out to grab others into its maw. We have to do something about it, it won't go away. The surrender-to-Iran deal is the exact opposite of what needs to be done.

THESE REFUGEES ARE A FIGMENT OF THE IMAGINATION
In the first phase of the refugee crisis the masses pushing into Europe were obsessively present, monopolizing newscasts, websites and one-sided debates. Their right of entry was established by the lethal narrative attached to the photo of the drowned toddler. Open-armed compassion was the only acceptable response. Above and beyond the destabilizing effect of the assault on Europe's borders and sovereignty, this "refugee crisis" campaign furthers the ongoing jihad conquest that is pushing Western societies to adopt en masse Islamic thinking and unquestioning obedience. No sovereignty but Allah, and the caliphate is his rightful transmission.

Rational thinking about the possibilities of integrating hundreds of thousands of immigrants is replaced by magical thinking. They've fled war, they've come for a better life, they are educated, skilled, they're not coming to take anything away from us. How disgraceful to try to keep them out. Though very few of the illegals want to settle in France— like their fellows in Calais, they are aiming for greener pastures—the discourse associated with their abrupt entry is dangerously unrealistic. How will the newcomers support themselves in a stagnant economy that has admittedly failed to integrate African and North African immigrants to the 3rd and 4th generation? A small minority, of course, are highly competent individuals that can get back on their feet rapidly and succeed in whatever they undertake. But the majority would be unable to master the French language and earn a living for the wives and children they will inevitably bring in their wake. It is no time for fairy tales in a country where wages are dismally low, discontent is at record highs, economic reform well-nigh impossible, populism gaining ground ...

The initial reaction of European leaders was dhimmitude submission, bowing to the will of the intruders, paying the *jizya* in the form of massive welfare payments in Europe and millions more to improve conditions in refugee camps in the Middle East. The extreme danger of Daesh operatives riding in on the human waves while raking in profits from smuggling people, selling counterfeit passports, and other illicit commerce is minimized or overlooked. This influx eats into developed economies in the same way that bloody attacks destroy tourism in Egypt and Tunisia. Channel traffic is interrupted for hours or days, rail service is disrupted, highways are blocked, city centers and peaceful villages are disturbed. But it was all papered over with the appeal to humanitarian selflessness.

Diversity is a hollow concept if people are all the same. Respecting every human being without prejudice is honorable but what happens when those we accept indiscriminately do not share our values? Our elevated principles clash with Islamic exclusion. The evidence stares us in the face. After getting rid of the Jews in all Arab-Muslim countries, they are now getting rid of the Christians and other minorities. Daesh goes one step further, destroying the vestiges of pre-Islamic civilization. It doesn't matter if this exclusion is done at the hands of a dictator, a nationalist, a caliph, warlords, or neighborhood thugs. When we welcome with open arms the Other that does not share our values, the gesture is nullified and the generosity dead-ended; society becomes less tolerant, less hospitable, more aggressive.

I WANT TO GO TO ~~AMERICA~~ GERMANY DA DA DA DA DA DA...

The concept of an Islamic population replacement strategy at work in the West is widely dismissed as alarmist Islamophobic conspiracy theory. The idea that Germany can take up to a million refugees because it has a vigorous economy and shrinking population was taken at face value in phase one of the refugee crisis. Instead of providing incentives to German women to have children, they'll bring in Syrian and assorted baby-makers. That's not population replacement? And you want Shoah analogies? Germany, beefed up with this new population, could develop an appetite for the conquest of Europe. Again. In fact, two days after trumpeting its welcome to all refugees the more the merrier, German authorities admitted their services were overwhelmed. Border controls were reinstated. Now there are reports of expropriation of private property to house refugees. The backlash is smoldering and percolating.

Hungarian Prime Minister Viktor Orban unashamedly declared that if other nations want to take in Muslims, that's their choice. Hungary does not. Big bad Hungary served to make everyone else feel virtuous. Strong arm tactics against the mob of intruders were scorned as gratuitous. In fact, the first clashes broke out when Hungarian authorities tried to register the incoming candidates, in conformity with EU rules that require asylum seekers to apply in the first Schengen zone country they reach. A well-spoken young man faces the camera and asks: "Why are the police going after us, we're not criminals!" They crossed the frontier illegally, but they do not recognize it much less respect it. Instead, they flood Italy and Greece with misery, thousands drown on the way, genuine asylum seekers mix with genuine illegals that count on the confusion to sneak in under the rope. Economic migrants are supposed to be deported. But in fact they are left to blend into the population. So why wouldn't they barge in?

Another example of the Zionist paradox: it's normal and even desirable for Syrian refugees to settle in far distant and radically foreign Germany but one cannot ask "Palestinian refugees" to settle in Jordan, Lebanon, or other sister nations. They must come "home" to Israel. This logic comes back to bite Europe today. If the refugees [Palestinians] misbehave it is because they are so oppressed so desperate and so overheated by 30°summer temperatures (sic). When Hungary [Israel] defends its territory, it is evil, uses excessive force, and deserves further, more violent revolt.

A HIJAB IS A HARMLESS PIECE OF CLOTH

A hijab is a piece of cloth and hundreds of thousands of people fleeing Muslim countries are a drop in the bucket compared to Europe's population (that already has a strong Muslim contingent). Hijab is a piece of cloth connected to a tightly woven fabric of political-religious ambition, and the intruders count for more than their numbers because their individual decisions to flee poverty, dictatorship, Daesh, and no-future add up to an assault on European sovereignty. Whatever their individual qualities and shortcomings, the impact of these intruders is not limited to their plight. They are human shields, pawns, a spinoff from the Islamic maelstrom.

In phase 1, the humanitarian jihad campaign flagellated the West. Zapping from channel to channel in the first week you found nothing but treacle taffy. Any objection to the bared breast was immediately denounced as indecent. Even while people drooling with humanitarian compassion were outpouring gifts, money, clothes, and food, they were scolded by news commentators and immigrant support groups for their stinginess. The operation was a bonanza for NGOs in France that have been trying for years to block all deportation of illegal immigrants. Aiding and abetting illegals was a misdemeanor. Now it is the *beau geste*. Against a background of enormous bags of donated clothing piled up in a refugee shelter in Germany, an anchor discreetly mentions a shortage of men's clothing and corresponding glut of cuddly toys. Obviously people thought they were contributing to a refugee population with a normal percentage of women, children, and the aged.

Why are "selfish" Europeans so generous? Why is the refugee welcome so overdone? Are they not behaving like a conquered population paying tribute to its new masters? I wondered how long the intruders would be satisfied with shabby hand me downs. A week later, in a report filmed at a shelter in the Netherlands, male refugees stepped up to the camera, one after the other, to broadcast complaints as if they were guests at a Club Med: not enough food, the internet service is too slow, nothing to do, and no cash to buy things.

The discourse that buoys up these illegal immigrants arriving in great numbers—an (under)estimated 700,000 already this year—is heavy on expectations, light on obligations. They want the good life. As if the good life were a box lunch we get at birth by virtue of living here in these good life countries. As if no efforts had been made to achieve it and maintain it, defend it when it was threatened, constantly revise the terms and the means. And what will become of a million people, mostly unaccompanied young men, when they discover that it isn't a box lunch, and they don't know how to get their share of it? How irresponsible to inject potentially violent discontent into societies that are weak on their foundations. The expectations are taken for granted by opinion-makers but not by exasperated, often hostile European citizens. Debt-ridden European governments that have been paring away at benefits suddenly open the treasure chests and pour out the gold coins. With at least 4 million unemployed and 2 million underemployed, France is in no position to offer jobs to the tens of thousands of refugees the government has promised to accept. Representatives of the French authority for resettlement actually went to Germany to seduce candidates away from El Dorado. One young man, filmed as he arrived at the airport, says he's going to learn French and find a good job. Does he know how many years it takes an adult to become fluent in French? What will he do in the meantime? Cuban lawyers fleeing Castro worked as gardeners. Jewish refugees who fled the Maghreb, leaving all their property behind, worked their way up to success in one generation. Too many Muslim Maghrebis are in trouble and making trouble. Will these able-bodied Syrian men volunteer to help the aged and the handicapped while waiting to be fluent in our languages and gainfully employed in high-tech jobs? In some quarters, it is indecent to even mention such practical considerations.

And heartless to ask who is pocketing the money generated by this traffic. Turkey, a member of NATO, facilitates the transit of weapons and foreign jihadis into Syria, contributing to the severe hardships that make people flee, while cashing in on the coming and the going. Civilians escaping from Daesh and Assad pass through Turkey, lining the pockets of assorted smugglers. We can suppose the government rakes off a percentage of the funds sent by European and Islamic countries to help sustain the refugees. The Erdogan government takes advantage of generalized violence to settle scores with the PKK and bombard other Kurdish fighters for good measure.

Crippled by perverse logic, the West hoists the "Palestinian" flag at the UN and snubs the Kurds on the battlefield and in the diplomatic arena. Why is there so little support for the force that is courageously fighting Daesh? Why aren't we pushing for an independent Kurdistan when other countries in the region are falling apart and the chunks and hunks are landing on us? Turkey is getting its way. Again. In a desperate attempt to stop the flow of intruders, the EU is asking Turkey for permission to create "hotspots" where asylum seekers can be weeded out from ineligible migrants before they set foot in Europe. Turkey does not wish to oblige. Tent cities in Turkey are overcrowded with women and children waiting to be shipped out by the hundreds of thousands to join the men under the family reunification provision for those who are granted asylum.

Why do these aberrations seem normal... at least at first glance...or to those who can't go beyond their warm tender feelings? It is not normal to judge harshly those who take care of their own, and uncritically embrace grown men who cannot defend their rights on their own ground. We should ask where they stand on our scale of values, we should know that if we do not defend our values we will be refugees within our own nations. It is not indecent to ask how this new population would be articulated with previous waves of immigration. Would they want to live in banlieue housing projects plagued by dysfunctional families, budding Salafists, merciless drug dealers, resentful garbage collectors, and impoverished law abiding citizens? Not exactly the good life.

How strange to hear apologists making comparisons with other waves of immigration—Polish, Portugese, Vietnamese etc.—without comparing the expectations of the host country and the newcomers in those days. Rejected, yes. Targets of prejudice, of course. But expected to respect their adopted country and be productive. In the present situation, an ideological leap has transformed hundreds of thousands of able-bodied young men into vulnerable toddlers like Aylan, to be cuddled and nurtured. How preposterous to promise them jobs that the native born can't find, plus subsidized everything for as long as necessary...while our military is fighting Daesh. These men could be organized in brigades to go back to Syria and free captive women. They could serve as anti-jihad ambassadors, rooting out and discouraging European candidates planning to join Daesh. If they are such an economic benefit they could settle in Greece and help solve that crisis. There has to be a reason why none of these possibilities are raised.

You can reject an aberration but it's hard to turn away the flesh and blood human beings that land on your doorstep, no matter who they are or how they got there. The problem is that this mass influx of illegal immigrants is an act of belligerence. They are sent (incited, if you prefer) with aggressive intentions and accepted with deliberate ignorance. European citizens are told this is a civilian operation, a human rights opportunity. In truth, our borders are erased (Islam does not recognize national borders), our values are trampled, our laws deliberately ignored; we are told to surrender our own human rights to brute force. And those who refuse to surrender are accused of being heartless.

THE 2015 *HAGIM* MURDER CAMPAIGN

The refugee crisis blossomed shortly after conclusion of the Iran "deal," and bloomed as the world's leaders congregated for the opening of the United Nations General Assembly in mid-September. Much to the disappointment of lifetime PA President Mahmoud Abbas, his conflict with Israel, upstaged by the wide scale savagery of Daesh, did not monopolize international attention. So, he dipped into his threadbare hat and pulled out Jew-killing rabbits that multiply and wreak havoc in the streets of Jerusalem and on the roads of Judea-Samaria.

The 1973 Yom Kippur War, the al Dura hoax of Rosh Hashanah 2000... once again, Islamic violence against Jews strikes on the *hagim*, the awesome days from Rosh Hashanah to Simhat Torah, known in English as the High Holidays. This year, Israeli Arabs and Palestinians in Judea-Samaria are going berserk. The sheer bestiality of these murders by knife, by meat cleaver, by car ramming, rock throwing, firebombing and gunshot aimed at young couples strolling with their children, at religious Jews in the old city of Jerusalem, at soldiers and policemen and random victims at bus stops and train stations, should have caused a gasp of horror from international onlookers. Instead of stubbornly, stupidly, mean-spiritedly misreporting the current raft of savage violence against Jews, the media should arouse the enlightened conscience of the West, so easily moved by the heart-rending photo of a drowned child, so heartlessly indifferent to the murder of peaceful civilians who wish no harm.

Ah but, you will say, the Jews are occupying the territories, the Temple Mount, the ancestral land of the ancient "Palestinians," the roads and streets and breathing space of the "rightful owners" of the land. Do you see the bloody irony of this logic? You in Europe should welcome any number of intruders and shower them with bountiful attention. Move over and make room for them. Don't be selfish and greedy. But an Arab who considers himself short changed can just pull out a knife and kill any Jew who happens to cross his path. Why didn't they open their arms, a century ago, to Jewish "refugees" returning to their ancestral homeland?

Conciliatory voices within and outside of Israel echo the latest justification for homemade genocide: The Muslims believe the Jews are going to destroy al Aqsa and replace it with the 3rd Temple. We must reassure them. Wouldn't it be better to remind them that Muslims built al Aqsa on the ruins of the 2nd Temple, destroyed by the Romans?

Here we go again: Cycle of violence, disproportionate reaction, excessive force, absence of a political horizon. When Israeli policemen shoot killers it's "revenge." The conscience of Europe, of the West, should not be justifying this hateful murder. Decent voices should call out with the force of a shofar, call the killers to order, place responsibility on Muslim political and religious leaders demand that they stop inciting their people to genocidal hatred.

October 12, 2015: Here's a selection of smirky headlines on a typical day of murderous assaults on Jews in Israel.

Channel 5, France: *C dans l'air* (serious round table news analysis) "...the cycle of murders and revenge in Jerusalem and the Palestinian territories..."

BFM TV, France, 24-hour news channel: "Two individuals wounded two Jews in a new knife attack in a colony of East Jerusalem"

[Here are details on the above incident from the *Times of Israel*: Pisgat Ze'ev—two young Arabs stabbed a 13-year-old boy, inflicting life-threatening injuries, and a 25 year-old man, in serious but stable condition.]

CNN: "Man shot and killed in Jerusalem"

[Click on the headline and it leads to a report on "the latest bloodshed in an intensifying spiral of violence": Israeli police say they shot and killed a young Palestinian who tried to stab a border patrolman in Jerusalem.]

BBC: nothing that day

France 24: "Israel: attacker shot dead in Jerusalem after stabbing"

Sky News "Mother and toddler 'killed in Gaza

THE AL DURA HOAX RECYCLED

Mainstream media switched cause and effect, social media bristled with truncated videos where Islamic stabbers were seemingly nnoent

victims of Israeli brutality, and Mahmoud Abbas acused Israel of executing a Palestinian youth in cold blood. His spokesman Nabil Abu
Rudeineh reportedly declared to the Palestinian *Wafa News Agency*:
"The execution [of the Palestinian teenager] in front of cameras is similar to the killing of a Palestinian boy Muhammad al-Dura during the
second intifada." Iseali authorities immediately released a video showing the entire sequence. Hassan Manasra, 15, and Ahmed Manasra, 13,
brandishing knives, stabbed an Israeli man who was able to run away
from them, and then stabbed a 13 year-old Israeli boy who is still fighting
for his life. Hassan was shot dead as he lunged at police, Ahmed was hit
by a car as he ran from the scene.

The difference is that this time Israeli authorities reacted immediately to squelch the blood libel. Abbas backtracked, claiming that the accusation was based on a slight information glitch: in fact the boy is brain
dead. Brainless, perhaps, but fully awake as he appears in a second video, comfortably ensconced in a bright clean room at Hadassah Hospital
where he is being treated. Alive and soon to be well. Like the iconic
model, Mohamed al Dura?

There will be no way of stemming the flow of refugees, no effective
defense against jihad conquest without a re-evaluation of the "Israel-
Palestine" conflict. It is not the cause of instability in the Middle East, it
is the launch pad for an assault on Western values. No degree of magni-
tude and horror of Daesh atrocities has yet untangled the twisted media
narrative. Faced with this flareup of murderous violence against Jewish
Israelis—again—media junkies indulge in the usual cheap tricks, revers-
ing chronology to switch cause with effect and turn the hate-filled murderer into a Palestinian victim "shot dead by the police." Day in day out
they spin the same tired tales to shore up their tumbling certitudes. "It's
all because of the colonization."

No. Frustrated national liberation is not the cause of murderous hatred against Jews. It is not anecdotal, not a side issue. Genocidal Jew-
hatred is the cause of the conflict. A hatred that knows no limits. This
hatred is drawn from a source that spreads beyond Israel and the Jews.
It stalks the journalist that turns the knife-wielders into little George
Washingtons fighting for independence. It will engulf the heads of state
that look down their noses at Israel and demand a "political horizon," an
end to "colonization." A smoldering substrate of hatred harbored in tens

of millions of hearts can burst into catastrophic flames anywhere, anytime. It is as ubiquitous as cell phones. The West that fails to recognize the nature of the one-sided, stoneheaded, ignoble, vicious assault on the Jewish State is helpless to combat the explosive hatred that perpetuates unspeakable acts in the region and turns entire populations into refugees.

The Syrians, I remind you, fleeing their war torn country via Turkey, come from a society that has always been in the camp of genocidal Jew hatred. Did their personal tragedy wash them clean? Is anyone asking? Does the question appear on the asylum application? The exquisite conscience of the West solicited by media that sprout angel's wings on demand must assume that Jews will accept any number of attacks, any level of violence, any death toll, and never react in a way that could disturb the peace of our self-righteous critics.

EUROPE WILL STUMBLE BACKWARD INTO WAR

Jihad does not look like war as we know it. Until it is too late.

Experts like to sing the lullaby: "The solution is not military, it is political." This means we will inevitably be drawn into limited military action followed by vain attempts to unite all factions in a peaceful compromise by means of international conferences and interim governments in suits and ties while, behind our backs, armed groups grab territory and slay their fellow countrymen. There is no solution to a problem that is misconstrued. The problem is not our failed interventions in the Middle East, it is not the lack of a political horizon for Muslims in Libya, Israel, or Paris. The problem is the free world's coexistence with a religion that is political, military, aggressive, and determined to conquer. Faced with lethal narrative warfare, the West makes sporadic, inconclusive military operations, and surrenders to the narrative without even recognizing its existence. This can be seen on every issue treated in this study. This is why it is of the utmost importance to understand the narrative and not just focus on concrete elements that, furthermore, are usually misrepresented. This problem is global and the response requires an intellectual and ethical re-examination.

Europe is falling backward into war. Political leaders maintain a compassionate front— human rights, our values, doing the right thing, hallowed asylum tradition —while trying to take serious protective and proactive measures to block the intruders. Border controls are more or less reinstated within the Schengen zone, hotspots will hopefully be established outside European borders to sort out asylum seekers, Daesh will somehow be smashed and, with a bit of luck, well, Syria could become livable again, yes? European countries are starting to deport dual nationals flagged as potential terrorists. The British forthrightly droned out two particularly boastful jihadis who were planning to kill the Queen of England. We won't mention the hand wringing when Israel took out Cheik Yassin. France has conducted two self-defense air strikes in Syria, reportedly aimed at jihadis plotting attacks in France. The Prime Minister has no qualms. "Terrorists don't have passports," he declared on a recent official visit to Jordan. Experts here and there are pointing out the obvious: Daesh won't be smashed without ground troops. But they are studiously ignoring the essential: What about Iran?

IRAN IS OFF THE HOOK

Can you see how the mass of intruders bursting into Europe drown the civilized conscience? A shady deal was made with Iran and suddenly the hordes escaping the war in Syria descend on us. The explainators tell us all this unrest is our fault for intervening here, not intervening there, thinking we could impose democracy, leaving before democracy took hold, supporting dictators, not supporting them when Islamists knock them down. And the Daesh caliphate? Our fault too. We didn't help the good guys right away so now it's only right to accept the spinoff refugees as brothers in our towns and villages. Daesh would never have reared its ugly head and chopped off so many others if we had helped the Syrian democrats to overthrow Assad and set up a democracy like...like what? Libya? Tunisia? Iraq? Afghanistan? Somehow they would have been the divine exception. But we didn't do the right thing. What they don't say is that the refugee-generating war might lose steam if Iran stopped supporting Hamas, Hizbullah, and Bashir al Assad. They won't say it because the P5+1 deal put Iran on the good side of the equation and shoved Israel definitively to the bad side. And now the whole of the West joins Israel in the dog house.

We can't smash Daesh? The US led coalition defeated the Iraqi army in less than 3 weeks and dethroned Saddam Hussein, but can't beat the Islamic State? Apparently not, unless we can get help from the Islamic

Republic of Iran. Senior French civil servants writing under the pen name Plessis publish a lucid analysis of the resistance of European citizens to a media concoction of irresponsible compassion and free entry for refugees. We must deal with the problem at its source, they write, and define a strategy based on rapprochement with Iran, concertation with Russia, and a "pragmatic" policy with regard to the Assad regime. With all these chums, who needs Israel? In fact, the Jewish State is evicted from the geopolitical debate these days in France. Traveling salesmen are creeping to Iran, on the prowl for lucrative business while the Islamic Republic proudly moves ahead with its nuclear arms program and genocidal ambitions.

Iranian leaders sincerely plan to exterminate the Jews. Those who think it is harmless rhetoric are either lying or tone deaf. The hostile intentions do not stop there, they extend to the United States of America, the West, infidels of all stripes, Muslims of insufficient submission, civilization in every nook and cranny of the wide world. The promises of destruction are repeated daily. Instead of pretending to have established a fantastic verification system that blocks Iran's path to nuclear arms, a genuine peacemaker would insist on an end to incitement. Instead of pretending that the raucous shouts of *Death to Israel Death to America* are the pale echo of a long gone silly notion that died away with the signature of the neat little P5+1 deal, honest statesmen would have demanded, before entering into negotiations, an end to genocidal incitement and proxy wars in alliance with genocidal allies like Hamas, Hezbollah and their fringes.

WE HAVE REACHED THE TIPPING POINT

We have reached the tipping point. The thoughtless open door policy triggered in Indian summer by the Aylan Shenu death photo has given way to hardnosed border controls all along the route from Turkey to Germany. Cold rain falls on the tens of thousands blocked in Croatia and Slovenia. Chancellor Merkel tiptoes over to Turkey and begs for respite like a vassal. She offers visa-free entry to the EU for Turkish citizens, accelerated negotiations for the integration of Turkey into the EU, and three billion euros to sustain the refugees that Turkey in its benevolence would agree to maintain. Europe applies to itself the logic it has been trying to impose on Israel since the Oslo Agreement. Erdogan pouts and says it's not good enough. PM Davutoglu declares "Turkey is not a concentration camp" where refugees will be held indefinitely.

The sheer brutality of Islamic knifings, rock throwing, car ramming is shocking consciences beyond the narrow limits of Zionism. The unspeakable barefaced amorality of media coverage of this gratuitous savagery is provoking protest in likely but also in unlikely places. More than ever, voices raised from within the Israeli Arab population declare outright rejection of this insane violence. Yes, because decent people know that Jewish patience, too, will reach its limits and the wrath that befalls murderous traitors will ultimately wither their entire community. Because there will be no other solution.

We have reached the tipping point in international relations, exasperated by the craven retreat of once benevolent American power, the absence of leadership and underhanded machinations of a cynical regime that lures America to act against itself.

The flames of usurpation are licking at the foundations of Judaism, the foundations of the West. Daesh dynamites Palmyra and a spiteful Palestinian Authority bites into the ankles of UNESCO, howling for more, for everything, the Temple Mount, the kotel, Rachel's tomb, Joseph's tomb. They aren't even trying to pretend that it's a secular issue of land and frontiers. They're foaming at the mouth and demanding international connivance in this insatiable bloodlust that bares its teeth. They've gone berserk.

The sheer quantity of murderous hatred pouring out of this corrupt source is enough to consume the face of the earth. It's there, one step away from me, one step away from you.

And this is its face.[3] Umm [*mother of*] Muhammad Shamasne. Interviewed by a young lady in flower-print hijab on Lebanese *Al-Quds TV*, the murderer's mother hopes her other sons will also kill Jews and die as shahids. Her only regret is that Muhammad did not take her to die with him when he murdered passengers on a Jerusalem bus on October 12th. The journalist wants to focus on the evils of the "occupation," but Umm Muhammad Shamasne has already made the leap from rhetoric to action. She pulls out a knife. Her eyes go dark and steely. The young lady gasps. "Please, we don't want that kind of thing on television." Too late. The image is indelible. This is the knife, these are the eyes, this is the poisoned heart and mind that kills "for Al Aqsa." Al Aqsa is her divinity.

Not the mosque, not the plaza, not the trumped up charges against Jews that defile it. Al Aqsa is the divinity that gives her permission to release the volcanic genocidal hatred planted in her womb, planted from womb to womb, giving birth to death, generating murder.

Why should the maternity of genocidal hatred prevail? Beneficial to no one, to no partisan interests, to no universal values. Sterile. Savage. Unspeakably cruel. The authentic united nations of decent freedom-loving human beings is infinitely stronger than the destructive forces riding high today in a brief flash of mistaken triumph, reducing every-thing they touch to stinking rubble.

Behold the beauty of our European world composed of overlays of greatness and tyranny, justice and abuse, animated by values that strive for elevation, that fall and reach upward again. Look at what these values have created in the Old World, the New World, to the ends of the earth, wherever humanity dominates base instincts. Look at what we have achieved, despite our failings.

We must not betray our heritage and abandon our generations. It would be the most senseless waste in human history. We are not the Roman Empire, we are free citizens of democracies. We are not sen-tenced to the deluge, not defenseless weaklings confronted by over-whelming force. We have achieved, by the creative powers of our intelli-gence, a portion of the divinity that inspires life.

If ever there were proof of the lifesaving potential of lucidity and el-oquence, it stands before us today. Despair is not an appropriate re-sponse dictated by the enormous challenge that confronts us. Despair is a tribute to fatality. It is a misconception.

Europe is not lost, Israel is not lost, the West is not lost. We have reached the tipping point and the tables can be turned.

JIHAD ATTACKS ON PARIS/2

November 14-17, 2015

It is like the death of a loved one. The death of our city that we love despite its failings, misdeeds, and particular misbehavior that I have been chronicling over the past fifteen years. A city is more than its cur-rent events. And today the heart of our city is broken. We do not have the fibre of Israelis who live with miraculous vitality in a permanent state of war & peace, but Parisians are not entirely devoid of courage and sharp instincts in the face of utmost danger. Anecdotes and eyewitness testimony are slowly emerging. The hard facts are at a minimum. A soft spoken young man in an elegant overcoat describes the scene at the café on Rue de Charonne. He was present, he saw people picked off like sitting ducks. "They didn't have a chance." And yet he himself cannot believe what he saw. The Public Prosecutor delivers official information in an appropriately neutral tone. A hundred shell casings are left at each of the cafés attacked. No one was spared. Those who are not dead are in desperate condition.

It was to be expected, but it is shocking, unreal. Friday night it seemed that the whole city was screaming with sirens. As you followed events on television you could hear the broadcast sirens echoing the wails that came from the streets and boulevards. Who doesn't have a friend who was in the Bataclan music hall or looking down from his apartment at dead bodies that only a short while before had been eating, drinking, laughing, enjoying life? In the global village, grieving families just a few days ago witnessed the massacre in Beirut or sobbed with the bereaved of the Sharm el Sheik-St. Petersburg flight. And now it is on their doorstep and has ripped apart their lives forever. We don't have to tell Israelis how it feels. But Europeans must wake up to the kinship they so earnestly tried to ignore.

Last week a French jihadi was arrested before going into action. He had ordered an army knife and two face masks from a firm in China. I suppose, in his infinite intelligence, he thought an order from a Chinese company would be undetectable. Or maybe he was attracted by the discount price? Well, the cheap packaging fell apart in transit, or so we are told, and a postal employee informed the police of the delivery of the killer knife. The young man intended to slaughter sailors at the Toulon naval base. A smartass TV commentator, implying that the police had over-reacted, shrugged it off. He said it was *la guerre des boutons* which, freely translated, means kids playing cops and robbers. "Like what's happening in Israel right now," he added. The knifings, firebombings, car rammings, and rock bashings... child's play to this snide observer. I honestly can't remember which anchor or expert it was, there are so many of the same stripe. Plentiful as the punk jihadis that poison our lives. The widespread consistent errors of appreciation on all that touches Israel and the Jews did not cause the November 13th Paris massacre; it was waiting to happen and nothing could have prevented it or another, similar one. But the massacre may well lead to the long awaited recognition that jihad strikes in Israel and in Europe with same genocidal hatred from the same source. The cold indifference to the wave of knife attacks in Israel this fall, the perverse reverse chronology that made Israeli forces guilty of gunning down Palestinians that (admitted in a whisper) had in fact tried or perhaps in some cases succeeded in stabbing...well, you know, a *colon*, or ultra-religious deserving victim... The tally of dead Palestinians was brandished with the righteous indignation that has been digging into our souls since the dawn of the 21st century. No gory details of the suffering inflicted on Jews in Israel were ever given in French media. Nothing that could make you taste the blood and feel the blade digging into your spine, your heart, your guts.

Now blood has been spilled in the streets of Paris. Except for the misfired explosive vests outside the soccer stadium, all the other attacks took place in the 10th and 11th arrondissements, on streets and boulevards in the vicinity of Place de la République. Sébastien Selam was slaughtered and mutilated in the 10th arrdt, Ilan Halimi worked in a cell phone shop on boulevard Voltaire in the 11th arrdt. The first recorded public cries of Death to the Jews were heard in October 2000 at Place de la République in a pro-Palestinian demonstration focused on the "death" of Mohamed al Dura. Last week a small clutch of Salafists shimmied one of those huge parallel-to-the-ground Palestinian flags and chanted "Arms for Hamas, Arms for Jihad." In the summer of 2014 pro-Hamas caliphators brandishing the black flag of jihad massed around the statue of Marianne in the Place de la République, screaming for Jewish blood.[1]

Marianne, the symbol of the French Republic, was defiled. The way Swedish women and forlorn British girls are defiled. Now, French people doing what French people do on a Friday night were mowed down. The way Jews in the Hyper Cacher were executed. Daesh has proudly signed the massacre of the "Crusaders," and promised more of the same if France does not cease and desist from meddling in Iraq and Syria. Ha! Sounds familiar. Muslims would stop stabbing Jews to death in Israel if the Zionists ended the Occupation. Don't bet on it. Cease and desist is the first in a long line of orders that will be barked at us in the coming months. Or years. Until we decide to go on the offensive.

The otherwise ineffectual President Hollande has promised a no holds barred fight against Daesh at home and abroad. French media, as far as I could see, have not dared to dissociate the massacre from the Islam that inspires it. The same media that were gushing over the refugees a few weeks ago are now reporting that one of the shahids who jumped the gun outside the Stade de France was carrying a Syrian passport stamped with a passage through Leros in Greece on October 3rd. Exactly what we expected.

A walk through the Marais early Saturday afternoon. Most of the shops were closed. Shabat, for some, the bloody events for others. So few cars in the streets, so few people strolling where on a normal Saturday afternoon the sidewalks would be overflowing. We had taken to joking about it: looking down the rue des Francs Bourgeois at the never-ending crowd, we would say "the refugees are coming." It looked so much like the human chain snaking through Slovenian fields. No soldiers, no police in the Marais this Saturday. So strange. Is it ominous? Does it mean there's no one left to protect the Jews now that the "Crusaders" are targeted?

Sunday morning shopping in an open market is almost a religion in France. This morning, heartbroken television cameras panned the dark empty alleys of the Marché Richard Lenoir where the ordinary cheerful bustle always impresses me as a model of peaceful coexistence. People of all origins and classes mingle and brush up against each other in the narrow aisles, all with the same goal of filling baskets and carts with good things to eat. Whether selling their own produce or stock that comes from the giant wholesale market at Rungis, salt-of-the-earth vendors, up since the break of dawn, exposed to the elements, lugging crates and arranging the merchandise with loving care, sell at a fast clip without a pause and never a complaint. The Richard Lenoir market is located in what we could call the massacre neighborhood, not far from the *Charlie Hebdo* offices, now vacated, and the modest restaurants targeted Friday night.

Eagles of death Metal, the American band that was playing at the Bataclan, has performed in Israel. The Bataclan was owned by Jews who sold it only two months ago. But let us take the mass murderers at their word: this time they were aiming at the Crusaders, the Christians. Most of the victims will turn out to be young people. Quite a few journalists enjoying a night out found themselves in "civilian garb" at the center of the action. It will change their world view and their discourse.

Though many French journalists (or is it coming directly from the infamous *Agence France Presse*?) have taken out of mothballs their al Aqsa Intifada misnomer, kamikazes, they are fostering no illusions about the legitimate aspirations of the shahids who have wreaked havoc in Paris. What a pity that it has taken so much bloodshed to ignite the spark that could bring together the decent citizens of the free world. Prime Minister Manuel Valls promises to annihilate, here and abroad, the forces that are attacking us. Public gatherings are prohibited at the moment, because of the security risk, but people come to city squares to light candles, shed tears, leave bouquets and messages of grief and defiance. Handmade signs declare *Même pas peur* (not even afraid), adding "We are Paris" to the *Je suis Charlie* stickers pasted to the base of the Marianne in January. "Pray for Paris" signs with the same funereal *Je suis Charlie* graphics are posted on the gates of churches.

The facts, as I said, are still at a minimum. The media have finally pronounced the name of the French shahid identified at the Bataclan by his severed finger: Ismael Omar Mostefai. A petty criminal convicted eight times but never sent to prison. Flagged but obviously not followed by security services. He went to Turkey in 2014 and, presumably, from there to Syria. Three alleged accomplices have been arrested in Molenbek (near Brussels), headquarters of some of our famous Islamic killers, platform of the weapons trade, cornucopia of Kalachnikovs. The thwarted Thalys train shahid set out on his mission with a suitcase full of weapons from his sister's apartment in Molenbek.

Flagged radicals, networks, cells, Daesh nomads, hate preachers, and manifestos of jihad conquest...it's all out there, all so familiar, so hotly active, toying with the soft underbelly of our democracies. Barbarians. And why are they getting away with it? We are not a decadent empire that deserves to be destroyed. They are not a daunting invulnerable gigantic monster gobbling us up like peanuts. Much is made today, by experts and commentators, of the military prowess of the three teams that shot up Paris Friday night. They're not bumbling amateurs like the Thalys jerk whose Kalachnikov jammed (but he managed to do quite a bit of damage with his handgun and box cutter). They're not clumsy fumblers like Glam who shot himself in the leg and only managed to kill one young woman but never made it to shoot up the Crusaders in the church at Villejuif. These guys were organized! It took planning. Nerves of steel to mow down people having a drink at a sidewalk café and pick off one by one almost a hundred in a concert hall. And the courage to blow themselves up for an encore.

I submit that there is hardly any difference between the bungling fools, the successful mass killers of Friday night in Paris, the Daesh savages spreading their caliphate like an oil spill in the Middle East, and the hordes that followed the enraged medieval prophet of Islam. When this light dawns on Europe the spirit of *résistance* will speak its mind. Instead of labeling products from the "colonies" like a snippety schoolteacher giving zeroes, Europe could begin to mobilize its resources and face the challenge intelligently. An enlightened Europe, battered by bitter experience, could draw the United States back into the concert of free nations where its indispensable military resources would finally weigh in the balance.

No, this is not the Third World War. This is the ongoing jihad conquest. And every magnificent European square is the gates of Vienna.

—Midah
—NER/The iconoclast

BONJOUR TRISTESSE
November 20-21 2015

Friday: Steady cold rain is falling as the truth starts to sink in. Rain extinguishes the memorial candles and flattens the bouquets in front of the grieving restaurants and the horrified Bataclan, and piled in terraces around the Marianne at Place de la République. The streets of Paris are forlorn, the boutiques are empty, there's no line waiting for a seat at the falafel joints, Christmas merchandise lies on the shelves, dumbstruck.

There was a brief moment of satisfaction at the news that the "mastermind" of last week's attacks was indeed dead several times over and beyond recognition after the 7-hour siege of his last hideout. DNA or some other tracer was matched to some shreds or drippings of Abdelhamid Abaaoud, junior Daesh executive in charge of planning jihad attacks in France and the Benelux countries. The so-called mastermind was caught by CCTV at the Croix de Chavaux métro station in Montreuil last Friday night at around 10 PM. The black Seat used by the easy riders who had finished executing people on restaurant and café terraces had been abandoned less than two blocks away. And the Big Chief ducked into the metro and jumped the turnstile. Punk!

I coined the term "punk jihadis" in November of 2005 when the banlieues went on a three-week torching spree. The pretext back then was the death of two youths running from the police; the boys took refuge in an electricity sub-station, and got electrocuted. Last Friday night punk jihadis killed 130 people in Paris, to punish them for being depraved Crusaders who listen to music, eat, drink, and make merry...

...for tomorrow we shall die? The truth sinks in and you assimilate it. In the immediate aftermath people light memorial candles...to forget the dread that has befallen them. They leave bouquets of flowers, hand scrawled notes, ribbons and flags and badges and other signs of life that will not die. After checking to make sure immediate family members are alive and intact, Parisians enlarged the scope and quickly touched the grief of bereaved friends and acquaintances. The media publish unbearable photos and accounts of first responders and survivors. The savagery screams in your ears like the sirens that wailed all night long.

Those columns of intruders marching into Europe on the tails of the Aylan Shenu photo are a living metaphor of our current situation. Savage killers were in fact embedded in the mass. Only a minority, you were reassured, as if that were an acceptable risk to take for the sake of not losing your humanitarian label. And now, and for decades, only a minority of ruthless mass murderers are hiding like squiggles in the wallpaper of Muslim communities in Europe. TV cameras pan the streets of Molenbek, base camp of the recent assault—all the women are in hijab. I am not the kind of journalist who pushes a microphone under someone's chin and asks a pointed question. What do you think about what happened? Who do you think did it? There is a different way of gathering and processing information. My memories of hundreds of man-in-the-street interviews play back today. I only have to look at the faces. The punks who actually grab the Kalashnikov and go on a killing spree, the punks that cheer them on, the nobodies with garbled minds that deplore the killing but deny its origins... Decent, perceptive, articulate Muslim intellectuals speak out too. These days they are more welcome than usual in the media. They are the real tiny Muslim minority. And most of them say, in measured voices: that's not the real Islam.

Writing close to the bone, I am overwhelmed by a flood of anecdotes and impressions. Reading distractedly the words of people commenting from a distance, I am close to infuriated by their flippancy. Some are so eager to latch on to a euphemism here, a sidestep there, and declare that the stupid French still haven't caught on that Islam is what's going on. Don't gloat. I happened to be in the United States on 9/11. When I returned to France a week later I was, yes, infuriated by their flippancy.

Countless hours of attention yield a full range of attitudes and analyses that can, however, be summarized. French people specifically and Europeans in general are on a learning curve. It is the difference that is notable, not the hangovers from an opaque recent past. Regional elections are coming up in December. Even though the issues are not technically international or even national, citizens will be voting on the question of Islamic jihad, for or against. That is, resist or fudge. And I still think that Marine Le Pen will not be the one to cash in the chips.

Saturday: The story line last night was: Parisians will not be terrorized. Here they are at Place de la République, lighting new candles to replace the ones that were rained out. Someone brought a piano to the improvised memorial near the Bataclan. People are singing and dancing, they went to the bistrots and had a drink. From screen to screen and one makeshift memorial to the other, correspondents served the plat du jour. "Hundreds are gathered" they said, confident that no one would notice the pitiful irony of it all. "Hundreds" means hardly anyone. So be it. People have to process this reality in their own way. Today a cold wind blowing directly from the North Pole (where there is apparently enough ice to chill us to the bone) is battering the memorial flowers as icy rain smothers the candles.

Last Sunday it was sunny and mild. I decided to jump at an exceptional opportunity to go face to face with *CNN*. First, I walked around the square twice to get the feel of things. My eye was caught by a small graffiti in the plaque marked 21 septembre 1792. *Flics, hors de nos vies* [cops, bug out of our lives]. Probably a remnant of the pro-Hamas rallies of the summer of 2014.

At the *CNN* tent, Hala Gorani said to a colleague, as she munched on a sandwich, "I've got to stop eating." Nice opening. I encouraged her to keep enjoying the best of the Paris... "Like you said this morning in your tribute to our city." She tells me she grew up here. And I show her a photo of pro-Hamas caliphators waving the black jihad flag right here in the Place de la République, right there on the pedestal of the Marianne, now decorated with flowers, candles, and *même pas peur* declarations. "Do you know what this is?" She doesn't know, but aha, she's no pushover. "This is photoshopped," she says with a wink of cleverness. "No, it's a collage. But this Palestinian flag, this Gaza Mon Amour poster, and this black jihad flag are at the same place at the same time. It was a banned demonstration. July 26th 2014. Israel was defending itself against attacks from Gaza." She looks uncomfortable. I give her a black & white photo of the cover of my forthcoming book, *The Black Flag of Jihad Stalks la République*. And my visiting card. "I'm available if you'd like to talk to me." The next day and ever since, Hala Gorani and her colleagues, all *CNN* BigShots, have been serving generous portions of Islamophilia. For example, an interview with someone from the Collectif Contre l'Islamophobie, who deplored the wave of house arrests as if it were worse than Guantanamo.

Radio Communauté Juive, one of several Jewish radio stations that share an FM band, could be fairly designated as "leftist, with highbrow aspirations." On a midday newscast last week, journalist Paule-Henriette Lévy, interviewing a high ranking military man, apparently wanted to query him on the real impact of air strikes against Daesh positions. "Thirty-three dead," she remarked, clearly swallowing the word "only" that gave meaning to her question. Then, her humanitarian reflexes kicking in, she blurted: "Of course every life matters...33 dead is 33 too many..."

I-télé broadcast an excerpt from an interview with the sister and brother of one of the Bataclan killers. They are horrified, simply horrified by what he did. He's not our brother, he's a monster, they sob. They repeat their horror, their sorrow, their distress, their stupefaction. And to think it was happening a few blocks away from the théâtre de la Main d'Or where they were watching Dieudonné perform. The interviewer is a bit stupefied himself. "You went to see Dieudonné's show? He's very controversial. Are you anti-Semitic?" And they reply, hidden behind the thickest biggest most checkerboard face blur I've ever seen, "No, we were just having fun, it's a comedy show."

I suppose most readers will have seen footage of the bespectacled guy who lent the apartment in St. Denis where Abaaoud made his last stand. Interviewed by *BFM TV* during the standoff, he could barely contain his arrogance and contempt for the journalist who dared to ask him how he came to give refuge to the notorious terrorist. "A *copain* asked me to lend the place to some of his *potes* for a few days. I said ok. I helped him out, monsieur, that's all, a helping hand." Of course he didn't know they came from Belgium, he didn't know they were terrorists. And perhaps he didn't see the policemen standing nearby that gently took him by the arm and led him to the paddy wagon. He's still in custody. According to an article in *Libération* the snooty chap subsequently identified as Jawad Bendaoud, is the goon of slum landlords that were renting apartments in the building, officially declared unfit for habitation. Bendaoud reportedly was sentenced to an 8-year term in 2008 for manslaughter. The victim was a friend. So I guess this wasn't the first time he helped out a *copain*. A cute young flirty looking friend of Bendaoud gives a different version. She says the apartment was abandoned. Her copain just broke in and expropriated it. He lent it to people who needed a place to crash. The downstairs neighbor of the hideout also told her story to TV cameras. The building was shaking, plaster was raining down from the ceiling. She didn't need to be blurred. She was in niqab.

Bendaoud was curiously precise in the pre-arrest interview: "I told the *copain* that there's nothing in the apartment, no mattresses, he said it's okay, all they need is water and a place to do their prayers." A few hours later, pieces of Hasna Aitboulahcen, identified as Abaaoud's cousin, were blasted out of the apartment, along with a bloody mattress [sic] that fell to the ground for all the eyes of the world to see. Just before Hasna was blasted by the suicide belt of the third fugitive, a policeman shouted up to her "Where is your boyfriend" and she replied "He's not my boyfriend." The confused young woman, who was a party girl until a few months ago, revealed in that brief exchange the juvenile stupidity of these mass murderers. She sounds like an 8 year-old girl with a ribbon in her hair meowing at recess. "Gna gna gna, Alhamid likes Hasna," chant les *copines* and Hasna stamps her foot and says, "He's not my boy-friend."

The enemy says we are racists, but when the savages shoot into the crowd, they murder people of all colors, creeds, and origins. The names of the dead are an international repertoire of contemporary French history. But they, the crazed killers, are all the same.

If going to cafés and bistrots is an act of résistance against the savage murderers, there are still some distinctions to be made. Go into any Muslim neighborhood anywhere in France and you will find men sitting in cafés and bistrots for hours on end.

— *NER/The Iconoclast*

WHAT DO THEY WANT?

December 2015

Our French feminine newscasters are attractive, charming, refined, and fashionably dressed. (Though a few have disfigured themselves with silicone lips that interfere with their ability to speak). Compared to their American and British counterparts, they are stunningly beautiful. And it just might have something to do with French culture, because women on the French channel of Israel's *i24 news* are in general better looking than their colleagues on the English channel.

I'm not sure of the appropriate vocabulary for their profession. Some are simple newsreaders, others are full-fledged journalists. They don't go into the grimy field like the American and British big names that stood up, rain or shine, at Place de la République for hours on end last week. Decades ago they were called *speakerines*, a word that has been dumped, along with *concierge* for custodian and *garçon* for waiter. For some reason that escapes me, our indoor journalists have taken to baring their arms to the shoulder when temperatures drop and normal people are bundled up in sweaters and jackets. In my experience, TV studios are more likely to be cool than overheated. But I was surprised to see a sweet young thing on the 14th of November dressed in a summery pastel sleeveless top reciting press releases filled with shock and gore. By the end of the day the word had apparently gone out. Since then, it's jackets or long sleeves, all black for the first week, now varied but still appropriate to a grieving nation.

Since Paris was attacked, these anchors have been asking invited guests, "What do they want?" Well, if they're terrorists it follows that they want to terrorize us and résistance consists of not being afraid. We'll go to concerts, restaurants, cafés, and shopping centers. The terrorists will not prevail. Then, since they are all Muslim, it means they want to divide our society, turn us against all Muslims, so we will resist by holding hands, forming human chains, and proclaiming friendship with our Muslim fellow citizens. TV cameras focused on a blindfolded man at Place de la République carrying a sign that said "I'm Muslim, give me a hug." Of course he got lots of hugs. No one seemed to notice that the blindfold was a keffieh... like the ones worn by the caliphators that brought the jihad flag to the statue of Marianne in the summer of 2014.

What do they want? From time to time, an enlightened Muslim guest responds: they want to establish a caliphate in every corner of the world. That leaves the newspeaker speechless. Of course, if you call them jihadis instead of terrorists, the answer is in the question. Today, words are increasingly calibrated with realities. French citizens demand decisive action, authority, power. They want to fight back individually and collectively, morally and militarily.

Every day there's a small increase in activity, more human presence, but far from normal. Shops are still empty. Concert halls and movie theaters are deserted as if they were all marked for death. None of the usual bustle in cafés and restaurants. Guards are posted at the entrance to supermarkets and shopping centers. Some have metal detectors. Nothing that could resist a commando armed with Kalashnikovs. The idea is to show their concern for public safety and their hope that business will pick up.

Last Sunday and Monday the weather was clear, crisp, and dry. I spent the day on Sunday at a colloquium organized by Shmuel Trigano, founding director of *l'Université Populaire du judaïsme*. A welcome relief from the all-day all-night news channels that we cannot bear and cannot escape. Attendance was weak...a handful of people in the morning, 50 or so in the afternoon. Speakers came from Canada, from Israel, from shell shocked Paris to share their deep thoughts with us--the heights of Judaism and its never-ending struggle to reach itself, the path to sovereignty, inner and outer obstacles. Surely a wider audience will catch the lectures on the UP site.[1] Thought is too precious to waste in these critical times.

Monday afternoon I met Shmuel in a café near Place de la République. Through the plate glass window we saw riot police coming and going past a long line of police cars parked in front of the café, a reminder that these vital moments of intellectual communion, as early winter darkness gathered, could be engulfed in the smoldering rage that he and I have been chronicling for fifteen years. Is night closing in on people like us who write real books, is it closing in on colleagues that are being hounded by the guard dogs against Islamophobia, are we left with the choice between being ignored or targeted?

On the way home I savored the fresh clear air. It is so good to be alive. Every day, every minute, every gesture is more delicious than ever before. The moon was plump and piercingly bright. The next day at the same hour all métro lines that converge on la République were stopped for an hour or more and the Place was evacuated. For verifications. Brussels was shut down for four days as the police combed through the city looking for the Most Wanted and the Also Rans. Paris had left itself wide open to attack; Brussels closed the metro, schools, shops, restaurants, streets and squares. They ordered a press lockdown too. No news reports or videos of police operations were allowed. A handful of suspects are in custody now, including the pair that drove to Paris after the attacks to bring Salah Abedslam back to Belgium. And the police can't find out where Salah is? How about some waterboarding, my friends?

PA President-for-life Mahmoud Abbas must be fuming. Not only does he have Hamas and Daesh in that order breathing down his neck, now Daesh has taken over the news cycle and no one cares about the Palestinians. Just before jihad hit Paris, Abbas was on his way to the ICC to accuse Israel of torture because interrogators yelled at a 13 year-old boy who had stabbed a Jewish boy his age nearly to death. On the video of the interrogation you hear one man holler at him in Hebrew, "Why did you do it?" and then another shouts the same question at him in Arabic. That's torture, in case you don't understand.

Today, the French population seems to be speaking with one voice. Wherever you turn you hear distress, defiance, and a demand for law and order. It's all common sense. You talk to repair men, store managers, neighbors, or read comments on newspaper articles. They understand the causes, they know what has to be done. But specialists and politicians are still promising to deliver...without committing evil. They have to round up some of the 10,000 flagged security risks, but "we're not going to create a Guantanamo." We're under a 3-month state of emergency, but "we're not going to make a Patriot Act." The police shot

5,000 rounds into the St. Denis hideout of the chief operator of the November 13 assault, Abelhamid Abaaoud, but no one is accusing them of using "excessive force." When you see the thickly clad Swat teams in France and Belgium you remember snide footage of t-shirted Palestinian shababs facing up to armored Israeli soldiers and tanks.

The commentators don't say "we're not going to do like the Israelis"— extra-judicial killings, preventive detention, security barriers, and guards at every doorway. They don't say it because Israel is absent from the debate. Israelis aren't invited to round tables, no comparisons are made, certainly not to say we have a lot to learn from them, they've been dealing with this for decades. Jewish thinkers and leaders aren't invited to the heated debates that make the screen shake. Unless you read "other" media, you don't know that Israeli intelligence informed German services that an ambulance filled with explosives was waiting to do its thing outside the stadium in Hanover where the chancellor was attending a life-goes-on soccer game. The stadium was evacuated before the opening play. Maybe the Europeans don't want to admit they were wrong about Israel but, behind the scenes, everyone with any sense is collaborating with Israeli security.

Update: I'm told that Pierre Servent said (in a *C dans l'air* TV debate that I missed) it was time we rethought our way of looking at Israel. While at the lowest point in the spectrum, a recently retired France 2 Jerusalem correspondent pissed into the gutter a pox on "racist" Israelis that, unlike dignified Parisians, don't know how to behave politely after a "terrorist" attack. I couldn't read past the first paragraph.

Iran, for very different reasons, is also nearly invisible. The idea seems to be "the less said the better." Who can keep track of our "allies" in the motley crew that is fighting Daesh or defending Assad, or both, while attacking each other? I like to hear or read a variety of commentaries by all sorts of specialists. They are so knowing...especially about the past. Full of hmph, it was obvious we/they shouldn't have done this/that. You know, the Kurds aren't interested in liberating the Sunnis from Daesh but the Sunnis will not be happy to see Westerners coming in, accompanied by Shia, to put their house in order. As for the present, they serenely spin new illusions: first we have to smash Daesh, then we'll have a provisional Syrian government that will organize UN-guaranteed elections open to residents and the Diaspora that will form a democratic pluralistic government, and...

Iran has one foot on the battlefield and the other standing in the shadows ready to pounce once Daesh is undone.

Abaaoud and his surviving team planned, we are told, to blow themselves up at la Défense, the modern business district just across the city line that looks like a cheap imitation of a 5th rate American downtown. The best bet to catch the crowd would have been the 4 Temps shopping mall. The jihadis would have hauled a lot of banlieue dudes and chicks in their explosive net; the business district is something of a Hebron, where a small minority of well-heeled executives and upper level employees is surrounded by a large population of the relegated disgruntled lower classes. Recent leaks suggest the killers also planned to hit a Jewish target. What else is new?

Paris prosecutor François Molins gave a long detailed update the other day. Every time I see him I am reminded of the press conference after the atrocious murder of Ilan Halimi, where he announced that the crime would not be qualified as anti-Semitic. The error was corrected shortly afterward, but the memory still has a sting.

In the present affair, the prosecutor sketched out a polka dot map of cell phone pings with blood- chilling implications—Abaaoud, after mowing down unsuspecting people in cafés and restaurants, abandoned the car, hopped into the metro without paying, and zipped down to the Bataclan where the victims of his co-killers agonized on a carpet of blood and the raid was still underway. The whereabouts of Salah Abedslam are also traced in a macabre hopscotch that night. His unexploded vest was discovered this week on a dead-end street in Montrouge. It wasn't in a normal garbage bin, where it would have been collected the day after it was chucked; it was on a pile of "objets encombrants," cumbersome objects like broken furniture and overworked mattresses. And, now, unused suicide vests.

Media coverage is thinning. Two weeks after the jihad outburst, the government organized a tribute to the victims at les Invalides. The ceremony was elegant and moving. The national anthem was honored by a resounding chorus of professional voices. La Marseillaise, composed by revolutionaries from Marseille that came up to Paris to overthrow the king, is so demanding that only a highly trained opera singer can do it justice. The president asked French citizens to adorn their façades with the national flag for the occasion. In neighborhoods I visited, flags are few and far between but the nationalistic fervor is in the air, awakened by the atrocious massacre. A sense of identity and pride that just a few weeks ago was decried as extreme right jingoism is embraced, with predictable exceptions, across the political and intellectual spectrum. The chord has been struck. It would be a mistake to underestimate the transformation of French society. In fact, no, it is not a transformation. It's a revelation of something that was always present but never recognized at its true value.

Pilgrimages to the murder sites continue. Volunteers clear away wilted flowers and burned out candles, quickly replaced by fresh ones. And the police are at work, searching for weapons, putting people under house arrest, gathering information, deporting imams. The French government informed the Council of Europe that it may have to infringe on human rights during the state of emergency.

Attention has finally turned to the lair of those not so lone wolves that have been spilling blood abundantly, but the glaring evidence of the articulation between "this is Islam" and "this is not Islam," has hardly been explored. The "white emir," a 69 year-old naturalized French citizen who goes by the name of Olivier Corel, has been running an Islamic academy in Lanes, a clump of rustic houses in the hamlet of Artigat in the Ariège hills outside of Toulouse. The Syrian Salafist Abdel Ilat Al-Dandachi aka Corel, is a sort of celestial body around which dozens of planets gravitate, wreaking havoc as they explode, immediately replaced by more of the same. Take a look at this graphic illustration of his galaxy:[2]

This week the emir was given a six month's suspended sentence for illegal detention of firearms, apparently an old hunting rifle, and allowed to return to his humble abode and chummy neighbors. Since 1987, when the steely-eyed Muslim Brother established his community in Artigat, his disciples have been implementing his spiritual message with Kalachnikovs and other murderous instruments. To mention only a few graduates of the self-styled academy:

Mohamed Merah, his brother Abdelkader, jailed as an accessory to the Toulouse-Montauban murders, and his sister Souad, believed to be in Syria.

Merah's buddy Sabri Essid, who has joined Daesh and recently appeared in a video with a kid-executioner who shot a man in the head. The victim, an Israeli Arab that had joined the caliphate, was accused of being a Mossad spy.

Fabien and Jean-Michel Clain, converts originally from Reunion Island, who recited the text taking credit for the latest Paris attacks. The brothers influence, organize and micro-manage activities from their base in Syria. Fabien was imprisoned in 2009 for his role in recruiting jihadis to fight in Iraq. Last spring the brothers piloted Sid Ahmed Glam's botched attack on a church in Villejuif. In 2009 Fabien Clain had personally threatened to punish the Bataclan for its Zionism. The Jewish proprietors, who sold the concert hall just a few months ago, hosted an annual gala concert—systematically hounded by raucous demonstrators—for the benefit of Israel's border police, the Magav.

The Clains, like almost every jihadi mentored by the white emir, have Belgian connections. They were involved with a commando that attacked French lycéens on a school trip to Egypt a few years ago... Corel/al-Dandachi has been detained several times for questioning and always released, because existing law denies the connection between "this is Islam"—self-styled or officially appointed imams preaching real Islam—and "this is not Islam"—the killers who activate their message. The emir doesn't fire a Kalchnikov and the mass murderers don't look "religious." The media and their experts report with a sigh of relief that Abaaoud's team was composed of petty to middling criminals, known more for taking drugs and womanizing than for praying at the mosque. One-eyed specialists prefer to implicate the Net as the untouchable radicalizer while ignoring one of the major sources of French jihadism.

September 21, 2001, a massive explosion at the AZF chemical plant in Toulouse left 31 dead and thousands maimed or injured. No "chemical" explanation for the blast has ever been found, but the possibility of a terror attack ten days after 9/11 has been stubbornly dismissed. Former anti-terrorist judge Jean-Louis Bruguière drafted a report on elements that were overlooked in the investigation. Without claiming to have found the cause of the accident, or the culprit, the judge details all the reasons why investigators should not have ignored troubling information about Hassan Jandoubi a truck driver killed in the blast. Jandoubi, an interim worker hired by an outside agency, allegedly had contacts with the Artigat Islamic community.[3] [

Two weeks after the attacks, Christmas decorations go up, the initial shock is no longer visible in the streets, the media have turned their attention to the COP21, leaving loose threads everywhere. The Green Summit is taking place at Le Bourget, where the UOIF, our Muslim Brotherhood affiliate, holds its annual Congress, a huge event chock full of hijab, inflammatory literature, sharia friendly speakers, and separation between men and women. The UOIF was conspicuously present at a summit meeting of French Islam held the other day to consecrate the fight against radicalization.

It's simply impossible to close a chapter in this ongoing drama. So much is left to be said: Samy Amimour, one of the 13 November executioners, worked for several years as a bus driver. It seems that Salafists have been ruling over certain depots in the Parisian transportation network. Political figures from all parties are now asking for a thorough review of flagged security threats employed in sensitive fields. Amimour's passport had been confiscated after he was caught trying to join the Caliphate. But his lawyer persuaded authorities to give it back to him so he could find employment. All of these murderous thugs have lawyers, usually young women with long blonde hair. Not court appointed lawyers, dedicated counsel that has been defending them for years. Why did the three shahids posted outside the soccer stadium jerk off without waiting for the crowd to pour out and get smashed? Who was their prompter? What language were they speaking? I don't know why they missed their cue, but they illustrate the idiocy of the refugee numbers game. What does it matter what percentage of the intruders are Daesh, when six weeks after the photo-choc of Aylan Shenu hit the screen, three unidentified men who came through Greece with false passports were in position to assassinate the president of France?

The squeaky clean intentions of the ecologists were brutally contested on the eve of the COP21 by another branch of the enemies of decency that, despite countless house arrests and a non-negotiable prohibition against demonstrations, made their contribution to the misery that assails us. Anarchists determined to impose their law, opportunists jumping at a chance to make trouble, extremist ecologists and, who knows, maybe some jihadis too, hiding under the same black hoods gathered at

Place de la République Sunday night to fight the police. In the heat of the battle the insurgents attacked the police with rocks, glass bottles, canisters, and candles grabbed from the memorial at the feet of the statue of Marianne. According to one eyewitness they used children's drawings as wicks to light candles. They even threw bouquets. More, I suppose, as a sign of contempt than with any illusion that the flowers could penetrate the riot policemen's shields. A dialogue between an assailant and a concerned citizen, possibly an ally in his combat shocked by the means he chose, reportedly went like this:

"How can you do this? [sacking the memorial] How can you disrespect the victims?"

"It happened in my neighborhood. I don't give a damn. I don't want a state of emergency, I don't want a state."

Like the caliphators of July 2014, the anarchists also took part in anti-Zionist anti-American rampages years ago. I wrote about them at the time—"Pitbulls for Peace"—when the mass media pretended they didn't exist. They were called peace marches back then. And now, the French president is doing his utmost to find allies in the war against Daesh. British forces are in position to strike as soon as the parliament gives the ok to David Cameron who has designated a prime target, Sheikh Abu Muhammad al-Adnani, the real mastermind of attacks in Europe.

And our charming newscasters have started alternating the term "Islamic State" with the Arabic acronym Daesh that, though accurate, has been used to avoid linking Islam to atrocities.

— *New English Review*

195

Appendix

DÉCALAGE HORREUR
[Death Lag]

Paris le 7 juillet 2014

Moi-même je suivais aux côtés de mon bien-aimé le match France-Nigeria—en pensant à Boko Haram—tout en redoutant le match suivant : si jamais l'Algérie devait vaincre l'Allemagne puis par la suite se faire battre par la France ce serait notre fête. Dans l'entre-deux matches comme entre deux guerres j'ai consulté mon inbox. Breaking news de la Metula News Agency. « Ils sont morts. » Tous les trois. Eyal Yifrah, Gilad Shaar, Naftali Frenkel. Depuis quand ? La semaine dernière des journalistes de i24 News notaient une lacune dans les déclarations officielles-- on parlait de retrouver à tout prix les kidnappeurs...pas les adolescents. Il y a deux semaines, en marge du colloque organisé par l'UPJF, Gladys Tibby a avoué, la voix cassée, que l'un des jeunes était mort, on ne savait pas encore lequel. On apprend maintenant que l'assassinat expéditif a été enregistré dans les minutes suivant le coup de fil à la police. « On m'a enlevé ». Suivi des cris rauques en arabe meurtrier ! Coups de feu ! Gémissements. La joie des tueurs. « Trois » ! Les parents le savaient. C'est

Israël. On leur avait fait écouter la bande enregistrée. Mais l'espoir contre tout espoir avait régné. On ne pleure pas la mort des vivants. Dix-huit jours. Notre peuple vivait au diapason des parents angoissés. Emmanuel Navon écrit, « ça pourrait être les miens ».[1] Oui, j'avais pensé à ma famille de cœur à Efrat ... sans me rendre compte que les ainés sont maintenant adolescents. La presse française, tout occupée à nous séparer de notre humanité. Enfants livrés à la sauvagerie des bêtes enragées ? Non. Des colons. Des jeunes dévoués à leurs études ? Humph ! En territoire occupée. Ce monde qui ne sait pas tirer une ligne rouge entre la barbarie et la civilisation s'amuse à tirer des lignes vertes pour se cacher la forêt d'arbres dressés contre nous tous.

Sébastien Selam, égorgé et mutilé au sous-sol de son immeuble dans le 10e arrondissement de Paris par son voisin musulman. Avec quels complices et quelle complicité ? Ilan Halimi kidnappé, torturé en banlieue parisienne au sein d'une cité subventionnée par le contribuable français dans un territoire occupé par des brutes minables et des indifférents coupables. Jonathan Sandler, ses fils Arieh et Gabriel, Myriam Monsonego exécutés par Mohamed Merah. De quel côté de la ligne verte se situe Toulouse, France, Messieurs les arpenteurs ? Emanuel et Miriam Riva, Dominique Sabrier, Alexandre Strens abattus par Mehdi Nemmouche qui exprime un seul regret : son GoPro, tombé en panne, n'a pas pu immortaliser son beau geste. Adel Amastaibou, Fofana et Cie, Merah, Nemmouche—de nobles Gaulois qui défendent leur patrie ?

On glisse de l'édition spéciale sur *i24 News* au match Allemagne-Algérie. J'évalue le fond et la forme des barbes à l'apparence salafiste, ne voulant rien savoir des qualités de tir des Algériens, me demandant tout simplement si leurs supporteurs ici dans nos villes occupées françaises brûleront plus ou moins de voitures s'ils perdent au lieu de gagner. Pas d'infidèles et un seul Noir dans l'équipe maghrébine-- le goal, barbu par ailleurs et super efficace. Ils nous laissent les bienfaits de la diversité et se concentrent sur leur quant à soi. Je compte sur la solidité germanique. Oublié *l'achtung*, donnez-nous du *blitzkrieg*.

Dernier tour à l'inbox avant l'extinction des feux. Un message d'X, qui a suivi le match dans un café de sa ville quelque part dans le sud de la France, devenue le nord du Maghreb : « Je suis rentrée avant la fin du match ». Ouf !

Lionel Messi, génie du foot, a soulevé son maillot pour dévoiler le t-shirt *≠Bring Back our Boys*. Michelle Obama, non. Son mari, le président des Etats-Unis exige de la retenue des deux côtés. Le Hamas menace de rouvrir les portes de l'enfer si jamais Israël ose réagir à l'exécution des « trois colons » par autre chose que des pleurs. Ah bon ? Je ne savais pas que les portes avaient été fermées du côté des territoires occupés par le Hamas. Depuis le kidnapping spectaculaire de plus de 200 cents filles, Boko Haram poursuit tranquillement ses méfaits-- enlèvements, barbecue de Chrétiens dans leur église, bombes au cœur des marchés... Les hashtaggeurs ont abandonné leur noble causette comme des vêtements qu'on donne aux œuvres charitables. Il ne faut pas leur en vouloir, juste comprendre pourquoi nous autres juifs ne sommes pas un plat convenable pour la consommation compassionnelle.

Le monde suivait le Mondial, les mères des jeunes otages allaient jusqu'à Genève plaider leurs cause devant la méprisante Commission onusienne des droits de l'homme. Par ailleurs des pourparlers interminables donnent à l'Iran toute latitude pour perfectionner son arsenal nucléaire. 2,400 morts comptés en Irak au mois de juin. Combien de milliers rajoutés en Syrie ? On va vers les 200,000. Le califat s'installe à cheval entre la Syrie et l'Irak en poussant vers la Jordanie car sa dague doit absolument viser le cœur d'Israël alors que mon pays natal, ayant choisi comme président par deux fois un ami des Frères Musulmans, se découvre, jusqu'aux milieux anti-jihad, suprêmement isolationniste. Qu'ils s'entretuent ! Ce n'est pas notre problème, on n'a rien à y faire, quelle folle idée de croire qu'on pourrait leur donner la démocratie comme on donne de la farine aux affamés (et encore elle se retrouve en vente au marché noir).

Les Américains, on nous dit, sont fatigués de la guerre. Les Européens ? Fatigués d'avance. Restent les forces françaises bel et bien engagées au Mali et en Centrafrique mais invisibles du grand public. C'est fou comme nos médias peuvent cacher un régiment derrière le sourire béat d'une animatrice, non, derrière le visage apprêté de toute une corporation, les meilleurs comme les pires.

Les soldats israéliens dépêchés à la recherche des jeunes, à peine plus âgés qu'eux, la population comme une seule mère juive mobilisée pour leur apporter un peu de confort, des lasagnes, des brosses à dent, le gîte.

Les maisons plus que confortables des résidents musulmans de Hébron. On ne découvre pas encore les adolescents qu'on espérait vivants mais on découvre l'implantation du Hamas à Hébron, là où 800 Juifs persistent à séjourner parmi plus d'une centaine de milliers d'Arabes. Extrémistes. Les Arabes, acquis on le sait maintenant à la cause de la destruction totale de l'Etat d'Israël et l'extermination des Juifs ? Non, les Juifs qui persistent à croire que le caveau de Machpela nous appartient sans partage (tout en acceptant de le partager). Caches d'armes, tunnels, caves et ordinateurs sont fouillés ou saisis. Le père de l'un des kidnappeurs-- Marwan Kawasme-- règne sur un clan de 10,000 hamasniks.

Je ne parle pas de deux poids deux mesures. Il n'y a ni poids ni mesure. Il faut savoir, même si on est journaliste, dire l'essentiel. Or, ce qui est passé sous silence c'est la source de lumière qui nous permet de comprendre. Mahmoud Abbas condamne l'enlèvement [les médias de l'AP s'en réjouissent], ses forces de l'ordre épaulent celles d'Israël [ses forces de propagande publient l'image de trois rats estampillés du *magen David* suspendus à une ligne de canne à pêche]. Mahmoud Abbas [qui vient de former un gouvernement d'union nationale avec le Hamas] met en garde les Israéliens contre les punitions collectives. Le gouvernement américain, l'ONU, l'UE [qui se sont hâtés de féliciter cette unification prometteuse] font comprendre que leur patience a des limites. De grosses bottes dans les maisons, des arrestations massives, des accusations sans fondement [dixit les familles des coupables] et puis de sourdes menaces contre le Hamas voire contre toute la population de Gaza et de la Cisjordanie, tout cela pour trois colons, ça commence à faire beaucoup.

Il faudrait plus qu'une vie entière pour conter l'histoire d'une seule vie, même d'un jeune de 16 ans. Infinitude de petites opérations, sollicitude de chaque instant depuis la conception et à longueur de chaque journée, la chaleur, la lumière d'un vivant, sa singularité miraculeuse, la physiologie d'un être vivant et les milliards de signes scrutés par un *yeshiva bocher*, le cœur à cœur qui nous lie, les rythmes et la musique de l'espoir en chair et os anéanti d'un seul coup de feu. Instantanée. Le mal, armé, agit, pam ! Ligne droite entre le projet diabolique et son accomplissement. Nous n'y pouvons rien.

Vient alors par ricochet un meurtre qui nous arrache de nos fondements. L'espoir, la déception, l'annonce atroce, le soutien d'un peuple uni dans une seule famille, la noblesse des endeuillés, le linceul, le corps sans vie, le kaddish, tout cela nous savons le faire. Un jeune musulman. De Jérusalem. Enlevé. Assassiné. Ce pourrait être un acte de vengeance. Commis par des Juifs. Non ! Pas ça. Pas de geste crasse et stupide. Non. On prie que ce ne soit pas ça. Des informations circulent sans qu'on puisse les confirmer. Ce pourrait être un crime d'honneur... il y a des précédents...brûlé ? Non, un Juif ne

9-11 juillet 2014 [2ème partie]

On a beau raisonner à partir de l'affaire al Dura, la Torah, les crimes d'honneur codifiés et typiquement islamiques, la vérité est implacable. Mohamed Abu Kheidr est mort, brulé vif. Celui ou ceux qui l'ont fait ne sont pas des personnages d'une œuvre en progrès. Ils existent. Les dents serrées on lit « la police penche pour le crime nationaliste ». Egale : « les coupables sont Juifs ».

C'est insupportable. Pourquoi ? Il ne s'agit pas d'une posture de supériorité morale ni d'une névrose de culpabilité. C'est que le judaïsme n'est pas un monument historique, ce n'est pas un édifice, c'est un système de valeurs qui vit par l'adhésion active renouvelée à chaque respiration de Juifs en chair et os, chacun totalement responsable.

Des Juifs qui s'emparent d'un Israélien musulman de 16 voire 17 ans, l'assomment, l'aspergent et mettent le feu sous prétexte de venger la mort de trois Israéliens juifs kidnappés et assassinés ? Je n'y crois pas un instant. C'est un prétexte. Comme les Israéliens dits arabes voire palestiniens qui lancent des rochers et des bouteilles incendiaires sur la police, saccagent des rues, des bâtiments, des stations du tramway à Jérusalem, scient les rails posés pour les inclure dans la collectivité, tout cela motivé par le meurtre du jeune Abu Kheidr ? Touchés dans leur for intérieur ? Plutôt ravis de l'occasion de pouvoir s'éclater en énergie destructrice.

Mais le cousin Tariq, que faisait-il dans cette histoire ? Le cousin d'Amérique, battu par des policiers israéliens, la vidéo le prouve, si c'est bien lui. Bel et bien battu, quand même. Le visage tuméfié, les yeux au beurre noir, il témoigne : « Je ne faisais rien, je regardais, c'est tout, la police est venue en courant, j'ai tenté d'échapper, ils m'ont pris, m'ont battu, je me suis réveillé à l'hôpital ». Sa mère en hijab, *American as apple pie*, rajoute : « On le fait tous les jours aux Palestiniens en Israël, eux, ils n'ont pas recours aux avocats, ne peuvent pas se défendre. Je veux qu'on sache : ce que mon fils a subi est infligé tous les jours aux Palestiniens. » Tariq est étudiant à l'Universal Academy of Florida, une école islamique liée au Tampa Bay Islamic Center, implantation notoire d'Islam tendance CAIR/Hamas/ Frères musulmans. Venu au mois de juin rendre visite à sa famille en Israël, le *typical American boy* a vécu— comment ? On ne nous le dit pas—le drame du meurtre de son cousin. Ils ont à peu près le même âge et se ressemblent comme des jumeaux. Selon la police, l'Américain, qui faisait partie d'une bande d'assaillants dont deux armés de couteaux, maniait un lance-pierre, refusait d'obtempérer ... Quoi qu'il en soit, notre jeune Tariq soutient l'équipe du Tampa Bay Islamic Society, aux couleurs du CAIR = Hamas= Frères Musulmans et à ce titre s'estime victime innocente de la brutalité israélienne notoire. Egale= j'ai le droit d'œuvrer à votre extermination, vous n'avez pas le droit de toucher à un cheveu de ma tête.

Enfin, non, ce ne sont pas des activistes « prix à payer », pas d'extrémistes de droite ni des collines, ce sont des « soccer hooligans » qui ont tué de façon atroce Mohamed Abu Khdeir. Leur forfait est devenu, une semaine plus tard, le Kristallnacht de l'extermination programmée des Palestiniens. Dans quelle équipe joue Mahmoud Abbas dont les médias officiels accusent Israël d'un génocide ? Egale 37 tués à Gaza, quasiment tous des *moudjahidin* et leurs familles. On commence déjà à jeter des bûches sur le feu, des enfants de Gaza heureux de mourir pour protéger la maison d'un cadre du Hamas. Pas vraiment pour protéger la maison. La preuve : elle a été détruite. Pour préparer la prochaine étape d'un scénario bien huilé. Incursion, kidnapping, meurtre, pluie de rockets, promesse de solution finale puis quelques pertes du côté des agresseurs, hurlements, appels à la communauté internationale, l'ONU, qu'on impose au plus vite un cessez-le-feu...qui leur accordera la victoire méritée. Nos oiseaux de paix tweet-tweet « solution politique » alors que leurs charognards tirent au-dessus de nos têtes un énorme linceul noir frappé du sigle *allahou akhbar* en invitant les instances internationales à tenir l'autre bout.

Ils préparent un massacre. Sommes-nous prêts ? Avons-nous l'équivalent d'un dôme de fer rhétorique pour parer leur *lethal narrative* [récit comme arme de guerre]? Souvenez-vous de Qfar Qana en 2006. Il leur faut un bataillon d'enfants morts pour enclencher la machine de la reddition imposée. Il faut comprendre que nous sommes toujours dans la sphère d'influence al Dura. Des enfants palestiniens déterrés, enterrés vifs dans des QG de Hamas, rapportés d'autres champs de bataille, de Syrie, de l'Irak, embarras du choix, des enfants morts déversés sur les écrans, un jackpot d'enfants morts nous attend. Il va falloir les enjamber et poursuivre l'opération de défense

Nous, qui suivons de près mais à distance la confrontation, résistons à la tentation de crier à chaque piqure de désinformation. Encore heureux de constater que nos médias français ne débordent pas d'enthousiasme pour la cause hamasienne. Le « printemps arabe » est passé par là, le jihad est entré dans le vocabulaire, les coupeurs de tête se répandent, le califat jette son ombre sur l'orientalisme frétillant, les anciens combattants européens du jihad nous guettent et tout le monde sait que les Juifs ne sont pas leur seule proie.

A nous de résister donc à la tentation de montrer une par une les énormités des reportages. Aux responsables israéliens de résister au qu'en dira-on de la communauté internationale.

Car, si je ne me trompe pas, la digue a déjà cédé. Un petit tour hier soir (10 juillet) auprès des luminaires de *SkyNews*, la *BBC*, *France 24*, *LCP* et j'en passe. Troisième jour, le seuil de tolérance est franchi. Bien entendu, Israël a le droit de se défendre, mais pas comme ça ! *Préparez les sacs poubelles, yahoud, on va vous déchiqueter.* Pardon, c'est une voix palestinienne. On cherchait les pleurs. Les morts et les blessés. Tous civils, tous innocents. Les voici. Ah, quel soulagement. On est enfin en terrain connu. Israël est fort, il a son dôme de fer, qu'on laisse tranquille ces pauvres Palestiniens démunis et occupés.

Des Musulmans prient dans leur mosquée sur le Mont du Temple, leur droit protégé par l'Etat d'Israël, sortent sur le parvis par centaines pour se réjouir du spectacle des roquettes tirées sur Jérusalem à partir de la bande de Gaza. Après le dôme de fer il nous faudrait un aspirateur géant qui les ramasserait, whoosh, pour les déposer doucement...à Alep, par exemple.

Les amis de mes amis sont là, mes amis sont sous le menace des roquettes, leurs enfants, leurs petits-enfants sont massés à la frontière prêts à entrer dans l'enfer de Gaza, ma famille est là, les enfants adultes de mes amis français sont là, mes souvenirs sont là, l'accueil, les repas, la chaleur humaine et du soleil, nuit blanche à Tel Aviv, shabbat à Jérusalem, colloques, conversations, jardins, l'intelligence délicieuse des esprits fins, mariages en plein air, dîner à la terrasse, collines de Judée, mer morte peuple plus que vivant, comment vous soutenir à présent ? On dépend de vous. Vous êtes la démocratie de toutes les démocraties. Ce ne sont pas « les Palestiniens » c'est le jihad qui avance. Le califat en Syrie-Irak sera le Gaza de l'Occident.

—Times of Israel

GAZA-ISRAËL : LE COMPTE N'EST PAS BON
[Gaza-Israel : it doesn't add up]

16 juillet 2014 (anniversaire de la rafle du Vel d'Hiv)

Israël, dit-on, un brin cynique, a le droit de se défendre, mais. Mais pas tout à fait. On demande de la retenue de part et d'autre. Car, il y a déséquilibre. La preuve : 37 puis 58 puis 102 et maintenant plus de 200 morts palestiniens. L'écrasante majorité, selon des sources palestiniennes, étant composée des civils. Femmes, vieillards, enfants, sans compter les milliers de blessés. De l'autre côté, que dalle. Ainsi la boucle est bouclée. Le récit comme arme de guerre [lethal narrative] est mis en place et alimenté quotidiennement, mécaniquement, sans gêne.

Or, il ne peut pas être question de retenue côté Hamas : son but est de tuer tous les Juifs et d'occuper tout le territoire de la vallée du Jourdain jusqu'à la mer. Tandis que les Israéliens souhaitent zéro mort, zéro blessé et l'intégrité de leur nation. Ce serait quoi, donc, la retenue? Le Hamas tuerait la moitié des Israéliens juifs ? Comment justifier cette vision comptable et totalement faussée d'une confrontation aux ramifications planétaires ? La ligne de partage entre la civilisation et la barbarie passe par la frontière Gaza-Israël.

L'armée israélienne pourrait écraser le Hamas de façon définitive en une seule journée, en faisant fi des civils pris dans les interstices d'une machine de guerre construite à la place d'une cité digne des êtres humains. Israël ne le fait pas.

Si, par malheur, les huit batteries du dôme de fer tombaient en panne, si jamais le Hamas prenait le dessus, les roquettes lancées de Gaza pourraient faire l'appoint. 200 victimes de chaque côté. Match nul ? Les deux équipes se serrent la main et repartent heureuses d'avoir bien joué ? Non. Le Hamas poursuivra sans retenue aucune son projet génocidaire. Que diraient alors le président des Etats-Unis, son secrétaire d'Etat, les chefs d'Etats européens, le Secrétaire Général des Nations Unies, les journalistes et les lecteurs avides de commenter le « conflit » ? Si jamais les Juifs d'Israël se trouvaient faibles comme les malheureuses populations d'Irak ou du Nigeria, que dirait l'opinion publique ? Qu'elle s'était trompée? Il aurait fallu frapper de toute sa force ? L'opinion publique contemporaine s'est très bien positionnée par rapport au génocide d'antan, la Shoah. Ce n'est pas sorcier. C'était une terrible tragédie qu'on regrette sincèrement Ou presque.

Trente-sept morts du côté palestinien dans les premiers jours de l'opération et rien dans l'autre camp, c'était scandaleux, non ? Un génocide, dit Mahmoud Abbas. Depuis lors, à chaque jour suffit sa peine, le compte est annoncé en fin de reportage sur les chaines du monde entier, la proportion de civils augmente de beaucoup à plus de la moitié jusqu'à quasiment la totalité. D'où viennent les chiffres ? Des sources palestiniennes. Qui pourra les vérifier ? Ce n'est pas la peine. A chaque confrontation c'est pareil. Un homme qui lance une roquette sur un quartier résidentiel d'Ashdod devient, si la riposte le touche, un civil. Alors que tous les Israéliens, tous les Juifs, y compris les trois jeunes assassinés en juin, sont des soldats.

Le Hamas n'est pas une organisation terroriste, c'est une force djihadiste. Il a la même idéologie islamique, les mêmes slogans, bannières, tenues et pratiques que ceux qui viennent d'établir sur une bonne partie de la Syrie et l'Irak les prémices du califat visant à s'étendre sur la terre entière. Que le Hamas soit en rivalité meurtrière avec d'autres factions djihadistes ne change rien à leur socle commun. Al Shabab, Boko Haram, ISIS, Al Nosra, Salafistes, Wahabis, Frères Musulmans et jusqu'aux soi-disant loups solitaires, tous sont des manifestations d'une seule et même force qui bouleverse notre monde aujourd'hui. Les parents des centaines de filles enlevées il y a trois mois déjà à Chibouk pleurent, les Chrétiens syriens, irakiens, libyens, pakistanais tremblent, des Musulmans égyptiens se sont révoltés et les Kurdes de Kirkuk se défendent fièrement contre les djihadistes qui exigent la soumission. Comme le Hamas à Gaza, comme le Hamas contre Israël. Comme les djihadistes qui ont assiégé la synagogue Don Isaac Abravanel rue de la Roquette à Paris le 13 juillet. De la retenue de part et d'autre ? Ils disaient clairement, tout comme le Hamas, qu'ils voulaient tuer des Juifs. Aurait-il fallu discuter avec eux les conditions d'un cessez le feu ? Les laisser entrer dans la synagogue ? Ou se battre de toutes ses forces contre les djihadistes de dimanche, comme ont fait les jeunes du Beitar, de la Ligue de Défense Juive et autres non-affiliés, épaulés plus tard par des CRS investis du pouvoir de la République? Pour s'assurer qu'il y aurait zéro mort du côté des Juifs.

Depuis le retrait unilatéral de Gaza en 2005 un total de 11,000 roquettes a été tiré contre Israël. Des roquettes éminemment concrètes. Il faut les fabriquer ou les importer clandestinement. Elles utilisent des matières premières, coûtent cher, prennent de la place, exigent des rampes de lancement mobiles ou fixes, installées dans des écoles et chez l'habitant, cachées dans des tunnels. C'est toute une entreprise, librement choisie. Notre ministre des Affaires étrangères exigent un cessez-le-feu immédiat. Notre président rappelle que la France cherche toujours le compromis, la bonne entente, la paix. Alain Juppé demande à quoi sert « la répression brutale [par Israël] ». Et le Hamas exige, aux dernières nouvelles, des conditions draconiennes : l'ouverture des points de passage des deux côtés—israélien, égyptien—la libération de tous les prisonnier relâchés lors de l'échange pour Gilad Shalit et arrêtés pendant les recherches des trois étudiants enlevés et assassinés. Ils demanderaient certainement, après et au-delà de l'accord de cessez-le-feu, d'autres fruits de leur victoire djihadiste du genre réparations, condamnations...ah, j'ai failli oublier...et la fin de l'occupation, d'Eilat jusqu'au Golan.

Autrement dit, en vertu d'avoir lancé plus de mille roquettes contre Israël le Hamas exige un retour au statu quo ante qui lui permettra de réapprovisionner et d'améliorer son stock d'armes en vue du prochain round et ainsi de suite jusqu'à la victoire finale.

Qui pourrait satisfaire ces exigences ? La communauté internationale pardi ! Composée d'une part, de leurs coreligionnaires et bailleurs de fonds et de l'autre de ceux qui, après Israël, à côté d'Israël, sont visés par le Hamas ou ses frères d'armes, voire ses rivaux plus djihadistes et plus puissants mais toujours sous la bannière noire du jihad, toujours aux cris d'égorger les Juifs, égorger les kuffars, allahou akhbar.

Il est obscène de dire « Israël as le droit de se défendre, mais... » Ce n'est pas un droit ça, c'est l'octroi d'une permission. Personne n'a le droit de l'accorder, ni de la nier, ni de la limiter.

DISPARITIONS INQUIÉTANTES
[Missing Persons]
1 octobre 2014

La décapitation des journalistes James Foley et Steven Sotloff puis celle de l'humanitaire britannique David Haines a fini par convaincre l'opinion publique européenne que nous sommes en guerre.

Malheureusement cette volonté tardive de confronter l'ennemi prend forme autour de la disparition inquiétante de l'Etat d'Israël, virtuellement évincé de l'actualité et de l'espace moyen-oriental.

Au mois d'août un millier de journalistes scrutait à Gaza le moindre faux pas israélien tout en servant un cocktail de drames palestiniens mélangés aux « informations » concoctées par le Hamas sous couvert de l'ONU (= UNWRA).

Interdit de filmer les combattants féroces en cagoule/keffieh (semblables à leurs coreligionnaires du Daesh). Le visage du Hamas était résolument civil.

Fin août le rideau tombe sur le spectacle Gaza-Israël sans présentation de l'épilogue qui aurait corrigé les fausses impressions savamment entretenues pendant l'opération. On joue maintenant tous unis contre l'Etat islamique.

Les méchants coupeurs de tête sont tellement affreux que le monde entier les vomit, y compris les bailleurs de fonds qui ne prennent même pas la peine de leur couper les vivres avant de se rendre en robe blanche à la Conférence de Paris où le président français et son homologue américain, en fins stratèges, rassemblent une trentaine de pays prêts à écrabouiller, éviscérer, éradiquer Daesh.

A-t-on jamais vu pareil spectacle ? Des bombardiers de toutes les Arabies côte à côte avec les Yankees en mission de sauvetage de la Civilisation. Pourquoi donc ? Parce que ces nations, toute la région, le monde entier est menacé par cette violence inqualifiable. La Turquie, le Qatar, le Bahreïn, les Emirats, la Jordanie, l'Egypte, l'Irak bien entendu, le Pakistan, l'Arabie saoudite, tous plus ou moins voisins de la bande de psycho-pathes qui ose s'appeler « Etat islamique. »

Voici les modérés, nos alliés dans le combat du bien contre le mal. François Hollande voulait aussi inviter l'Iran mais Barack Obama a mis son véto, provocant l'exaspération d'un tas de spécialistes.

Marine Le Pen et son lieutenant Florian Philippot refusent cette soumission aux diktats américains qui nous empêchent d'entretenir de bonnes relations avec l'incontournable Iran. Et Israël dans tout cela ? Voisin menacé par les djihadistes ? Allié fort et fiable ? Non. Israël dispa-raît de la configuration.

On fait de la géopolitique en mangeant des petits fours comme des joueurs de Mah Jong. On retrouve le plaisir de dire du mal de l'Amérique de G. W. Bush. Tout cela, dit-on avec une certitude joyeuse, est la faute à l'invasion illégale de l'Irak en 2003 et gloire à la France de s'être abste-nu. D'aucuns rajoutent la Libye en donnant un coup de pied à BHL et à Nicolas Sarkozy.

Comme c'est agréable de participer à une guerre humaniste ! Les na-tions menacées par Daesh sont tendrement dénommées et prises sous notre aile. Toutes sauf Israël. On félicite les aviateurs arabo-musulmans, on se félicite de savoir agir en concert avec eux, preuve qu'il ne s'agit pas d'une guerre de l'Occident contre l'Islam. On dit Daesh car, voyez-vous, ce n'est ni un Etat ni islamique. En fait c'est un califat mais chut ! ça touche un nerf sensible.

L'un après l'autre les gouvernements occidentaux se décident à parti-ciper aux frappes aériennes en promettant, comme le séducteur d'une vierge, de ne pas aller plus loin. Mais... est-ce possible de venir à bout de ces fanatiques sans invasion terrestre, sans une vraie sale guerre? Où sont les journalistes fraichement sortis de Gaza ? Ne peuvent-ils pas rappeler le dilemme posé au gouvernement Netanyahou? Le guet-apens, les soldats tués, l'opprobre jeté sur Tsahal, le réseau diabolique de tun-nels, le massacre de Rosh Hashana déjoué, les roquettes importées, l'argent détourné, le chef intraitable confortablement installé au Qatar...

C'était quoi au fait ce truc à Gaza ? Une branche du mouvement glo-bal djihadiste qui attaque pour la énième fois l'Etat d'Israël en vue de sa destruction ! Israël, le seul pays de la région qui sait se défendre. Le seul pays occidental qui accepte courageusement la charge de la guerre comme prix de sa liberté et de sa survie.

Israël, le seul allié fiable dans la région est écarté de la photo de famille à la faveur d'un méli-mélo de dictatures cyniques et manipulatrices. A quoi sert cette coalition factice ? A jouer en temps réel la partition : sans Israël on s'entendra à merveille au Moyen Orient. Ce n'est pas l'islam c'est la barbarie ! La décapitation en Algérie du guide de montagne Hervé Gourdel a plus choqué en France que les meurtres en masse des populations chrétiennes et yazidies dans le califat en formation. C'est culturel. Le pays des droits de l'homme s'émeut pour un seul homme, une star et surtout un baroudeur. Les précédentes victimes exhibées en tenue orange crûment improvisée étaient déjà abimées par des années de captivité cruelle. Hervé Gourdel est passé en 24 heures de la virilité de l'alpiniste à l'abîme de l'égorgé.

Les drapeaux en berne, les marches silencieuses, la France frappée d'effroi...et on dit au bon peuple que ce n'est pas ça l'Islam. Comme une armée de meurtriers frottant furieusement sol et murs pour effacer toute trace de sang, nos médias jurent que ce n'est pas l'Islam. Petites journalistes à la coiffure soignée, spécialistes-apologistes de l'Islam, philosophes, sociologues, criminologues, hommes et femmes politiques s'improvisent théologiens d'un Islam imaginaire. Ce n'est pas ça l'Islam, égorger un brave montagnard qui adorait le Maghreb. Ce n'est pas l'Islam ce sont des criminels, des terroristes.

Ce n'est pas l'Islam c'est la barbarie ? Lisez *L'Exil au Maghreb* du regretté David Littman et Paul Fenton. Pendant des millénaires l'Afrique du Nord était dénommé la Barbarie. Parmi les supplices imposés aux Juifs figurait le salage des têtes découpées. Ce n'est pas l'islam ?

Lisez *The Legacy of Jihad* d'Andrew Bostom MD, le récit documenté de la conquête islamique, des origines à nos jours. Les tours de dizaines de milliers de têtes découpées montées sous les ordres de Tamerlan au XIVe siècle. Mohamed, vénéré comme prophète par tout musulman, a participé à la décapitation de 600 à 900 hommes de la tribu juive des Bani Quraizah établissant ainsi le modèle éthique pour ses fidèles à travers les siècles. Les Musulmans qui prétendent aujourd'hui que la décapitation n'est pas islamique descendent eux-mêmes des survivants—ou des auteurs— des massacres et atrocités de la conquête islamique.

Cet été à Londres, le Nigérian Nick Salvadore, converti à l'Islam, a décapité Palmira Silva, une grand-mère d'origine italienne, dans son jardin. L'autre jour, Alton Nolen / Yah'keem Yisrael, américain noir converti à l'Islam, a décapité une collègue dans une entreprise d'agroalimentaire à Moore Oklahoma. En 2009, Muzzamil Hassan, fondateur de la chaine de télévision *Bridges* dont le but était de donner une image positive de l'Islam véritable, a décapité sa femme Aasiya dans les locaux de la chaîne.

Dalil Boubaker, recteur de la Grande Mosquée de Paris, a réuni une petite foule pour dire que décapiter n'est pas l'Islam. Surtout pas d'amalgame, ça non. Les musulmans venus partager la peine de la famille d'Hervé Gourdel cherchaient surtout à mettre en garde la société française : pas d'amalgame. Nous n'y sommes pour rien. Le recteur a lu des versets du Coran dont certains sont pris de nos écritures judaïques mais passons. Il a convaincu la journaliste de *BFM TV* qui déplorait le détournement de la religion de la paix par des voyous sans foi ni loi.

C'est tout simplement faux. D'ailleurs, ce n'est pas présenté comme un argument mais comme une évidence. Il n'y a pas de débat. Des esprits autrement plus exigeants tombent raide mort dans la pensée unique : ce n'est pas l'Islam, c'est sa négation. Que valent les versets du Coran égrenés ? Les versets de paix et de tolérance ne sont pas seulement abrogés par des versets de haine ils sont contredits par la réalité historique et actuelle. Les déclarations des musulmans européens sincèrement choqués par la brutalité des djihadistes sont des paroles de circonstance, bonnes à entendre en Occident, sans valeur de remise en question de la sharia.

La mise en cause des Juifs est la contrepartie d'un vivre ensemble conçu autour de la négation de la haine génocidaire des kuffars enseigné par l'Islam. En effet, l'Emir du Qatar, grand allié de la coalition, accuse Israël de crimes contre l'humanité commis à Gaza. Que valent les centaines massées devant la Grande Mosquée à côté des dizaines de milliers qui ont déchiré la paix civile avec des émeutes pro-Hamas cet été?On dédouane l'Islam de tout lien avec les « terroristes » en faisant abstraction d'innombrables agressions commises, depuis l'an 2000, par des Musulmans contre les Juifs et ponctuées par des meurtres d'une cruauté ahurissante.

Sous prétexte d'éviter le piège d'une guerre contre les musulmans on cautionne le lethal narrative [le récit comme arme de guerre] de la coalition œcuménique qui affaiblit notre défense contre le jihad, entretient l'animosité contre l'Etat d'Israël, fragilise la sécurité des Juifs en Europe et trahit la petite minorité de musulmans épris de liberté qui n'ose pas se révolter contre l'Islam tyrannique.

— *Times of Israel*

ÉTAT PALESTINIEN : LA LIGNE VERTE DU DJIHAD

[Palestinian State: the green line of jihad

24 novembre 2014

On voudrait nous faire croire que la création d'un Etat palestinien serait la réponse adéquate aux attaques lancées contre Israël depuis l'enlèvement et le meurtre de trois yeshiva bochers au massacre des Juifs en prière dans une synagogue à Har Nof.

Or, l'Etat-palestinien dont on parle n'a rien à voir avec une entité politique située dans un espace géographique. « Etat-palestinien » est un mot valise, un mot de passe, une arme. L'appel à la création de cet Etat-là se situe du même côté de la ligne verte du jihad que les atrocités commises depuis le mois de juin. La façade innocente du mot « Etat » cache un projet génocidaire.

D'ardents défenseurs d'Israël soutiennent, eux aussi, comme preuve de bonne volonté la solution à deux Etats.

Il faudrait plutôt chercher à comprendre pourquoi on relance cette « solution » à l'heure où les « partenaires pour la paix » rivalisent en atrocités.

Le Fatah n'est pas seulement uni avec le Hamas, qui avoue sans vergogne sa volonté d'exterminer les Juifs, il a pris le relais en démarrant la bataille de Jérusalem au lendemain du cessez-le-feu à Gaza. Après les roquettes et les tunnels viennent les voitures assassines, les meurtres à l'arme blanche et la campagne de reconnaissance auprès de l'ONU et des Etats européens sous la bienveillance ambiguë du président américain.

18 novembre 2014, Kehilat Bnei Torah, Har Nof, Jérusalem : deux Musulmans armés de haches, de couteaux et d'un pistolet, criant allahou akhbar, massacrent des Juifs en prière.

Quatre sont morts sur le coup, d'autres sont blessés grièvement voire mutilés. Une nouvelle étape est franchie. Certains médias, déstabilisés, se ridiculisent. *CNN* nous donne un attentat dans une mosquée, 2 Palestiniens tués.

Sur *BFM TV*, le bien-nommé Emmanuel Faux, fils de Gisèle Halimi, glose sur la judaïsation de Jérusalem et les provocations des extrémistes juifs.

Si le conflit, au demeurant territorial et politique, est devenu religieux, dit-il, ça a commencé quand des Juifs voulaient prier sur l'esplanade des mosquées.

Alain Gresh (*Monde diplomatique*) rajoute la colonisation, l'Occupation, l'injustice, l'unification illégale de Jérusalem.

D'ailleurs, Har Nof se situe pour les uns à Jérusalem Est, alors que d'autres comptent les assassins parmi les victimes des attentats de cet automne, y compris les cousins qui ont fait couler le sang sur les livres de prière, fendu des crânes et découpé un bras enroulé de tfilin.

Du côté de *Sky News* et de la *BBC*, on demande comment la destruction des maisons des criminels—morts de surcroît—pourrait mener à la réconciliation.

Des sympathisants offrent des sucreries en l'honneur des shahids Ghassan et Uday Abu-Jamal de Jabel Mukaber. Chez les gens polis, on sert le plat du jour : processus de paix, solution à deux Etats, fin de colonisation, division de Jérusalem.

Or, une vidéo diffusée par Daesh deux jours avant la tuerie dans la synagogue met en scène de fiers Européens à visage découvert tenant dans une main un couteau de boucher et dans l'autre le cou qui sera bientôt séparé de la tête d'une victime.

Maxime Hauchard, un converti français de 22 ans qui a abandonné ses vaches normandes pour les sables du Califat est identifié. Lui aussi, il crie avec ses camarades allahou akhbar.

A Jérusalem des Juifs d'origine canadienne, britannique, américaine sont sauvagement attaqués parce qu'ils priaient dans une synagogue alors que dans le Califat des décapiteurs de nationalité européenne et américaine invitent leurs compères à suivre leur exemple en Occident.

Ils soutiennent, eux aussi, une solution à deux Etats—dar al harb et dar al islam—en vue de la création d'un seul et unique Califat soumis à Allah et à sa loi, la sharia.

Ceux qui veulent se placer du bon côté de la ligne verte des atrocités jurent que couper des têtes n'a rien à voir avec l'islam. Le conflit israélo-palestinien non plus. Il n'est pas religieux ou ne le serait pas si les extrémistes juifs ne troublaient pas les Musulmans sur « l'esplanade des mosquées ».

Ainsi, des Juifs sur le Mont du Temple sont extrémistes et les Musulmans qui massacrent des Juifs en prière sont des victimes « abattues » par la police.

Quant à l'héroïsme du jeune policier druze Zidan Saif mort de ses blessures, les médias généralistes n'en ont pas fait grand cas![1] Arrivé avec un collègue en premier sur les lieux, Saif a tiré sur l'un de tueurs qui est sorti de la synagogue et lui a tiré dessus à bout portant.

Des Juifs qui veulent vivre dans des quartiers de Jérusalem décrétés « arabes » par l'opinion internationale sont des criminels.

Un gouvernement qui construit des logements pour résidents juifs dans des quartiers étiquetés « colonies » par les bien-pensants est d'extrême droite. Israël, avec 20 % de population non-juive, est un Etat d'apartheid mais la détermination — curieusement noble — de Mahmoud Abbas de construire un Etat palestinien libre de toute présence juive mérite le soutien des parlements européens. C'est une logique génocidaire !

Gérard Marx [loge hatikvah du B'nai B'rith] se demande pourquoi le *Times of Israel* omet de citer le rôle de la sénatrice écologiste Esther Benbassa,[2] foudroyer notoire des Juifs « complexés » et fière d'avoir déposé une proposition de résolution sur la reconnaissance de l'Etat de Palestine : « Reconnaître l'Etat de Palestine est une manière de dire clairement non à l'idéologie messianico-expansionniste qui anime une partie de la population israélienne ainsi que la coalition formée autour de Benyamin Netanyahu».

Plus d'une centaine de parlementaires annonçant leur intention de voter contre la résolution nous rassurent : ils soutiennent bel et bien la solution à deux Etats. Seulement il faudrait y arriver par la négociation.

On est tenté de citer une à une les énormités vues et entendues ces derniers jours. Tenez, par exemple, l'émission « On ne va pas se mentir » du 19 novembre. Sous la houlette d'Audrey Pulvar, quatre intervenants d'une ignorance-arrogance éblouissante —Philippe Bilger, Anne Giudicelli, Claude Guibal et Myriam Benraad—montent une construction proche orientale dont chaque brique d'agression musulmane est jetée à la tête d'un Israël coupable.

Quelques perles : Le gouvernement israélien se radicalise depuis l'assassinat des trois adolescents au mois de juin. La population palestinienne voit les attentats comme une réaction normale aux crimes des colons. On assiste à un retour aux fondamentaux de part et d'autre : les attentats, le siège de Gaza ; les Palestiniens séduits par le débat sur l'Etat islamique, les Israéliens par le débat sur un Etat juif. Pour prévenir [ces attentats] mieux vaut ne pas provoquer. Israël instrumentalise ces actes isolés pour se dédouaner de sa politique...

Si on suivait jusqu'au bout la logique de ces spécialistes, le bain de sang à la synagogue de Har Nof est la faute des Juifs : ils n'avaient qu'à ne pas saigner.

C'est quoi le « end game » de ce discours ? Quel est l'élément qui justifie la punition d'Israël ? C'est l'échec du processus de paix qui devrait aboutir à la solution à deux Etats.

Une solution totalement, absolument et résolument divorcée de toute réalité factuelle. Il ne s'agit ni d'un processus ni d'un Etat mais d'un écran de fumée destiné à cacher les horreurs qui se produisent devant nos yeux tout en les attribuant à l'Etat juif coupable du péché originel : ne pas être l'Etat islamique, ne pas se soumettre.

Tout comme le Mont du Temple est travesti en « esplanade des mosquées » l'Etat d'Israël devrait être, par une stratégie de Djihad déguisée en processus de paix, transformé en état soumis à la sharia.

Zvi Mazel, de passage à Paris, me montre une brève du *Figaro* où on annonce que les autorités israéliennes, pour la première fois depuis longtemps, autorisent sans restriction d'âge l'accès à l'esplanade des mosquées. « Notre ambassade ne fait rien, dit Zvi. Il faut dire au *Figaro* que c'est le Mont du Temple. »

En effet, quelques jours plus tard, Michal Philosoph, porte-parole de l'ambassade, laisse dire sans broncher [*I Télé*] « l'esplanade des mosquées » en assurant l'engagement ferme du gouvernement de respecter le statu quo. « Une toute petite mosquée de 600 mètres carrés au coin d'une étendue de 14,5 hectares, s'insurge Zvi, et il n'y a pas de place pour des Juifs ? Et maintenant ils appellent toute l'étendue du Mont du Temple al Aqsa. »

Pas religieux, le conflit ? Et « l'Intifada al-Aqsa » déclenché en septembre 2000 par la visite dite provocatrice d'Ariel Sharon sur le Mont du Temple et la mise en scène de la « mort » du shahid Mohamed al Dura ?

Ce n'est pas religieux, on insiste, c'est politique, c'est territorial. Et L'Islam ? N'est-il pas politique, territorial, djihadiste ?

On s'épuise à signaler l'aveuglement volontaire des spécialistes, dirigeants politiques et journalistes, à leur dire le mal qu'ils font. Savent-ils seulement le mal qu'ils se font ? Ils baissent la tête devant le décapiteur, épousent la stratégie du djihad qui les condamne, mettent le couteau dans la main de leur compatriote à peine sorti de l'enfance et tout fier de devenir bourreau. Ils se radicalisent, nos commentateurs, ils se radicalisent tout seuls.

Aucun discours, aucune résolution parlementaire de reconnaissance ne changera la réalité du sang qui coule, de la main qui tient le couteau, de l'esprit qui la dirige et qui les vise, eux aussi.

— *Times of Israel (français)*

Notes

Introduction
1. Landes, Richard. "Anti-Zionism: Soft Underbelly in Jihad's Cognitive War on the West." *Journal for the Study of Antisemitism.* (forthcoming)
2. Charlesworth, Marcus. *Operation Protective Edge: Qualitative Analysis of Canadian Media Coverage.* Ottawa: Carleton University Ottawa, 2015

Chapter 1 Prelude

Flashback
1. Poller, Nidra. *Al Dura: Long Range Ballistic Myth.* authorship international. Paris 2014

Attacking Israel with genocidal intentions
1. "Communiqué de la direction de l'université Paris 8 Vincennes – Saint-Denis," February 17, 2012.
2. Efraim Karsh, "The Middle East's Real Apartheid," Jerusalem Post, March 5, 2012.
3. Latma TV, "Benjamin Netanyahu's letter to the Flytillistas", http://www.jpost.com/DiplomacyAndPolitics/Article.aspx?id=266012
4. http://jssnews.com/2012/04/19/lettre-ouverte-a-charles-enderlin-par-pierre-rehov/.

Death Lag (Décalage horreur)
1. http://navonsblog.blogspot.fr/2014/06/israels-hierarchy-of-error.html

Anti-Israel Protestors
1. http://www.chabad.org/library/article_cdo/aid/111855/jewish/Don-Isaac-Abravanel-The-Abarbanel.htm

217

Chapter 2 Gaza-Israel Dateline Paris /July

Dispatch 1
1. Cessez-le-feu humanitaire (info # 022007/14)
2. Jewish men defend the synagogue on rue de la Roquette :
https://www.youtube.com/watch?v=geye3CS3eoA
Esti, artist and film maker. Video of the start of the July 13th hate-fest:
http://www.youtube.com/watch?v=TkWefM_qd7o&list=UUIMw2qukP-
6g2HdP_gaU4Sg&index=1
Guy Sauvage. Video of selected moments from the beginning of the July 13th hate-fest to its
endpoint at the Place de la Bastille, plus interviews with people who were in the don Isaac Abravanel synagogue rue de la Roquette during the siege: http://ripostelaique.com/jai-pu-filmer-la-
manifestation-palestinienne-puis-rentrer-dans-la-synagogue-attaquee.html
3. *Le Nouvel Obs* spins a blame-the-Jews tale for the battle at Don Isaac Abravanel synagogue:
http://tempsreel.nouvelobs.com/faits-divers/20140715.OBS3748/synagogue-de-la-rue-de-la-
roquette-ce-qu-il-s-est-vraiment-passe.html?xtor=RSS-17
4. *Huffington Post* (France) report on the July 13th demonstration:
http://www.huffingtonpost.fr/2014/07/14/israel-palestine-manifestation-gaza-
paris_n_5583340.html?utm_hp_ref=france
5. Report on the battle at Barbès: http://www.lepoint.fr/societe/manifestation-pro-palestinienne-
scenes-de-guerre-a-barbes-20-07-2014-1847574_23.php
6. Dispatches 1-10 published by New Englsh Review / The Iconoclast

Dispatch 2
1. http://www.lefigaro.fr/actualite-france/2014/07/20/01016-20140720ARTFIG00158-barbes-
sarcelles-la-contagion-de-la-violence.php'

Dispatch 3
1. http://www.lemondejuif.info/2014/07/exclusif-videos-paris-manif-anti-israel-mort-israel-au-
quartier-juif
2. http://ripostelaique.com/cetait-une-manif-palestine-bon-enfant-puisquon-vous-le-dit.html

Dispatch 4
1. http://madame.lefigaro.fr/societe/letat-islamique-ordonne-lexcision-de-toutes-femmes-
mossoul-240714-899278

Dispatch 5
1. http://www.lefigaro.fr/actualite-france/2014/07/26/01016-20140726ARTFIG00149-les-
images-du-rassemblement-pro-gaza-a-paris.php

Dispatch 6
1. https://twitter.com/Pauluskupa
2. http://shoebat.com/2014/07/26/muslims-take-fifty-innocent-people-cut-heads-place-heads-
poles-throughout-area/
3. http://www.lefigaro.fr/vox/monde/2014/07/25/31002-20140725ARTFIG00233-pour-sortir-
du-conflit-israelo-palestinien-une-seule-solution-la-laicite.php
4. http://miami.cbslocal.com/2014/07/25/ambassador-rips-media-for-coverage-of-israel-gaza-
conflict/
5. http://www.imra.org.il/story.php3?id=64492

Chapter 3 Gaza-Israel Dateline Paris / August

Dispatch 7

1.[http://www.thomaswictor.com/two-pallywood-duds/].
2.http://www.tomgrossmedia.com/mideastdispatches/archives/001475.html

Dispatch 8

1. update: finally identified as Mohammed Emwazi in February 2015
2. http://www.gatestoneinstitute.org/4645/foley-beheading

Dispatch 9

1. http://www.dailymail.co.uk/news/article-2738805/ISIS-beheads-terror-chief-guarded-U-S-journalist-James-Foley-s-prison-accusing-spying-M6.html
2. http://www.liberation.fr/monde/2014/08/27/on-n-a-plus-de-maison-mais-je-ne-partirai-pas_1088266
   3. http://www.ibtimes.com/sotloff-family-statement-journalist-beheaded-isis-was-no-war-junkie-1677914

Dispatch 10

1. cf Richard Landes "from Palestinian sources" http://www.commschool.org/page.cfm?p=648)
2. http://www.thomaswictor.com/two-pallywood-duds/

Chapter 4 Epilogue

Palestinian State (Etat palestinien: la ligne verte du jihad)

1. http://fr.timesofisrael.com/une-video-montre-le-role-cle-du-policier-druze-tue-a-har-nof/
2 http://www.huffingtonpost.fr/esther-benbassa/reconnaissance-de-letat-palestinien_b_6091908.html

Now Look what they've done

1. L'esprit de l'escalier, Radio Communauté Juive, 23 November
http://radiorcj.info/diffusions/27585/
2. http://www.timesofisrael.com/police-bust-massive-shipment-of-firecrackers-knives-bound-for-jerusalem/

Chapter 5 Jihd Attacks in Europe

Head-on Collision

1. http://www.newenglishreview.org/custpage.cfm/frm/25151/sec_id/25151-
2. http://www.newenglishreview.org/blog_email.cfm/blog_id/38896/Auto-da-fe-in-Paris-its-no-joke

Prologue True & False Notes

1. http://www.d-intl.com/2014/05/08/the-national-fronts-dark-underside-2/?lang=en http://www.newenglishreview.org/blog_direct_link.cfm/blog_id/54197/cat_id/326/Marine-Le-Pen-is-Shopping-for-Allies-at-the-EU-Parliament]
2. http://www.timesofisrael.com/swedish-far-right-leader-jews-are-not-true-swedes/

True & False Notes

1. http://www.israelhayom.com/site/newsletter_article.php?id=22867
2. http://www.huffingtonpost.fr/2015/01/29/frederic-chatillon-mis-examen-faux-marine-le-pen_n_6571766.html
3. http://www.standard.co.uk/news/london/law-trainee-says-kuffar-who-killed-our-people-are-to-blame-for-paris-terror-in-online-video-rant-9987500.html

Jihad attacks in Denmark
1. http://www.algemeiner.com/2015/02/15/defiant-mother-who-hosted-bat-mitzva-as-terror-struck-copenhagen-synagogue-recounts-harrowing-ordeal-no-one-can-tell-me-where-i-can-live-my-jewish-life-interview/
2. http://www.memritv.org/clip/en/4783.htm
3. http://www.lefigaro.fr/international/2015/02/17/01003-20150217ARTFIG00108-copenhague-des-fleurs-deposees-devant-l-appartement-du-suspect.php

Chapter 6 Acquiescence
P5 + 1 & the Pope submit
1. http://www.weeklystandard.com/blogs/media-gets-pope-s-abbas-comments-wrong_948653.html
2. http://mondafrique.com/lire/decryptages/2015/02/04/polemique-sur-charles-enderlin-entre-le-syndicat-national-des-journalistes. Leconte, who played a very minor role in casting doubt on the authenticity of the al Dura news report, was misrepresented by Mondafrique as a prime mover.
3. http://www.theatlantic.com/international/archive/2015/05/obama-interview-iran-isis-israel/393782/
4. http://www.washingtonpost.com/news/volokh-conspiracy/wp/2015/05/22/obama-is-nostalgic-for-white-israel/
5. http://mfa.gov.il/MFA/AboutTheMinistry/Conferences-Seminars/Pages/5th-Global-Forum-for-Combating-Antisemitism.aspx

Humanitarian Jihad
1. http://www.lejdd.fr/Medias/Television/Charles-Enderlin-prend-sa-retraite-apres-30-ans-en-Israel-Il-n-y-aura-pas-deux-Etats-743702
2. http://www.newenglishreview.org/blog_print_link.cfm/blog_id/62112#CurDomainURL#/blog.cfm
3. http://www.memritv.org/clip/en/5128.htm

Jihad attacks on Paris/2
1. https://twitter.com/frhaz/status/493047182065684480
http://www.europe-israel.org/2014/07/manifestation-pro-hamas-paris260714-compilation-dimages-a-voir-pour-savoir/
https://www.youtube.com/watch?v=rozngjznLts

What do they want?
1. http://www.unipopu.org/
2. http://www.lefigaro.fr/actualite-france/2015/11/27/01016-20151127ARTFIG00226-15-jours-apres-les-attentats-le-point-sur-l-enquete.php
3. http://www.v921.net/ACTUALITE/2011-03-01%20Rapport%20Bruguiere/2011-03-01%20Rapport%20Bruguiere.pdf]

www.ingramcontent.com/pod-product-compliance
Lightning Source LLC
Chambersburg PA
CBHW031429270326
41930CB00007B/625